CALL HANDLING OPERATIONS S/NVQ

LEVEL **2**

Candidate Handbook

Keith Bowen

Yvonne Munn

Peter Richardson

D0316006

Heinemann Educational Publishers,
Halley Court, Jordan Hill, Oxford OX2 8EJ
A division of Harcourt Education Ltd

Heinemann is a registered trademark of Harcourt Education Limited

OXFORD MELBOURNE AUCKLAND
JOHANNESBURG BLANTYRE GABORONE
IBADAN PORTSMOUTH NH (USA) CHICAGO

First published 2002
2006 2005 2004 2003 2002
10 9 8 7 6 5 4 3 2 1

A catalogue record for this book is available from the British Library on request.

ISBN 0 435 45561 3

British Library Cataloguing in Publication Data is available from the British Library on request.

Typeset by J&L Composition, Filey, North Yorkshire

Printed and bound in Great Britain by The Bath Press Ltd, Bath

Please note that the examples of websites suggested in this book were up to date at the time of writing. It is essential for tutors to preview each site before using it to ensure that the URL is still accurate and the content is appropriate. We suggest that tutors bookmark useful sites and consider enabling students to access them through the school or college intranet.

Acknowledgements

To our long suffering partners, David, Marion and Carol for their support, cajoling, understanding and encouragement. To Rachel, Carol and Carolyn who proof read the initial drafts and helped knock them into shape.

The authors and publishers would like to thank Keith Waudby, in particular, for his enthusiasm for the project. We would also like to thank the following for permission to reproduce photographs and screen shots:

Alamy page 147; Arriva page 152; Gareth Boden page 63; Trevor Clifford page 279; Epsom page 279; Getty Images pages 51, 263, 307, 78, 199; Antony King/Medimage pages 279, 280; Lloyds TSB pages 188, 189, 190; Microsoft Corporation pages 296, 286, 287, 296; Photodisc pages 113, 279, 287; Peter Richardson pages 3, 10, 60, 71, 138, 152, 156; Tropical Places page 155; Yiorgos Nikiteas page 126.

Peter Richardson would like to thank the following companies for their co-operation: DVLA; Livingstone; Powergen and Redcats.

Every effort has been made to contact copyright holders of material published in this book. We would be glad to hear from any unacknowledged sources at the first opportunity.

Tel: 01865 888058   www.heinemann.co.uk

Contents

Candidate Handbook

Foreword	iv
About the CD-ROM	v
Introduction	1
Skills Scan – Choosing your option units	10

MANDATORY UNITS

Unit 1 – Contribute to developing and maintaining positive caller relationships	15
Unit 25 – Contribute to an effective and safe working environment	55
Unit 26 – Contribute to improving the quality of service provision	111

OPTIONAL UNITS

Unit 2 – Address the needs of callers	131
Unit 6 – Make arrangements on behalf of callers	161
Unit 7 – Authorise transactions using telecommunications	183
Unit 9 – Offer products and services over the telephone	223
Unit 11 – Enter and retrieve information using a computer system	277
Unit 17 – Process telephone calls	307
Test your knowledge – Answers	343
Glossary of call handling terms	355

CD-ROM

OPTIONAL UNITS

Unit 8 – Generate sales leads for follow-up calls

Unit 10 – Undertake telephone research

Unit 12 – Communicating information using email facilities

Unit 18 – Provide information and documentation to meet requirements

Unit 21 – Contribute to the handling of incidents and resources

Unit 47 – Remotely provide, modify or cease telecommunication service

Assessment Toolkit

Glossary of NVQ terms

Additional resources for Units 25 and 26

Foreword

Call Handling has continued to grow as an emerging sector throughout the 1990s and into the new millennium. It is anticipated that the sector will continue to grow, with over 1 million people employed in contact centre related activities by 2005! In the early days of call centres, coping with call volumes and call-handling capacity has been the main priority; to this end the quality of calls became, in some cases, the casualty. This has been widely reflected in the tabloid press as being the 'Sweat Shops of the 90s' giving contact centres a less than favourable reputation. A call centre is seen as a low paid – high pressure environment in which to work. In the majority of instances this is not the case, contact centre working conditions tend to be modern, purpose built facilities with excellent call handling applications and technology, with high team morale and management support.

The first call handling occupational standards were developed as early as 1995 and the second generation superseded them in 2000, with the result that a new suite of National Vocational Qualifications became available in 2001.

These new qualifications cover call handling operations at levels 2 and 3, supervising call handling at level 3 and managing call handling at level 4. This candidate guide is designed to support candidates who may wish to take an NVQ at level 2 in call handling operations.

The purpose of the candidate guide is to help new entrants to the sector, or people working in the sector to enhance their call handling skills and techniques. The learning exercises in the workbook and the additional materials on the CD-ROM have been specifically designed to encourage candidates to explore how they work and interact with their organisation and improve their existing call handling skills. The guide is designed so that candidates can 'dip in and out' as required depending on which option units they choose as part of their qualification. The most popular option units have been included in the book with the remainder being covered on the accompanying CD-ROM.

The CD-ROM also contains a valuable 'Assessor's Toolkit', providing assessors and internal verifiers with ready-made assessment materials in order to assist them with their assessment strategy.

I am happy to endorse this candidate guide and CD-ROM as adding significantly to the learning and assessment materials available within the contact centre sector and feel that it will enhance knowledge and understanding of call handling at all levels.

Keith Waudby

e-skills Manager
Communications Technologies

e-skills UK is the sector skills council recognised by the government with responsibility for information, communications and electronics technologies.

About the CD-ROM

The CD-ROM contains a library of resources that accompany the *NVQ2 Call Handling Operations* book. It has been divided into five areas:

How to use this CD-ROM – detailed help files that explain how the CD-ROM works, what computer specifications you need, and how to access the files that you want to use.

Option Units – detailed outlines of the five optional units not covered in the book.

Assessment Toolkit – the assessment documentation for you and your assessor relating to *all* units of the qualification are included under this topic heading.

Additional resources for Units 25 and 26 – additional exercises and tables for you to complete and print out. They will help you complete the various tasks in Units 25 and 26. Throughout these two units you will see the 'link symbol' which indicates that there is an additional resource on the CD-ROM.

⊙ LINK

Glossary of NVQ terms – this glossary will help you get to grips with some of the most commonly used terms that relate to National Vocational Qualifications (NVQ).

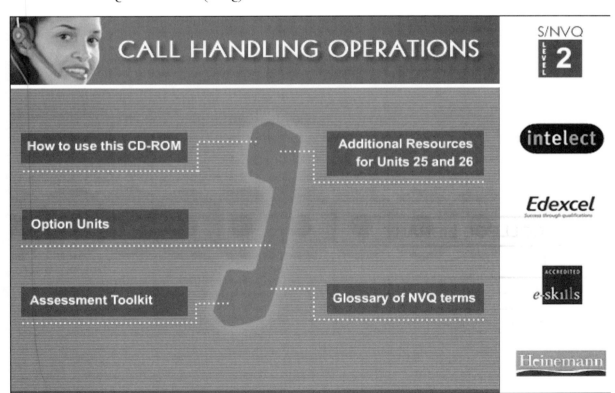

Opening screen of the CD-ROM

Running the CD-ROM

Note: You may be required to restart your PC after running the CD-ROM for the first time.

♦ Insert the CD into your CD-ROM drive.
♦ The CD-ROM should run automatically.

If your PC does not support autorun:

♦ Go to 'My Computer' and double-click on your CD-ROM drive.
♦ The CD-ROM should run.

If it does not run, but instead displays a list of the files on the CD-ROM, then:

♦ Double-click on the file *start.exe*.

Introduction

This book provides detailed information about the National Vocational Qualification, Call Handling Operations at level 2. It is aimed at:

- candidates who want to work towards or who are working towards this qualification
- assessors who are responsible for assessing this qualification
- organisations who wish to or are already offering assessment for this qualification
- other readers who wish to know more about this qualification.

The S/NVQ system
What are S/NVQs?
National Vocational Qualifications (or NVQs) and Scottish Vocational Qualifications (or SVQs) are qualifications which reflect the skills, knowledge and understanding that an individual possesses in relation to a specific area of work.

S/NVQs are all about being able to do a job well. They are based on occupational standards developed by industry with the help of a Standards Setting Body. This makes them relevant to the workplace and valued by both employers and employees.

Each S/NVQ is made up of a number of separate units, which means that they can be achieved 'bit by bit'. These units set out:

- what the candidate must be able to do
- how well the candidate must be able to do it
- the knowledge and understanding that the candidate needs to have.

What is a qualification level?
When a qualification is developed, it is allocated a level within the NVQ framework depending on the:

- range of work activities within the occupational role
- range of contexts in which the work is performed
- responsibilities associated with the job role
- extent of the autonomy or control of others that is involved.

The NVQ framework has five levels, which are defined by the Qualifications and Curriculum Authority (QCA) as:

- **Level 1** 'competence which involves the application of knowledge and skills in the performance of a range of varied work activities, most of which may be routine or predictable.'
- **Level 2** 'competence which involves the application of knowledge and skills in a significant range of varied work activities, performed in a variety of contexts. Some of the activities are complex or non-routine and there is some individual responsibility and autonomy. Collaboration

with others, perhaps through membership of a work group or team, may often be a requirement.'

♦ **Level 3** 'competence which involves the application of knowledge and skills in a broad range of varied work activities performed in a wide variety of contexts, most of which are complex and non-routine. There is considerable responsibility and autonomy, and control or guidance of others is often required.'

♦ **Level 4** 'competence which involves the application of knowledge and skills in a broad range of complex, technical or professional work activities performed in a wide variety of contexts and with a substantial degree of personal responsibility and autonomy. Responsibility for the work of others and the allocation of resources is often present.'

♦ **Level 5** 'competence which involves the application of skills and a significant range of fundamental principles across a wide and often unpredictable variety of contexts. Very substantial personal autonomy and often significant responsibility for the work of others and for the allocation of substantial resources feature strongly, as do personal accountabilities for analysis and diagnosis, design, planning, execution and evaluation.'

Did you know?

The fastest growing NVQ level is currently level 5. The number of NVQ certificates awarded in the 12 months up to 30 September 2001 was 9 per cent higher than the number awarded in the preceding 12 months.

What are the benefits of S/NVQs?

With S/NVQs, it does not matter if you have developed your competence all at once, in stages, at work or at college. If you can prove to your assessor that you can meet the required standard then you can gain an NVQ as they are *not* course-dependent or course-based. S/NVQs can help you to make sure that your competence is recognised by allowing you to get credit for the skills that you may already have.

If you gain an S/NVQ, it shows that you have acquired the skills and knowledge that your industry needs and it proves that you can do your job to the right standard. Having your performance assessed whilst you are actually carrying out your job benefits many people who are deterred from taking qualifications by the thought of sitting exams.

Today, the QCA (SQA in Scotland) works together with the Department for Education and Skills (DfES); National Training Organisations; Sector Skills Councils; and Awarding Bodies to ensure that:

♦ qualification standards are derived from approved National Occupational Standards
♦ qualification standards meet the needs of employers and employees
♦ candidate assessments are rigorous and consistent.

By meeting both the needs of industry and individuals, S/NVQs offer opportunities for everyone. They help employers to identify 'skills needs' and meet such needs through effective training. In addition, they show that a company is committed to quality and 'investment in people'.

What is assessment?

In order to obtain a unit or a full S/NVQ award, a candidate must demonstrate their ability to consistently meet all the criteria specified in the national standards. Evidence of competent performance must be supported by evidence of underpinning knowledge and understanding.

Assessment is a process of collecting evidence of competence and judging it against the national standards. In S/NVQs, the standards for competent performance are clearly defined and are available to both the assessor and the candidate. Assessment decisions are therefore a matter of judgement as to whether the standards have been met and whether the evidence is sufficient to confirm that the performance can be consistently maintained.

Evidence can be derived from many sources, so the assessor must ensure that each candidate is given the best opportunity to provide the right mix of evidence in order that a fair judgement can be made. Evidence used in an assessment must be: valid, reliable, authentic, current and sufficient.

Did you know?

The total number of NVQ certificates awarded up to 30 September 2001 was 3,488,656; an increase of 13 per cent on the total awarded to 30 September 2000.

The assessor should work with the candidate to develop and agree an assessment plan which identifies what evidence is required; what already exists; and how, when and where the additional evidence required to demonstrate competence will be collected.

Work closely with your assessor

It is possible that one performance criterion could be supported by several pieces of evidence, and that one piece of evidence could support several performance criteria. These cross-referencing opportunities should be identified within the assessment plan, which should be regarded as flexible and should be continuously reviewed by both the assessor and the candidate.

Assessment of S/NVQs is conducted through Approved Centres by assessors who are appointed by the Awarding Body. Candidates can enrol for one or more units or a full S/NVQ. During assessment, the candidate will provide evidence to the assessor who will record this evidence and the judgements made.

The candidate may also contribute to the evidence required by building a portfolio of evidence. This can contain various articles (including training certificates, records of achievement and witness testimonies) but it is stressed that this evidence can only play a supporting role to that gained from performance and other sources. It must also satisfy the criteria of validity, reliability, currency, sufficiency and authenticity.

The four steps that make up the assessment process

1 Assessment planning.

2 Evidence collection.

3 Judging evidence.

4 Making an assessment decision.

When carrying out assessment, the assessor should take account of the following points:

♦ assessment must be based directly on the performance criteria, range statements and knowledge specifications in the qualification standards, and must comply with the specified evidence requirements
♦ performance evidence must feature in the assessment of all elements
♦ performance must be demonstrated and assessed under realistic conditions, preferably in the workplace. Where assessment in the workplace is not practicable, alternatives used must enable the full requirements of the qualification standards to be met and confirm that the competence can be sustained in employment. Alternative assessment methods must be agreed with the External Verifier
♦ there must be evidence that the candidate possesses the specified knowledge and understanding
♦ candidates must meet all performance criteria consistently, and cover the full range of circumstances in which competence must be applied, as specified in the evidence requirements
♦ access to assessment for an NVQ or units must be available to all with the potential to reach the required standard; be affordable; be free from unnecessary barriers; and independent of age, the mode or location of learning and timescales (unless legal/statutory constraints make this necessary)

- alternative forms of assessment must be made available, if necessary, to increase access to the qualification for candidates, including those with special assessment requirements
- some of the assessment may be conducted in a language other than English, provided there is clear evidence that the candidate's competence in English meets the standard required for competent performance throughout the UK. Assessment may be carried out entirely in Welsh and, for NVQs offered outside the UK, in other languages; this fact will be noted in the resulting certificate
- a reliable system must be in place for recording evidence, assessment judgements and decisions in relation to the award of NVQs and units.

Possible types of evidence

There are many sources of evidence, but in general they fall into the following classes:

- observation reports
- documented processes and procedures
- accreditation of prior learning (APL)
- questions and answers
- tape recordings
- work product evidence
- photographs
- witness testimonies

Observation reports

These are reports where your assessor records the details of their observations of you achieving the outcome of the S/NVQ elements or units. The report records the location; under what circumstances you were performing the tasks, and record how your performance met the defined standards.

The assessor will record how each of the performance criteria for each of the elements was met and how you applied your skills, knowledge and understanding of the processes and procedures to achieve the knowledge specification. The assessor will also record how you achieved any range of activities required to meet the evidence requirements. Your assessor may well observe you undertaking similar, or the same, tasks several times whilst you are working towards your S/NVQ; this is to prove the consistency of your performance.

Questions and answers

Although your assessor may have gathered some evidence of your knowledge and understanding during any observations, he or she may still need to ask you questions to confirm you have the depth of knowledge and understanding needed to meet the requirements. This can be achieved by asking you questions while you continue working, by setting written questions that you are required to answer in writing, or by conducting a professional discussion with you away from the workplace. Whichever method your assessor adopts, the discussion should be fully recorded as evidence, either as a written report or tape recordings of the discussions.

Work product evidence

Work product evidence is the outcome of your work activity. It may be in the form of screen dumps of information that you have input into the computer; transaction slips you have completed; documents you have prepared; messages you have sent; etc. This evidence must be attributed to you, either by your personal computer ID, or witnessed by someone in a responsible position (or your assessor).

When you use any product of your work activity as evidence you must ensure that all personal details of any customers or clients have been deleted before it is included in your portfolio. This will ensure customer confidentiality.

Documented processes and procedures

Although these can be vital pieces of evidence to prove that you are following the processes and procedures expected by your organisation, it is not recommended that you photocopy any of these for inclusion in your portfolio. Instead include them on your supporting evidence location summary sheet and clearly mark their location in the column provided. This means your assessor will be able to consult the most up to date copy of the document instead of referring to a photocopy you made sometime in the past.

Tape recordings

A large number of call handling operations monitor or record the calls you handle. These resources can be used as a source of evidence for your portfolio. If you intend to include this type of evidence in your portfolio, it is essential that you discuss this with your assessor and team leader or line manager and get their agreement before proceeding any further.

Photographs

Photographs can be useful evidence so long as they record an actual event. To prove their validity they will need to be authenticated by a responsible person who was present when the photograph was taken. Today with the widespread use of video and digital cameras you may want to record your actions using this equipment.

Accreditation of prior learning (APL)

Accreditation of prior learning (APL) is the name given to the process within assessment whereby experienced candidates are given credit for their previous experience. Evidence of this experience may take many forms, such as: products or artefacts; reports; projects; certificates of achievement; or letters of validation from employers, customers, etc. In fact, it could be anything that attests to your achievements and competence.

APL does not allow you to by-pass the assessment process, but it does allow you to move directly to assessment when you are already competent.

In considering a candidate's APL, assessors and verifiers will need to address the:

- validity of the evidence
- authenticity of the evidence
- currency of the competence
- reliability of the evidence
- sufficiency of the evidence

APL can provide a cost-effective method of collecting evidence. However, it must not be used to provide an exemption route to the S/NVQ. The candidate will always be required to provide sufficient, valid and reliable evidence to demonstrate their *current* competence, as required by the competence standards in the S/NVQ.

Witness testimonies

Evidence may be provided by witnesses, such as a manager, colleague or customer, or an accredited assessor, in the form of a testimony. A witness should ideally be competent in the candidate's occupational area, and be familiar with the standards required. It is the responsibility of the assessor to determine the reliability and value of witness testimony.

Witnesses should be asked to:

♦ endorse a candidate's own reports and evidence records (signature, date and status) **or**
♦ provide a signed and dated account of the candidate's performance **or**
♦ provide an oral account of the candidate's performance to the assessor **and**
♦ sign the candidate's Witness List.

Candidates should prepare witnesses by:

♦ providing them with a copy of the standards for which they are providing evidence
♦ explaining how, what the candidate will be doing is related to the performance criteria and evidence requirements
♦ explaining why the candidate needs a testimony and how it will be used
♦ making sure they know when and where they are required to observe the candidate.

In considering using witness testimonies as evidence, candidates should appreciate that the assessor has to ensure there is sufficient authentic and reliable evidence, before making any judgement. This evidence must confirm the candidate's *current* competence in meeting the required standard.

Portfolio building

A good portfolio of evidence is a comprehensive record of the evidence that exists to support your ability to perform to the standards defined within the S/NVQ that you are working towards. You will find that there may be many occasions when it is not appropriate to remove evidence from the workplace so that it can be included in your portfolio. For example, where personal information about someone (which is protected under The Data Protection Act 199) is involved or the material is part of a work-based record system. Where this is the case, leave the evidence in the workplace where it belongs (there is no need to produce a copy of it for the portfolio either) and reference it within your portfolio. The portfolio MUST contain sufficient details of where to find any evidence not contained within it, to enable anyone connected with the assessment process to track down the actual evidence at a later date.

Assessors must be aware of, and take care to avoid, the danger of judging the quality of a portfolio rather than the quality of the evidence that it contains or references. It must be remembered that it is not how well the portfolio is put together that matters (although it is true that a portfolio that is put together well can make an assessor's life easier!) it is the currency, validity, reliability and authenticity of the evidence that matters.

The diagram below shows a suggested layout for a portfolio of evidence.

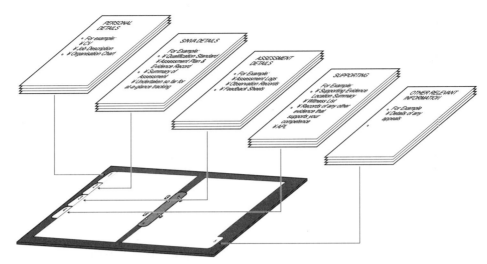

A typical portfolio of evidence

Did you know?

As at the end of September 2001, there were 743 different NVQs within the Framework.

The call handling sector

The call handling sector includes all operations that involve call centres and also where the use of the telephone constitutes a significant proportion of the activity undertaken. It therefore covers a wide range of services, such as: customer service; direct sales; technical support; emergency call handling; customer care lines; telephone switchboards and reception desks; telephone research; and direct handling from advertising.

The use of call centres by organisations of all kinds (in both the public and private sectors) has grown dramatically in recent years. This has been due to a combination of competitive pressures, increased customer expectation, fewer resources and technological developments. A combination of these factors has promoted the use of call centres as a means by which businesses can interact with their customers.

The modern call centre has its roots in two distinct business movements:

◆ direct marketing
◆ the philosophy of gaining competitive advantage by being customer centred.

Financial services gave the biggest boost to call centre growth when deregulation, rising costs and intense competition forced companies to look at other ways of dealing with customers. The use of call centres was seen as a low cost way of interacting with customers.

Did you know?

It is estimated that over 5 million people are engaged in telephone-based work.

Developments in information and communications technology have enabled this dramatic growth to take place, particularly the increasing availability of cheaper products that have greater power and functionality.

Call centres are part of the rapid expansion of the service sector in the UK, and are a major contributor to the economy. However, despite the growth in the number of call centres, and their economic significance, there is still widespread ignorance and misunderstanding about the value of telephone-based business and of call centre work. A typical view is that the work is narrow in scope, intellectually undemanding, of low status and marginal to business success. This negative view of call centres has been fuelled, in part, by media reports of 'sweatshops' and 'battery farm' conditions. People see call handling work as easy because they think it is only answering the telephone – and everyone can do that. However, it is in fact as specialised a skill as any other in business.

The reality is that it can require extensive product knowledge, knowledge of legislation and services and the ability to work with computer equipment. In addition to this, well developed interpersonal skills are required as well as the ability to process information, solve problems and work as part of a team.

The call handling sector is one of the most exciting and demanding of sectors. Companies and people entering this sector for the very first time often under-estimate the amount of time, effort and investment it takes to develop a highly successful operation.

With nearly 70 per cent of costs going on personnel, training has always been an important factor in UK call centres, both as a tool to improve quality and as an aid to staff retention.

Skill scan – Choosing your option units

How do I choose the option units that best match my job role?

In order to achieve the National Vocational Qualification 'Call Handling Operations at Level 2', you will need to prove your competence against the three mandatory units:

♦ Contribute to developing and maintaining positive caller relationships
♦ Contribute to an effective and safe working environment
♦ Contribute to improving the quality of service provision.

In addition to the three mandatory units above, which all candidates have to take, you must also achieve three option units from the twelve option units that are available.

If you are working towards your qualification because your employer has encouraged you to do so, your employer may well have already indicated which option units they want you to do. However, if they have left the choice up to you and you are not sure which units are best for you, working through this section should help you to decide. Work through the questions on pages 10–11 and decide which things you do: often within your job role; only do sometimes; or never do. This will enable you to decide which option units are most suitable for you.

Choosing the right option units ensures you develop the most appropriate skills for your job

In response to each of the questions below, tick the column that best describes how frequently you carry out the task.

Do you do the following things?	Do you do them?			Which option units should I choose?
	Often	Sometimes	Never	
1 Find out what the caller wants from your organisation?				If you do 1 and 2 often, then you should choose Option Unit 2 – Address the needs of callers.
2 Take steps to ensure that the caller's needs are met?				
3 Decide what arrangements you need to make as a result of the customer's call?				If you do 3 and 4 often, then you should choose Option Unit 6 – Make arrangements on behalf of callers. This could be reservations and bookings, or routing calls around your own organisation.
4 Make the necessary arrangements?				
5 Deal with financial transactions such as debiting credit cards, transferring money between accounts, or transferring money to pay bills and invoices?				If you do 5 often, then you should choose Option Unit 7 – Authorise transactions using telecommunications.
6 Make calls to potential customers to generate sales leads?				If you do 6, 7 and 8 often, then you should choose Option Unit 8 – Generate sales leads for follow-up calls.
7 Assess the customer's level of interest in your organisation's products/services?				
8 Arrange follow-up activity with potential customers?				
9 Speak to customers over the telephone to find out if they are interested in your organisation's products/services?				If you do 9, 10 and 11 often, then you should choose Option Unit 9 – Offer products/services over the telephone.
10 Promote the features and benefits of your organisation's products/services in order to generate interest?				
11 Gain the customer's commitment and complete the sale?				
12 Carry out telephone research and customer satisfaction surveys?				If you do 12 often, then you should choose Option Unit 10 – Undertake telephone research.
13 Use a computer system to enter, retrieve and store information as part of your call handling activity?				If you do 13 often, then you should choose Option Unit 11 – Enter and retrieve information using a computer system.
14 Send and receive emails as a routine part of your job?				If you do 14 often, then you should choose Option Unit 12 – Communicate information using email facilities.

Do you do the following things?	Do you do them?			Which option units should I choose?
	Often	Sometimes	Never	
15 Regularly make and receive telephone calls on behalf of your organisation as a telephone operator, in a front office reception area, control room, call centre or similar call handling facility?				If you do 15 and 16 often, then you should choose Option Unit 17 – Process telephone calls.
16 Report any faults that may occur in the telephone equipment that you use?				
17 Obtain information from or provide information to colleagues or customers?				If you do 17 and 18 often, then you should choose Option Unit 18 – Provide information and documentation to meet requirements.
18 Draft and prepare documentation?				
19 Handle incidents and events within a communications centre or control room?				If you do 19, 20, and 21 often, then you should choose Option Unit 21 – Contribute to the handling of incidents and resources. This unit is mainly for the emergency services and CCTV control rooms.
20 Review, prioritise and monitor incidents?				
21 Allocate, monitor and control the resources required to deal with incidents?				
22 Change customers' telephone services from a call centre, by starting or stopping telephone services or adding new telephone facilities?				If you do 22 often, then you should choose Option Unit 47 – Remotely provide, modify or cease telecommunications service.

Now look at how frequently you have indicated that you carry out the above tasks and use this to help you decide which of the option units best suit your job role. In addition, please bear in mind the following.

It is always best to choose the option units that are made up of the things that you do most frequently. If you often do the things that make up any of the option units above, then you should have plenty of opportunities to gather enough evidence to show that you can carry out the tasks to the required standard.

If you only sometimes carry out any of the things that make up a unit, then you may still wish to consider doing the option unit that the task is part of. However, it may make gathering sufficient evidence to prove your competence more difficult.

You may well find that you do a lot of these things everyday, in which case you should decide which tasks are most relevant to your job role and highlight those. You should then look to see which units these tasks are part of – this will indicate which units you should do. Remember that you only need to do *three* option units.

You should not choose option units that contain tasks that you do not carry out as part of your normal job role, unless your employer is willing to offer you the opportunity to perform these tasks so that you can broaden your abilities. It is possible that your employer may be willing to do this if they want you to become more multi-skilled.

If you still feel unable to choose the option units that will suit you best after having worked through the table above, then consult your assessor. Your assessor is not only there to judge your performance against the standards that make up the qualification, but also to mentor and coach you through your qualification. Discuss any option units that may be suitable with your assessor and ask for help to decide which ones will be best for you.

As the qualification consists of such a large number of possible option units, this book only contains the most popular option units within the qualification framework: namely, option units 2, 6, 7, 9, 11 and 17. If the option units that you have identified as the best for you are not those that are contained within this book, you can obtain further information regarding the remaining option units from the CD-ROM. See page vii for more details on how to use the CD-ROM.

UNIT 1

Contribute to developing and maintaining positive caller relationships

This module is one of the three mandatory units. It is all about interacting with the caller in a way that presents the organisation and yourself in a positive and friendly manner whilst maintaining the organisation's service standards.

This unit has three elements:

♦ promote a positive image for the organisation by telephone
♦ communicate effectively by telephone
♦ manage difficult customers effectively.

After you have completed this unit, you will be able to:

♦ be an ambassador for your organisation – by being polite, courteous and, above all, professional
♦ take control of calls at the earliest opportunity – by assuming responsibility for any action points, encouraging the caller to take an active part in the conversation, addressing them personally, and confirming that you have accurately identified the caller's needs
♦ handle callers who have hearing or language difficulties with patience and understanding.

The case studies in this chapter are based on a fictitious office supplies company – 'Calhand Direct'. Examples from other sectors such as banking, insurance, telemarketing and travel will be covered in later chapters.

Case study 1 – Andy's experiences

The caller had placed an order with Calhand Direct for a particular length computer lead. He had ordered the 3-metre printer lead, catalogue number PL17285, and had been sent the 2-metre lead, PL17284. I agreed with the caller that this must have been very annoying and told him that I would sort it out straight away. I sent an immediate dispatch through to the warehouse for the lead to be sent out that day with guaranteed delivery before 10 a.m. the next morning. I also added a note that the wrong lead should be collected at the same time for return to stock.

The caller – Mr Davis – had been quite angry when I answered the call, but after I had apologised and explained that it was probably an error in dispatch, where the wrong lead had been picked up, Mr Davis accepted that this was the most likely cause. I informed Mr Davis that I would be entering him in our free draw for the Pentium 500 Desk Top System for his inconvenience (this is normally only open to customers who spend more than £50 in one order).

A week later I was called to my manager's office, where she explained that Mr Davis had written to customer relations saying that he was surprised at the speed the error was corrected and pleased with the professional way that I had dealt with his problem.

1 Did Andy take control of the call?
2 How did Andy balance the needs of the caller with the needs of the organisation?
3 By entering Mr Davis in the free draw did Andy actually give him anything extra?
4 Is it likely within your organisation that the wrong item could be collected at the same time as the correct item is being delivered?

1.1 Promote a positive image for the organisation by telephone

WHAT YOU NEED TO KNOW OR LEARN

◆ How to be prepared
◆ How to introduce yourself to callers
◆ How to demonstrate your listening skills
◆ How to create a positive impression
◆ How to promote a professional image
◆ How to handle callers with hearing or language difficulties
◆ How to close calls.

How to be prepared

'Be prepared' may be the motto of the scouting movement but it is also good advice for whatever role you play in life. If you are a decorator, the more thoroughly you prepare a surface before you start painting, the easier the painting will be and the better the results. This also applies to the call handling sector, where the more thorough your preparations are, the easier the work will become. When everything is to hand and you have confirmed that all the information you are likely to use is current, you can be confident that any information or advice you give is correct.

Without adequate preparation, you put yourself under pressure from the start. As soon as a caller asks for information that is not immediately to hand, you begin to founder. You start by delaying your response, or make excuses to the caller while you search for the information. If you cannot find it immediately, it is very likely that you will distract a colleague from his or her work in order to help you find the information.

If you have prepared well, then your self-confidence will be high and you will be convinced that you will be able to deal with the majority of calls without referring to anyone else. When all these factors come together you are off to a flying start in your contribution to developing and maintaining positive caller relationships.

What can you do to prepare for handling calls?

First, you should ensure that you know exactly what your areas of responsibility are and what targets, if any, you are expected to achieve. If this includes selling, you will need to know the range of products and services you are dealing with and whether there are any specific target areas and promotional or special offers available. If part of your responsibility is handling queries or requests for information you will need to know what information you are likely to require, and where it can be found.

You may be employed by an organisation that operates and runs call centres for other organisations. If so, you will need to be familiar with the products and services offered by each of your client organisations. You may even have to represent a different client's organisation every time you answer a call.

Second, you will need to ensure that all the reference material you are likely to use for information is current and up to date. You should also be aware of any memos or updates that may have been issued to correct information in your reference material.

Preparing your work area

Third, if you use computer databases as reference information or to record details of calls, you must have the necessary computer access to enable you to carry out your work. If this is not correct, you will need to speak to your supervisor or team leader to have your computer access amended by your local IT specialist.

Next, you need to ensure that you have all the consumable items you might need during your work period or shift, such as paper, pens and pencils. You can then make notes or jot down details during calls. These usually end up as scrap paper but can be invaluable at the time, especially to make a note of the caller's name.

Finally, you should ensure that your headset is working and adjusted correctly so that the microphone is not directly in front of your mouth, or too far away, so that your speech is clear and unmuffled. You may also need to adjust the headset volume control to a suitable level so that you can hear clearly.

Did you know?

When people experience difficulty hearing during a telephone call they have a tendency to raise their voice, assuming that the person at the other end is also experiencing the same problem.

Check it out

Do you need reference material to carry out your job? What reference materials do you use in your every day job? How do you ensure that the material is up to date?

How to introduce yourself to callers

Today everyone expects an excellent standard of customer service. How you greet the caller is an introduction to your organisation and yourself. Your introduction is the first contact that the caller has with your organisation and the old saying that 'first impressions count' is as important as ever, even when contact with the customer is not face to face. When you make or receive a call, you are representing your organisation. Competition across all sectors is such that if you upset a customer or fail to meet customers' expectations, even in your introduction, they are likely to take their business elsewhere.

Your greeting should be made in such a way that it captures the caller and leads them naturally into the body of the call. This is sometimes referred to as 'the verbal handshake'.

A 'verbal handshake' is a good way to start a call

Many organisations will expect you to demonstrate your friendliness and answer calls by thanking the caller for phoning your organisation. Other organisations will expect you to be very concise and to the point, an example of this is the emergency services, where time could be of the essence if it concerned a life or death situation.

If you are involved in initiating outbound calls your introduction has to hold the recipient's attention and allow you to explain the reason for making the call. If your job involves you in cold calling then it will require a lot of preparation and practice if you are to be successful at the task.

What makes a good verbal handshake?

As in everything we do or say, there are degrees of acceptability in a verbal handshake. Most people would agree that an inbound call that is left to ring without answer for several minutes and then answered with an incorrect or broken salutation is unacceptable – both to the caller and the employer. The minimum requirement for a good verbal handshake is usually a call that is answered within a certain number of rings, the person answering then gives the correct salutation in a positive, clear and concise voice that leaves the caller in no doubt that this person is there to deal with their call. To improve further, you will need to demonstrate your enthusiasm, sincerity and show a willingness to accept responsibility for the call and any actions that may result. If you can demonstrate all of this for every call, you will have achieved an excellent verbal handshake.

This should put the caller at ease, dispel any misgivings they may have, and make them feel that their call is important and not just another call for you to deal with.

Here are a few examples of typical introductions for inbound calls:

◆ *Thank you for calling Calhand Direct, my name is Jenny. How may I help you?*

- *My name is Andy, thank you for calling the flood line; can I take your postcode?*
- *Thank you for calling the order line, can I please take your account number?*
- *Emergency services, which service do you require?*

If your calls are outbound you will need to get over all the necessary information in a friendly, courteous and business-like manner without rushing, while still holding the attention of the person you are calling. You will need to maintain the goodwill of the person you have called during your introduction in order for that person to allow you to continue into the body of the call. We have all come across callers whose main aim is to get all the information over in the shortest possible time before the person being called has time to respond. In such cases the person is usually out of breath before they have finished and it is very obvious that they were ill prepared and had not practised what they had to say.

Your introduction for outbound calls should also put the person at ease, dispel any misgivings and make that person feel that he or she is an important part of the call. Here are a few examples of typical introductions for outbound calls:

- *Good evening, my name is Jenny. I am calling on behalf of Calhand Direct, we are conducting a survey into customer satisfaction. Could you spare two minutes?*
- *Mr Jones, my name is Andy, I am calling in response to the message you left the hospital appointment department. How may I help you?*
- *My name is Paul Edwards, I represent a company called Thermal Windows, have you seen our advert on the television?*

Identifying the caller

Another important part of any introduction is to establish the identity of the person you are talking to. This is best achieved in the early stage of the introduction as it personalises the conversation and brings the person directly into the conversation instead of having an unidentified voice at the end of the line.

Most people automatically give their name at the start of the calls they have originated, but there are others who will wait until asked. Asking can be as simple as, *'Who am I speaking to'* or *'Could I have your name please?'*. Always be in a position to write the person's name down whenever it is given.

If there is any doubt about the name don't be afraid to ask the caller to spell it for you. This could avoid problems later. It is always advisable to ensure that you have recorded the name correctly by repeating it back to the caller using the Phonetic Alphabet.

The Phonetic Alphabet is given below.

A	Alpha	N	November
B	Bravo	O	Oscar
C	Charlie	P	Papa
D	Delta	Q	Quebec
E	Echo	R	Romeo
F	Foxtrot	S	Sierra
G	Golf	T	Tango
H	Hotel	U	Uniform
I	India	V	Victor
J	Juliet	W	Whisky
K	Kilo	X	X-ray
L	Lima	Y	Yankee
M	Mike	Z	Zulu

Figure 1.1 The Phonetic Alphabet

You must make sure you are extremely familiar with this so that you can use it instinctively.

Try it out

Look at the following examples of the phonetic alphabet.

Adams   = ALPHA, DELTA, ALPHA, MIKE, SIERRA

Bramhall = BRAVO, ROMEO, ALPHA, MIKE, HOTEL, ALPHA, LIMA, LIMA

F362PXT = FOXTROT, 3, 6, 2, PAPA, X-RAY, TANGO

1 How would you use the phonetic alphabet for these three words: Liquor, script, vehicle?

2 Now try this out for the names of your family or your address. (Practice makes perfect!)

When you have confirmed the person's identity you should address them by name at every possibility. You should ensure you address them personally:

♦ at the beginning, '*What can I do for you this morning, Mr Jones?*'
♦ the end, '*Thank you for your order, Mr Jones. If I can be of any further assistance please call*'
♦ at all other relevant times throughout the call.

This is especially important when you find it necessary to demonstrate to the person that you are in control of the call, or when you are trying to overcome the person's objections.

Beware of possible dangers

If your organisation is one that encourages you to adopt a very friendly attitude to all callers you will need to be aware of possible cultural differences between yourself and the caller. Although the modern trend is towards adopting a less formal attitude, using first names or showing unnecessary familiarity to someone of a different gender, age or ethnic group may be viewed as disrespectful or unacceptable to some people. Many of the older generation were brought up in an era where the respect you received was in direct proportion to your age.

Set scripts

In order to portray themselves in the most advantageous light, some organisations employ experts to write set scripts that you are expected to follow throughout the call. These scripts usually highlight the organisation's name and usually lead the caller through all the products and services offered by the organisation. There are two main reasons behind such an approach. First, it educates the caller to all the products and services offered by the organisation. The majority of the callers to any organisation are usually only aware of a few of the services on offer, but by leading them through all of the products and services it can help stimulate demand for the full range. Second, by adopting a set script, the organisation maintains continuity in the way calls are handled.

Some organisations demand that the scripts are strictly adhered to, while others adopt a more flexible approach and allow agents freedom to make changes if this is advantageous to the organisation. Some are designed to capture all of the caller details, such as name, address, telephone number and in some cases personal details, before proceeding into the body of the call. In a few cases the system will not allow you to proceed further until all the details requested by the system have been supplied and entered into the database.

Example of a set script

Beverley	*Thank you for calling Caldirect, my name is Beverley, how may I help you?*
Mrs George	I would like to place an order.
Beverley	*Could I have your customer details please?*
Mrs George	Gave customer details and customer reference number.
Beverley	*Could I have details of your first item?*
Mrs George	Gave details of the first of seven items.
Beverley	Confirmed the details and entered the order into the computer system. Next item.

Mrs George	A new printer item number …………
Beverley	Confirms and enters details, at which point the screen flashes 'offer insurance'. Mrs George, as a company we have started to offer an extended warranty on all our electrical goods. Our terms are extremely competitive; can I interest you in taking it out.
Mrs George	How much is it going to cost?
Beverley	Gives details and convinces Mrs George to take out the extended warranty.

Check it out

Do you have one or more standard greetings within your organisation? Make a note of these.

How to demonstrate your listening skills

Whenever we hold any conversation, whether one to one or as part of a group, it is a natural instinct to look for indications that the person or persons you are talking to are interested and listening to what you are saying. When the conversation is taking place face to face, you are able to see the other person's body language, their facial expressions, and the amount of eye contact they are making with you. If the other person is

You can tell a lot about a person's attitude from their body language

interested and listening to what you have to say then they usually stand face to face near you (but not too close so as to infringe on your personal space), where they can hear clearly and be in a position to openly demonstrate that they are interested and listening.

Where the other person is not particularly interested in the conversation, they try to arrange their position so that their body language is hidden from the speaker. In this situation, it is common to find the parties side by side so that they hide the look of boredom from the other party. This position also allows them to be free to look around and focus on anything else that may catch their eye.

When the conversation is conducted by telephone the speaker has none of these clues to work out whether the other person is listening or not. We therefore have to find other methods.

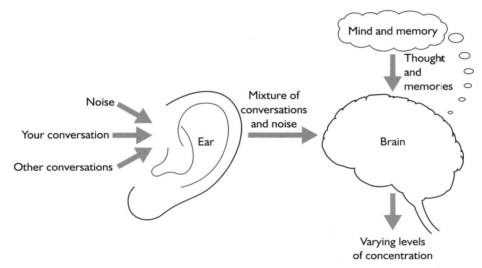

Causes of lack of concentration in conversation

The first and most important method is to listen actively to what the caller is saying. When we listen to a normal conversation, there are times when our concentration is not fully on what is being said and our minds often drift off for moments at a time. As the majority of conversations we hold in normal life are not of supreme importance, we can usually pick up the thread of the conversation quickly. When you are employed to answer calls and deal with requests for information and services, you need to concentrate and actively listen fully to what is being said. You will also need to be in a position where you are able to demonstrate to the caller that you have been listening and that you are interested in what they have said.

There are several techniques that you can adopt to demonstrate that you are listening. The first and easiest of these is to simply say *um, yes,* or *I understand* at appropriate moments during the conversation. These simple phrases have the same effect as a nod or shake of the head in a face to face conversation. They indicate that you are listening and understand what is being said, but not that you necessarily agree with the sentiment. The use of these words not only shows the caller that you are listening but also indicates that you are participating in the call.

Mrs Francis	*My name is Mrs Francis*
Sally	*Hello Mrs Francis, how may I help?*
Mrs Francis	*I ordered a self-assembly computer desk from you three weeks ago, and was told it usually takes two weeks to deliver.*
Sally	*Yes.*
Mrs Francis	*On Tuesday I received a call to say they would deliver it on Thursday morning. As I work on Thursday I arranged for my son to be there to take the delivery. The person who rang said they would call again just before they were due to arrive to get final directions.*
Sally	*Um.*
Mrs Francis	*He stayed in all day and heard nothing from them. I tried to call last night but you had already closed for the day, so I am ringing from work now to find out what is going on.*
Sally	*I'm sorry, if …*
Mrs Francis	*I'm not interested in how sorry you are, I want to know what you are going to do about it.*

Another technique is to paraphrase what the caller has said. This not only shows that you were listening but also demonstrates that you understand and can interpret what you have heard. When paraphrasing, you take whatever the caller has said and repeat it in a slightly different way. It also gives the caller the opportunity to correct any errors you have in your interpretation of what was said.

Mr Edwards	*I would like to place an order. I've got your catalogue in front of me. I want 24 black pens, item code number WK 2423; I also want 24 red, they are the same code number.*
Richard	*Can I repeat your order to you to confirm my understanding:* *Pilot Hi-Tecpoint Pen / Black / code number WK 2423B quantity 24, Pilot Hi-Tecpoint Pen / Red / code number WK 2423R quantity 24.*
Mr Edwards	*That is correct.*

Both these techniques can be used to demonstrate to the caller that you are listening and are a willing participant in the call. They also have the effect of encouraging the caller to continue with their participation in the call.

No matter how well you listen, there will be times when you will still be unsure what the caller is requesting. In such cases, you are within your rights to ask for details of the request to be repeated in order for you to clarify your understanding.

Beware of possible dangers
Continuous requests from you for the caller to repeat information or details will show that you are not listening properly.

How to create a positive impression

Your behaviour and telephone manner will not only affect the outcome of the call but can affect the person's perception of your organisation as a whole. If your attitude is positive, the person's impression is more than likely to be positive, but if your attitude is negative, the person is left with a negative impression of the organisation. To create a positive impression you will need to adopt a positive attitude and make a conscious effort to avoid taking any negative emotions forward from previous calls.

You will need to show that you are articulate by choosing a tone and pitch for your voice that will demonstrate to the caller that you are motivated and enthusiastic about answering and dealing with their call. You will need to demonstrate good listening skills and be able to convince the caller that you are courteous, friendly, honest and sincere. Your approach should be disciplined and sensitive to the needs of the caller and, where necessary, you should be able to empathise with the caller. You should demonstrate good common sense throughout the call, and where appropriate be willing to accept ownership of any actions that are necessary. All information you give should be accurate and all responses given by you should be consistent. You should always be positive and tell the person what you *can* do for them, not what you cannot do.

Having adopted the positive points you must avoid the negative points such as indecision, insincerity, indifference, apathy and disinterest. You should avoid interrupting the caller unless absolutely necessary and never patronise, be rude or get angry with the caller.

How to promote a professional image
What is a professional image?

A professional image is the overall perceived image of yourself and the organisation in the way that you deal with customers, your attitude towards them, and the effective way in which you achieve their requirements. It is the overall professionalism you display in your dealings with customers. This will include how you build up and maintain a rapport with the caller and how you overcome any opposition they may have to what you say or propose. It will also include how you leave them at the end of the call – was it on a positive or a negative note? Have you fulfilled the reason for their call and left the caller with a positive impression of yourself and the organisation?

How to achieve a professional image

One of the first requirements is to be well prepared and have a thorough knowledge and understanding of the products and services offered by your organisation.

Second, build on the relationship you start with the caller during your introduction and verbal handshake. With some practice you will be able to lead them into the body of the call where you allow them to identify their requirements or to explain the reason for making the call. Your contribution to the call should involve words and phrases they understand and should be positive throughout the call.

You should set the pace of the call so that it suits the needs of the caller, but at the same time be aware of the quality and level of service targets you are expected to achieve by your organisation. At times this may appear quite a juggling act, but it is important to balance the needs of the caller against the needs of your organisation.

Case study 2 – Jenny's experiences

The caller had been told to 'get some paper' by her boss. She didn't really know what she wanted. I asked the caller if they had used us before to supply their requirements, she confirmed they had, so I asked for their account number. I was then able to look back over the last three orders to see what had been ordered. I could see that they used a lot of copier paper, so I asked if their usage was the same as before and this was confirmed. I was able to inform her of the type and quantity they usually ordered, and she agreed to order the same amount this time. I also told her that they usually ordered toner for the copier at the same time. She checked her stock and said she would like to order three cartridges.

By looking at their previous orders it was easy to identify what they might need.

1 At what point did Jenny take control of the call?
2 Was effective use of questioning made? If so, what types of questions were used?
3 Do you look at previous caller contact within your organisation?
4 Did Jenny leave the caller with a positive image of herself and the organisation?
5 What do you think will be the caller's assessment of Jenny's professionalism?

Think about it

Think about the last few calls you have handled.

♦ Did you leave the callers with a positive image of you and the organisation?

♦ How would the callers have assessed your professionalism? If not, what could you have done differently?

Check it out

What are the main products and services offered by your organisation? Make a note of them all.

How to handle calls where the caller has hearing or language difficulties

People who experience difficulties with their hearing or language are usually very sensitive about the fact. Some will not accept they have a problem and will blame everyone and everything else rather than acknowledge it. Others appreciate they have a problem and will take steps to limit or overcome the effects. However, whether they accept they have a problem or not, they would still like to be treated in the same way as everyone else.

As you are the first point of contact that people have with your organisation, the onus is on you to be patient and try to identify the problem. This may involve you in asking some very sensitive questions to identify the problem and then to implement one of the procedures your organisation has already put in place for dealing with such a situation.

Hearing difficulties

The natural reaction of both the person who is beginning to experience hearing difficulties, and the person who is dealing with people with hearing difficulties for the first time, is to raise the voice in the hope that it may solve the problem. This usually makes matters worse instead of better. It is better to be patient, talk normally and discuss with the person the problems you are both experiencing.

People who appreciate and accept they have a hearing difficulty usually make arrangements to limit its effect or overcome the problem with the use of a hearing aid or a loud speaking telephone. In this case, all you have to do is to be patient and possibly speak more slowly while the instrument is being adjusted. Callers with major hearing difficulties are usually well prepared and may use a third person to make the call and translate the conversation into sign language. This allows the deaf person to be a full participant in the conversation. If you encounter such cases you will need to be very patient, limit the amount you say each time, and allow time for the third person to make the translation and receive the reply.

Some organisations have installed systems such as *Minicom* or a *Typetalk Service*, where people with hearing difficulties can ring dedicated telephone numbers and can be connected to an operator who will communicate via text messages.

Language difficulties

People with language difficulties may well suffer from the same frustrations as people with hearing difficulties, and again you may be required to be patient and speak slowly.

Organisations that receive significant numbers of calls from foreign or second language speakers usually employ people fluent in these languages in order to provide the required level of service. If you work for such an organisation you will normally be expected to try to identify which language the caller is using and transfer the call to a person within your organisation that speaks that language.

Some callers who expect to experience difficulties may come prepared with a third person to translate for them. In such cases the same principles apply as for the deaf person who uses a translator. You will need to be very patient, limit the amount you say each time, and allow time for the third person to make the translation and receive the reply.

There may be times where the caller knows that he or she has difficulty, but unfortunately a third person is not available to carry out the translation. In such cases you will need to use simple language and phrase questions in different ways so as to give the caller a better chance of understanding.

Check it out

Find out if your organisation has a policy for dealing with people with hearing or language difficulties. If so, what does it say? Where is this policy kept? Do you speak any other languages?

Case study 3 – Neema's experiences

The caller was partially deaf and this had left him with a speech impediment. He knew exactly what he wanted and got straight down to business. He had made a list from the catalogue and went through it methodically, he even asked me if I had understood or did I require him to repeat anything. Most people with hearing difficulties tend to use our fax facility, the catalogue has a section at the rear where you can pull out an order form and fill it in. You can then fax it direct to our free-phone fax number.

1 In the case study above the caller was very helpful, but what could have happened if he was not so helpful?
2 How would you have solved the problem if the caller had not been so helpful?

Think about it

Find out all you can about the Disability Discrimination Act 1995. See how the Act relates to how you should treat deaf people.

♦ What is the role of the RNID and how could they possibly help the situation?

How to close calls

Having led the caller through your introduction and the main body of your call, you will arrive at the point where you need to close the call. It is usually good to close on a high note. The use of, *'Thank you; bye'* will be seen as rather lame and lazy. The use of, *'Goodbye Mr Jones, thank you for calling'* may be better but it is well short of a high note; it is the minimum you should use for closing a call.

Ultimately you should be aiming to finish on a positive note where you summarise any key points or actions, thank the person for calling and leave them with the feeling that something has been achieved.

It is also helpful to remind the caller of your name and contact number should the person require any clarification or assistance with the content of the call. This implies to the caller that you are personally willing to accept responsibility for any future actions or queries he or she may have as a result of the call.

Below you can see how Andy from Case Study 1 may have closed the call to Mr Davis.

Case study 1 – continued

Mr Davis, before I close, I would like to summarise what we have agreed.
First, I will arrange for the new lead to be delivered by 10 a.m. tomorrow and at the same time have the other lead collected.
Second, I will arrange for you to be included in the prize draw I mentioned if you are happy with that.
Third, if you have any other queries please don't hesitate to call me, Andy, on the usual number; and finally I would like to apologise for the inconvenience you have been caused.
Goodbye Mr Davis, thank you for your call.

As you can see, Andy managed to satisfy all the above and add value to the call as far as Mr Davies was concerned.

You should always try to close calls on a positive note by confirming that the caller is satisfied with the outcome of the transactions you have made, thanking them for their custom and encouraging them to call again.

Some organisations will provide a set script for closing calls, with words that they have specifically chosen for this purpose, for example, the closing words used by one major fast food outlet, 'Have a nice day'. This may appear very corny or contrived but as an advertising gimmick, it has brought the company name to the fore. It is these ideas and innovations that bring customers back to the organisation. Striving to improve customer service is a constant activity.

Check it out

♦ Does your organisation have a closing statement? If it does, what does it say?

♦ Can you think of any other closing statements, such as 'Have a nice day'? If so, what are they?

♦ Which organisations use them?

Keys to good practice

✓ Be an ambassador for your organisation. Be polite, courteous and above all be professional.

✓ Confirm the details of people's name and address by repeating the details back using the Phonetic Alphabet. This can save confusion or even embarrassment later.

✓ Take control of the call at the earliest opportunity.

✓ Always assume responsibility for action points.

✓ Encourage callers to take an active part in the conversation.

✓ Address callers by name whenever possible.

✓ Always confirm your understanding of the caller's requirements before taking action.

✓ If callers have hearing or language difficulties be patient and understanding.

✓ Remember – when **you** take the call *you* are the organisation.

1.2 Communicate effectively by telephone

One of the dictionary definitions for the word *communicate* is 'succeeds in conveying information to evoke understanding'. The definition implies that there must be two or more people involved to be able to communicate: one passing the information and the others listening and understanding what is being said. In reality it is rare for information to flow in only one direction, it usually passes both ways, i.e. there is a conversation.

We all use conversations to tell others about our likes and dislikes. We also use them to inform others of our views and to tell them what we want. This is usually very easy when we are talking to our families and friends, but it may be different when we have to communicate with strangers. While most people are able to communicate effectively most of the time, others have difficulty explaining what they want and will need to be encouraged and directed in order to have their needs satisfied.

In this section we will look at what you will need to learn in order for you to communicate effectively by telephone.

WHAT YOU NEED TO KNOW OR LEARN

◆ Use of appropriate questioning techniques
◆ How to handle calls
◆ Transferring calls
◆ The effective use of resources
◆ Organisational requirements and responsibilities.

Use of appropriate questioning techniques

Before looking at the different types of questioning techniques, you need to understand why we ask questions.

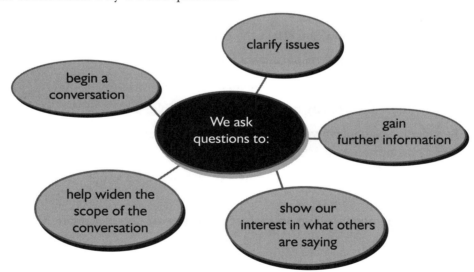

Figure 1.2 We ask questions for a number of reasons

There are only two basic types of questions: closed and open questions. You will need to identify which type of question is the most appropriate to use in the above situations.

Closed questions

Closed questions require a limited response from the recipient. The answer to a closed question will be 'yes' or 'no', or you present the caller with a number of options and ask him or her to select the appropriate one.

Examples of closed question include:

♦ *Which of the following options would you like to choose?*
♦ *Will you be able to attend on that day?*
♦ *Is that correct?*
♦ *Did you fill in the details first?*
♦ *Shall we leave this until later?*

Open questions

Open questions are designed to encourage the caller to talk and give as much information as possible in answer to the questions you pose. They are worded in such a way that the caller is not given the option of just saying 'yes' or 'no'.

Open questions usually begin with words like: *how, what, where, when, which, who and why.*

Examples of open questions include:

♦ *how did that work?*
♦ *what do you use your present machine for?*
♦ *where do you find the time to do that?*
♦ *why did you consider that option?*

If we now look back at why we ask questions you should be able to see which type of question will the be most appropriate in each case.

To begin a conversation

If you ask a closed question to begin a conversation you will probably find that it limits the conversation and may kill it dead. If you are trying to engage someone in conversation and you ask a simple question that only requires the other person to say yes or no, then in effect that exchange has ended and is unlikely to go any further. But if you ask an open question the other person has the opportunity to answer with as much detail as he or she likes. This response gives you the opportunity to ask further questions to expand on the details or submit differing views.

To gain further information

You can use either closed or open questions to gain further information. If it is your initial request for further information it may be more appropriate to ask an open question and allow the other person to give as much detail as he or she likes. But if you are attempting to home in on specific information, it may be more appropriate to ask a closed question. Where you have been given most of the information, and it is only necessary to confirm which of the options is correct, a closed question is the most appropriate.

To clarify issues

You are more than likely to ask a closed question to clarify an issue. You are likely to be asking for confirmation of your understanding of what the other person has said. If the other person's answer is positive, the issue is clarified; but if it is negative, you may need to pose an open question in order to satisfy your needs. In some situations you may have asked a closed question, and only be expecting confirmation, but the other person may try to expand on the reply. In such cases you may have to politely stop the other person, to avoid wasting time.

To help widen the scope of the conversation

This is very similar to the question that you use to start a conversation; if you choose a closed question the conversation is very likely to die. However, by using an open question you can lead the other person into other fields, which leaves them with very little option but to answer and widen the scope of the conversation.

To show interest in what others are saying

You can use either an open or closed question to show your interest in what the other person is saying. It will all depend on whether you are attempting to confirm your understanding, in which case it is likely to be a closed question similar to those used for clarifying issues. However, where your requirement is to obtain further information it is likely to be an open question.

Having looked at the two basic types of question, it is time to look at a third type – a probing question.

Probing questions

These are usually open questions, but they can be either open or closed. Probing questions are where you use information already given to you by the caller to target areas where you require additional information. They can be used to take you deeper into the subject you are already discussing, or to leave that subject and consider something outside the present discussion. They can be useful to lead callers into products and services that they had not previously considered.

Here are a few examples of probing questions that a person may use when trying to complete a sale of computer equipment. You should try to devise similar questions for the products and services your organisation has on offer:

♦ *There are several types of PC available that will meet the specification you have given, but they vary in speed and performance – what do you think you will use it for the most?*
♦ *You expressed an interest in publishing documents. We have several software packages available but can I ask you some more questions before I can advise which is best for you?*
♦ *At present we are doing a special deal on printers for people that purchase that type of machine. There are several models available. What quality and volume of printing do you intend to do?*

All three questions make use of information already given by the person. In the first, we have asked an open question to take the person deeper into the subject, but in the second we used a closed question to the same effect. The third demonstrates how a probing question can be used to lead the person to consider an item outside his or her original request.

Case study 4 – Winston's experience

The caller wanted one of our special offers that we had been promoting in the supplementary brochure, 'Everything you need for the office at home'. Fortunately the script took us through everything that needed to be considered.

Some of the questions went like this:

Q1　How big is the room?

Q2　There are several types of desk available and we have several that have space for a PC work station built in. Which do you think would best meet your needs for the space you have?

Q3　Would you like that in black or white?

Q4　Have you considered what type of answering machine you want? Digital? Tape with date and time stamp? Fax memory or straight to print?

Q5　Would you like an extension telephone to go with that?

Q6　We have that in cordless digital and analogue fixed line, do you think you will want to walk around whilst talking?

Look at the six questions above and note down whether you think each is an open, closed or a probing question.

How to handle calls

How you handle calls will depend on how well you have prepared. This is where you bring together your salutation, listening skills, questioning techniques and your professionalism. When applied together they will show you how well you have handled any particular call.

Having successfully completed your salutation and led the caller into the body of the call, it will be necessary for you to ask the caller appropriate questions which should be clear, concise and in a language that he or she understands. You should allow the caller sufficient time to answer the questions you have posed, giving verbal nods and paraphrasing where necessary. A verbal nod is where you simply say *um, yes,* or *I understand* at appropriate moments during the conversation. Paraphrasing is where you take whatever the caller has said and repeat it in a slightly different way.

You should seek clarification where required and ask probing questions if further information is required to identify the caller's requirements. You should remain totally in control of the call throughout, setting a pace that is comfortable for the caller, but remain aware of the organisation's standards and requirements. The call should follow its natural flow, with you regularly confirming your own and the caller's understanding. In general, you should avoid the use of jargon or abbreviations unless you are absolutely confident that the person you are dealing with has the same level of knowledge and understanding as yourself.

During the call you should always keep the caller informed of any actions you are taking. This is particularly important when you are updating screens, waiting for the computer system to display the information you have requested relating to the call or seeking advice or information that could occupy you offline. During the periods where you are inputting or checking data on your computer system it is an ideal time to ask the caller to confirm the details as you are inputting or checking.

If you have achieved all of this and generated a rapport with the caller so that the call sounded natural and you have remained in control of the call throughout – you have successfully handled the call.

See how successful you have been handling calls by assessing yourself against the following criteria. Think of your last call.

How well did you listen and ask questions?

Assess yourself now.

Assessment criteria	Quality of service	Your assessment
You are not listening to the caller; this is demonstrated by you asking the caller to repeat information already given.	Your handling of calls is poor and unacceptable	
You demonstrate you are listening by giving verbal nods.	Your handling of calls is acceptable	
You ask questions and demonstrate you are listening by giving verbal nods. You also use paraphrasing to confirm and demonstrate your understanding.	Your handling of calls is good	
You ask probing questions to gather additional information or lead the caller in the required direction. You also use verbal nods and paraphrasing to demonstrate you are listening and to clarify your understanding.	Your handling of calls is very good	
You achieve a quality of performance in excess of the above and you build a rapport with the caller so that the call sounds completely natural.	Your handling of calls is excellent	

How well did you control the call?

Assess yourself now.

Assessment criteria	Amount of control	Your assessment
The caller has to push and ask you for information.	Poor and unacceptable ☹	
You are asking questions but are not probing deeply enough to fully identify the caller's requirements.	Acceptable 😐	
You are controlling the questioning and using the caller's name to demonstrate authority. Your line of questioning is such that you have been gathering the facts and identifying the caller's requirements from the start of the call.	Good 🙂	
You achieve all the above and in addition identify solutions and make recommendations.	Very good 🙂🙂	
You remain solidly in control throughout the call and achieve a quality of performance in excess of the above. You also build a rapport with the caller so that the call sounds completely natural.	Excellent 🙂🙂🙂	

Don't be too disappointed if you cannot achieve the excellent standard immediately. You will need some experience and practice to achieve that standard, and even then it will be unlikely you can maintain it with every call. Callers can be very different and there will be times when you will have difficulty building a rapport with some of them.

Transferring calls

For the sake of simplicity we will consider the people who handle calls in three distinct areas: those that operate call handling facilities where callers can seek advice or help, order goods or services, or make appointments or bookings; telephone operators who man switchboards for connecting calls; and office receptionists who deal with office visitors and answer incoming telephone calls. The person who mans the call handling facility will usually deal with the calls from start to finish and will only consider transferring them if the caller asks to speak to someone personally or the call requires the authority of someone senior. However, the transferring of calls is a major part of the call handling function of telephone operators and office receptionists.

Call handling facility agents

If you are employed as an agent in a call handling facility, your organisation will expect you to be able to deal with the vast majority of calls without reference to anyone else. The callers themselves will also expect a 'one-stop shop' to deal with all their enquiries and problems. Therefore transferring calls should only be considered as a last resort.

Telephone operators and office receptionists

The call handling of the majority of the people working in this area will involve answering calls, identifying who the caller would like to speak to, and connecting them to the appropriate person or department. As more and more organisations introduce modern telephone facilities even this is quickly coming to an end, as companies can publish the extension telephone numbers of their employees and expect outside callers to ring the person or department directly.

How to transfer calls

This is one of the areas of call handling which can cause most annoyance to callers and be responsible for many of the problems associated with call handling if it is not carried out correctly. In order for you to identify a necessity to transfer the call, the caller will have given you a lot of detail and information as to the reason why he or she is calling. If you just transfer the call without any explanation, the new recipient of the call will expect the caller to start all over again. The caller will find this extremely annoying and frustrating. It is therefore up to you to pass on as much information as possible to avoid the caller having to repeat all the details.

Whenever you are transferring a call, you should always ensure that the caller is kept informed of what you are doing. If you have to place the caller on hold while you explain the reason to the other person, it is advisable to update the caller periodically if there is some delay in completing the transfer.

It is not unknown for calls to fail during the transfer process, therefore it is advisable to inform callers where they are being transferred to. You should always give the name of the person and the telephone number so that, should the call fail, the caller has the opportunity to call the person direct without having to go through the same process.

Some organisations have set procedures for transferring calls between people or departments, in which case these should be followed.

An example of a typical procedure for transferring a call
1 Only transfer calls when it is absolutely necessary – transferring should be seen as the last resort. Try to own the call, it will help build your confidence.
2 Explain to the caller that it will be necessary for you to transfer the call to a colleague and you will be placing them on hold while you check if they are available.
3 Check if the colleague is available and willing to accept the call.
4 Return to the caller, thank them for holding and explain that you are able to transfer the call; give the name, department and telephone number of your colleague; and then explain that you are going to place them on hold while you explain the details to your colleague.

5 Return to the colleague and give them the following information:

   a customer's name

   b customer company name, if applicable

   c exact details of the request

   d any account reference numbers, if applicable

   e any other relevant facts.

6 Return to the caller, thank them for holding and tell them that you are about to transfer their call.

Check it out

♦ Does your organisation have a procedure for transferring calls?

♦ What does it tell you to do? Make a note of this.

♦ Where is the procedure documented within your organisation?

♦ Write it down and keep it as evidence.

Case study 5 – Andy's experiences

The caller, Mr Johnson, told me that he telephoned yesterday and spoke to Jenny; she couldn't answer his questions regarding his last invoice but transferred him to the accounts department. The lady there was kind enough to explain his invoice to him and explained what the item codes meant. Since then he had thought of a couple more questions he would like to ask, and wanted me to put him through to accounts again.

I said, 'Of course, sir, please hold whilst I transfer you. There may be a slight pause while I pass on your details to accounts, so that you don't have to repeat them again.'

I What else would it be useful to ask Mr Johnson so that a seamless transfer can be implemented (e.g. invoice number)?

2 What other key information should you obtain from the caller before attempting to transfer the call?

3 What would you do if the caller were lost whilst on hold?

4 What would you do if you couldn't transfer the caller to the accounts department because all lines are busy?

The effective use of resources

The resources available are the tools of your trade and it is your duty and responsibility to make efficient and effective use of them. If they are physical resources you will need to know how to use them, and what they are capable of doing. If they are reference material you should know what information they contain, how they can be accessed, and where they can be found. This is especially so in the call-handling sector where information can change on a daily basis as organisations fight to survive.

Examples of some of the resources you may be using include:

♦ communications systems, such as telephones, fax and email
♦ information screens, directories and catalogues
♦ materials such as stationery and office equipment
♦ information, both internal and external to the organisation
♦ time – both organisational and personal.

Many of you will be using computer systems at work to run software applications that contain information you will need or that require you to input data. You have a responsibility to be fully conversant with these applications and the information they contain. It is likely that your organisation will update these applications on a regular basis, but there will be times between the regular updates when they may need to implement changes for immediate effect. The issue of information sheets, which they expect you to action immediately, usually does this. It is therefore an essential part of your job to familiarise yourself with the changes to the software applications and to read, digest and action all information sheets released in the interim.

Many of you will also use publications such as timetables and catalogues which you may only use infrequently; therefore the requirement for them to be included as a computer application will be a low priority. In such cases it is your responsibility to check and confirm that the issue you are using is current and the information up to date.

You must also remember that your time is a valuable resource. You are employed by your organisation to carry out a particular function for which you are paid; therefore, your employer will expect you to carry out that job in a professional manner.

Organisational requirements and responsibilities

Whatever the nature of your organisation's business, it is almost certain that it will have some form of controls and restrictions – whether mandatory or advisory – recommended by the government or the laws of the land. As an employee of your organisation these controls and restrictions also apply to you in varying degrees. These could include the Data Protection Act or legislation restricting the sale of certain products to people under a certain age.

Check it out

♦ Are there any controls or restrictions imposed that affect your job role?

Your employer will also impose rules and responsibilities which you will be expected to obey and accept, and which will normally form part of your terms of employment. These could include:

♦ working within your authority
♦ meeting targets set by the organisation
♦ maintaining the quality standards imposed by the organisation
♦ balancing the needs of the caller with those of the organisation.

Working within your authority

Your organisation may stipulate levels of authority over which you cannot go when handling calls. These may be financial limits, above which you cannot authorise transactions, or it may be a contractual limit above which you cannot commit the organisation.

Where limits to the level of authority are imposed, organisations have usually put in place procedures where these limits can be exceeded with the agreement of a manager or team leader. However, it should be remembered that your manager or team leader will also have a limit imposed to his or her level of authority, which they cannot exceed. There will be times when you consider the level of authority to be an inconvenience, but you would need the wider picture of the organisation's overall commitments and strategy to understand its necessity.

Meeting targets set by the organisation

Targets will vary considerably across the whole of the call handling sector so all we can do here is to consider some of the basic ingredients of the targets.

The majority of organisations set targets based on:

◆ your rostered hours
◆ the number of hours you are logged onto the system ready to accept calls
◆ the number of calls you deal with
◆ the amount of sales you achieve in the period.

As you can see from the example below, using these basic ingredients your organisation can produce a series of targets to measure your performance. These could include:

◆ calls handled per hour
◆ average duration of calls
◆ sales per hour
◆ sales per call
◆ percentage of time spent on Not Ready
◆ percentage of hours logged on against calculated hours.

| TEAM | | TRAIL BLAZER 2 | | | | | | | | | |
| DATE: | | Aug-01 | | | | | | | | | |

SALES REVENUE

Name	Total Sales Week 1	Total Sales Week 2	Total Sales Week 3	Total Sales Week 4	Total Sales Week 5	Total Sales Month	Monthly Target	Percentage of Target	Total No of Calls	Total No of Sales	Av Value / sales call
Abel	£ 4,234.24	£ 5,267.19	£ 5,367.89	£ 5,201.93	£ 4,893.56	£ 24,964.81	£ 25,000.00	99.86%	2278	492	£ 50.74
Ben F	£ 4,196.23	£ 4,896.34	£ 5,189.45	£ 5,027.89	£ 5,023.40	£ 24,333.31	£ 25,000.00	97.33%	2014	463	£ 52.56
Clair H	£ 4,563.50	£ 4,924.50	£ 4,907.45	£ 5,010.23	£ 5,184.70	£ 24,590.38	£ 25,000.00	98.36%	2301	460	£ 53.46
Donia F	£ 4,489.23	HOLS	£ 5,401.16	£ 5,398.07	£ 5,390.87	£ 20,679.33	£ 20,000.00	103.40%	1834	342	£ 60.47
Ethel	£ 4,747.46	£ 5,367.00	£ 5,367.19	£ 5,298.54	£ 5,421.92	£ 26,202.11	£ 25,000.00	104.81%	2178	473	£ 55.40
Fiona	HOLS	£ 5,456.00	£ 5,567.05	£ 5,023.60	£ 5,100.34	£ 20,946.99	£ 20,000.00	104.73%	1934	372	£ 56.31
Gary	£ 5,056.98	£ 5,567.67	£ 5,341.80	£ 5,401.28	£ 5,402.80	£ 26,770.53	£ 25,000.00	107.08%	2376	501	£ 53.43
Henry	£ 2,567.78	£ 5,217.56	£ 5,301.23	£ 5,807.90	£ 5,428.34	£ 24,322.81	£ 25,000.00	97.29%	2287	482	£ 50.46
Ian	£ 5,102.62	£ 5,498.50	£ 5,502.68	£ 6,002.12	£ 5,692.05	£ 27,797.97	£ 25,000.00	111.19%	2367	532	£ 52.25
Janet	£ 5,069.23	£ 5,336.67	£ 4,587.27	£ 5,601.73	£ 5,707.90	£ 26,302.80	£ 25,000.00	105.21%	2398	498	£ 52.82
Keith	£ 4,879.45	£ 5,476.01	£ 5,601.00	£ 5,790.34	£ 5,512.83	£ 27,259.63	£ 25,000.00	109.04%	2401	518	£ 52.62
Leane	£ 4,962.90	£ 4,956.03	£ 5,004.98	£ 4,997.23	£ 5,017.90	£ 24,939.04	£ 25,000.00	99.76%	2257	467	£ 53.40
Mary L	£ 2,989.38	£ 4,735.94	£ 4,867.95	£ 4,946.21	£ 5,000.78	£ 22,540.26	£ 23,000.00	98.00%	2149	429	£ 52.54
TOTAL	£ 52,859.00	£ 62,699.41	£ 67,807.10	£ 69,507.07	£ 68,777.39	£ 321,649.97	£ 313,000.00	102.76%	28774	6029	£ 53.35
TARGET	£ 59,600.00	£ 59,600.00	£ 64,600.00	£ 64,600.00	£ 64,600.00	£ 313,000.00					
% Achieved	88.69%	105.20%	104.96%	107.60%	106.47%	102.76%					

Figure 1.3 An agent league table

Maintaining the quality standards imposed by the organisation

Nearly all organisations involved in the call handling sector will have quality standards, which they will expect you to maintain. There are basically two ways in which any organisation can measure whether you are achieving these standards.

The first is by carrying out a customer satisfaction survey with a proportion of the callers you have dealt with. Such surveys usually involve asking the callers whether they were satisfied with the way in which you handled the call; whether you were courteous; answered their questions directly; and achieved what they required from the call. These surveys can provide valuable information about the callers' perceived quality of the organisation, but they can be time consuming. They also show callers that, as an organisation, they are interested in the views of the caller.

The second method of ensuring that quality standards are being maintained is to monitor or record calls. Some organisations will monitor or record all calls, while others will only cover a percentage.

The monitoring and recording of calls

Apart from quality control, there are many reasons to monitor and record calls, including establishing facts, or to prevent or detect crimes. Although the majority are legitimate there could be others, which could be considered dubious. In order to prevent illegal use of monitoring and recording of calls, the government has implemented laws to protect the public. The following law applies – see below.

Telecomms Regulation/Telecomms Licence/Lawful Business Practice Regulations state that:

Businesses will be authorised to monitor or record all communications transmitted over their systems without consent for the following purposes:

a Establishing the existence of facts

b Ascertaining compliance with regulatory or self-regulatory practices or procedures

c Ascertaining or demonstrating standards which are achieved or ought to be achieved by persons using the system

d Preventing or detecting crime

e Investigating or detecting unauthorised use of the business's telecoms system

f Ensuring the effective operation of the system.

The regulations also allow businesses to monitor, but not record, communications for the following purposes:

g Checking whether or not communications are relevant to the business

---

h Monitoring calls to confidential, counselling helplines run free of charge.

The regulations also authorise public authorities to monitor or record in the interest of national security.

In all these cases, the regulations require the businesses to 'make all reasonable efforts' to inform those people who use the organisation's telecoms systems that interception may be taking place.

If your organisation is one of the many that records calls, it should be doing so only for one of the above reasons and it should be making all reasonable efforts to inform the callers that it is happening.

Some organisations will instruct you to inform all callers that conversations may be monitored or recorded, as part of your introduction to the caller. Others may pre-empt this by preparing a recorded message that is automatically played to all inbound callers before the calls are answered by an agent or operator.

These messages usually thank callers for calling the organisation and inform them that they are at present in a queue waiting for an agent or operator to become free to answer their call. The message continues to inform the caller that calls may be monitored or recorded, and usually explains the reason why. This is usually either for security reasons or training purposes.

If your organisation is one that monitors or records conversations and it adopts either of the two methods of informing callers then it can be deemed as complying with the law and no further action is required. This is a matter for the organisation and not yourself.

Check it out

♦ Does your organisation record calls? If so, does your organisation inform the callers?
♦ What does your organisation say? Make a note of this.
♦ Does your organisation explain to the caller the reason for monitoring or recording the calls?

Balancing the needs of the caller with those of the organisation
Beside the requirements your organisation will impose on you, you will also have responsibilities to the caller. In the majority of cases you are the person your organisation has selected to accept the responsibility to accept orders, give advice or make arrangements on behalf of the caller. Therefore *you* are responsible for ensuring that the customer's request is dealt with fairly and promptly within your authority and responsibilities. In the process of you handling calls, you are gathering information from the caller, which they have a right to expect you to treat in confidence.

The importance of confidentiality

No matter which part of the call handling sector you work in, there will be times when you will be given information by a caller that they will expect you to treat as given to you in confidence. This could include information about their bank account, credit card, health, relationships, or personal preferences; the list is endless. Callers not only expect you to treat this information in confidence but also have a right to expect you to do so.

Callers can expect you to limit your collection of information to that which is relevant to the purpose for which it is to be used. This purpose should be specified at the time and its subsequent use limited to the fulfilment of that purpose.

Information you collect in this way should be held in confidence and used only for the business of the caller and should not be disclosed to anyone other than the officers, directors or employees of your organisation with a specific need to know.

1.3 Manage difficult callers effectively

Here we will look at what constitutes difficult callers, try to understand what causes them to be difficult, suggest ways in which to handle them, and identify possible further actions if all else fails.

It is inevitable that at some time in your life you will come into contact with someone who is difficult to handle, whether it is over the telephone or face to face. In general, people are more likely to be aggressive or abusive over the telephone than they are in a face to face confrontation. In a face to face confrontation everything is more personal, the comments and verbal abuse are being directed at you, and there is always the danger that things can get out of hand and verbal abuse turns into physical abuse. Over the telephone people are freed from the direct contact and probably see you as just a voice at the other end of the line. The aggression or abuse is directed at the system or the organisation and very rarely at you, even though you are in the direct line of fire.

WHAT YOU NEED TO KNOW OR LEARN

♦ Different types of difficult callers you may encounter
♦ How to handle difficult callers
♦ How to remain calm when faced with a difficult situation
♦ Possible further actions when dealing with difficult callers.

Case study 7 – David's experiences

The caller was absolutely fuming. She had taken the day off work to stay at home to accept delivery of the PC workstation – catalogue number PCW2294. It goes out as a flat pack system for home assembly – well you can't exactly get it through the letterbox.

Anyway by 4 p.m. it hadn't arrived and Mrs Edwards wanted to know where it was and what we were going to do about it. I immediately took responsibility for the problem and told her I would try and find out what had gone wrong.

Rather than keep her hanging on the telephone I took the order number she had been given and said I would call her back within 20 minutes. I put the order number into the system and it immediately brought up Mrs Edward's details; she was correct in that it was listed for delivery today, 22 January. I got onto warehousing and distribution to find out what had gone wrong. Having unique order numbers makes cross-referencing easy; dispatch identified which van it had gone out in within 5 minutes. Unfortunately, the van had been involved in a major pile up at junction 10 on the M6 at about 11.30. Everything was a complete write off. Fortunately, the van driver was OK with only minor abrasions but everything in the van was damaged.

I got back to Mrs Edwards and explained what had happened. She could see that this really was beyond our control but that we still needed to deliver the goods. I suggested that we could list the workstation for delivery Saturday morning (she works Monday to Friday, 9 to 5), or if that wasn't possible did she know a neighbour who would accept it on her behalf? Mrs Edwards said that next Saturday morning would be fine. I thanked her for her call and told her I would get straight onto dispatch and arrange for another one to arrive Saturday morning. I made sure that I told her my name and the reference number relating to the actions I had taken and that she should contact us if she had any further problems.

1   Do you have unique identifying numbers within your organisation?
2   Could this order have been organised so that it was delivered on a Saturday in the first instance – to avoid the caller having to take the day off work?
3   Would you have sufficient authority to be able to reschedule transactions?
4   Do you think David could have handled this any differently?

Different types of difficult callers you may encounter

There are five types of difficult callers that we are going to consider here. They are:

♦ aggressive
♦ abusive
♦ confused
♦ distressed
♦ insistent.

Aggressive callers

There are three basic types of aggressive people: people who are aggressive by nature, people who show aggression as a driving force and people who become aggressive as a result of drink or drugs. The people who are aggressive by nature take us back to the evolution theory where aggression allowed the fitter and stronger animals to carve out larger areas of territory or have a greater number of mates, therefore ensuring their genes survived into the next generation. Today, direct aggression is not normally tolerated by society; the majority of people who are aggressive by nature are usually highly competitive.

Aggression as a driving force occurs when frustration and tension builds up as a result of a grievance of some kind. Aggression is not the first reaction of this type of person. They have usually had a problem or complaint which they have tried to sort out, but their attempts have been thwarted by the lack of action by the organisation or system. The build up of frustration and tension continues until the person becomes aggressive and releases them.

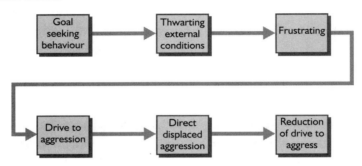

Figure 1.4 The different stages of aggression

Most people who become aggressive as the result of drink or drugs are also not aggressive and abusive by nature. The effect of the drink or drugs helps them lose any fear or misgivings they may have had and feeds their bravado. It also makes them argumentative. Their aggressiveness can be triggered by a relatively minor thing that they appear to blow up out of all proportion, and in a few cases the original cause is long forgotten.

Abusive callers

Abusive callers usually start by being aggressive but, when they think their grievance is not being dealt with as they would like, they turn abusive. This can be the result of frustration or an inability to express themselves.

Confused callers

Confusion is not just the domain of the old and infirm – anyone can become confused. Even some of the younger generation can be very unsure and confused when they are required to talk to anyone other than their friends. When pushed to make a call to someone unknown they will ask for help and assurance as to what to do and say.

Some people are not comfortable using the telephone. They have to build themselves up before attempting to use the telephone, even to the extent of preparing a list of things they have to do and say. When you answer their call and you ask for details or information that is not readily available, they can become very confused and even have a panic attack. Thankfully this is a rare occurrence.

Your attitude can also make callers confused. Callers can become flustered and confused if you demand information that is not readily to hand. This type of confusion is common when organisations give you a script to follow and you doggedly follow it without regard for the requirements of the caller. Also some callers can be easily intimidated and if you start the 'hard sell' they will become flustered and confused.

Distressed callers

Some of you will rarely have contact with callers who are distressed while others will be dealing with them on a regular basis. If you are involved with any of the emergency services, vehicle breakdown services, doctors or hospitals, it is likely that a high proportion of your calls will involve callers in a distressed state. Anything out of the ordinary that happens to a person has the ability to make them distressed. This could include becoming ill or feeling unwell, being involved in accidents or fires, becoming lost, or being bereaved.

Insistent callers

Insistent callers are people who feel they have a point to make and they are going to make it regardless of anyone else. They are usually articulate and can make their case forcefully. Their grievances may be genuine, in which case they will demand reparation; or they may be the result of a misunderstanding, in which case this can be explained or corrected.

Think about it

Think of a situation where you have dealt with a difficult caller.
♦ How did you deal with the call?
♦ How did you feel immediately after you had dealt with the call?

How to handle difficult callers

From the last section you can see that there are five basic types of difficult callers that you may need to deal with: aggressive, abusive, confused, distressed and insistent callers.

Aggressive and abusive callers

The first step in dealing with these types of callers is to try to avoid a situation arising where they can become aggressive or abusive in the first place. Remember the saying, 'Prevention is better than cure'.

Most callers will appear normal when you first answer the call and it is only when you have talked to them that the frustration and tension builds up to the extent where it has to be released by an outburst of aggression and possibly abuse. It may not be your fault that the person became frustrated and tense, it is likely that it has been building up over a period of time and you were the catalyst to trigger the explosion.

In order to prevent this happening, it is essential that you are fully trained regarding the products and services offered by your organisation and are very familiar with the company's procedures. This will mean you handle calls more efficiently and answer all the caller's questions satisfactorily, which is less likely to add to the caller's frustration and tension.

This is not a panacea for dealing with all aggressive and abusive callers. There will always be some who will still get aggressive and/or abusive no matter what you do or say.

When faced with this situation the following advice should be helpful:

♦ try not to panic or close the call immediately
♦ try not to lose your temper
♦ don't be tempted to react in a similar way
♦ try not to take the remarks personally
♦ don't become upset
♦ remain patient
♦ listen to what the caller is saying; giving verbal nods to reaffirm you are listening
♦ try to calm the situation by addressing the caller by name
♦ if the caller does not calm down, clearly advise them that unless they are prepared to continue the discussion in a civil manner, you will have no option but to terminate the call
♦ if the caller calms down and you are able to continue, but he or she is not satisfied with your answers to their questions, offer to pass the call to a colleague or supervisor, or offer to call them back when you have investigated further
♦ if, despite a warning the aggression and abuse continues, then you may have no alternative but to terminate the call.

It is possible that your organisation will have policies and procedures for you to follow in cases where you are subjected to aggressive and or abusive calls. If available these should be followed.

Such policies and procedures usually include when and under what circumstances you can terminate or transfer a call to your supervisor. This may include your responsibilities as a call handler and those of the supervisor and manager. They may also detail how and when you should report such calls to your supervisor. Whether or not your organisation has such policies and procedures in place, it is always good practice to report any incidence of such calls to your supervisor as soon as practically possible.

At the end of a call where aggression and or abuse has been used towards you it may take some time for you to calm down. No matter how experienced you may be, there will be times when you will feel upset by what was said. If this is so then you will need to take a break away from handling calls to collect your thoughts or to speak to a colleague. If you don't there is a great danger that you will carry forward the effects on to your next and subsequent calls.

Case study 8 – Fiona's experiences

About six weeks ago I took a call from a Mr Stephens. He seemed polite. I asked for his customer reference number and called the screen up. A message flashed up saying, 'don't accept any further orders, refer all enquiries to the Credit Control Department'.

I politely explained this to Mr Stephens, at which point he started to become aggressive saying organisations like ours had it in for small businesses like his, and we are trying to put him out of business. I tried to explain that was not the case and if he would allow me to transfer him to the Credit Control Department the matter could easily be resolved.

At this point he started to get abusive, calling me names and casting doubts about my parentage. I remember saying, 'Mr Stephen, if you don't calm down and act in a civilised manner I will have no option but to terminate the call'. There was then a pause after which I repeated the fact that if he allowed me to transfer the call the matter might easily be resolved. He grunted OK. I transferred the call.

After I had transferred the call I was visibly shaking, so I logged off and went to the toilet and had a drink of water. After 10 minutes I was feeling better and went and logged on again.

About three weeks ago on the Wednesday I answered a call in my usual way by saying, 'Thank you for calling the organisation, my name is Fiona, how may I help you'; when I heard his voice again. I felt the colour drain from my face. He asked if there was anyone else called Fiona working for the company, I said no. He explained who he was and said he hoped I would forgive him for the outburst he had put me through three weeks previously. He explained that the person who worked for him had been taken ill and had been off work for 4 weeks prior to the outburst. He said things had built up to the point where he was working 18 hours a day to try to fulfil the orders. I accepted his apology.

On the Friday after, at about 11 o'clock, someone came into reception and asked for me. It was the local florist, with a large bunch of flowers that had a message attached, thanking me for my understanding and saying it would never happen again.

My colleague and friends gave me some stick, trying to find out who was sending me flowers at work. I never explained, I just left them wondering.

1 Do you have policies and procedures in place for dealing with such incidents?
2 Did Fiona do the right thing in accepting Mr Stephens's apology so readily?
3 How well do you think Fiona handled the situation?
4 Do you think Fiona could have handled this any differently?

Confused callers

Some callers will be confused when you answer their call, being uncertain about what they require and hoping you will be able to tell them. Others will appear calm and in control at first but may become confused and flustered when you start asking questions to discover their requirements.

When faced with either of these situations the following advice should be helpful:

◆ remain calm
◆ be patient
◆ explain calmly the options available to them
◆ where possible ask closed questions, giving the caller options to choose from
◆ give reassurance, where necessary.

Hopefully, confused callers will respond to you and you will be able to provide the service they require.

Distressed callers

Callers can be distressed for many reasons and it is possible that they may need to be handled in different ways. Callers who report accidents, fires, or emergency situations will need to be handled calmly, sensitively, and firmly until you have gathered all the facts and been able to dispatch the necessary services. Until this point there will be no time for niceties if a life or lives may be in danger. Once the facts have been determined, and the appropriate service dispatched, the caller may require your calm support and reassurance until the dispatched services arrive.

Callers who are distressed as a result of illness or being bereaved will need to be treated calmly and sympathetically while you question them to discover what is the matter and how you can help. You may need to avoid empathising too much as it may result in the person becoming very emotional. In general distressed people respond favourably if they are supported and the cause can be identified and procedures quickly put in place to solve or alleviate their problems.

Insistent callers

Probably the best way to handle an insistent caller is to remain calm and let the person have their say. Usually there is little point in attempting to stop the person as it may well inflame the situation. The person is usually determined that he or she is going to tell you what they think. Listen and try and discover what is the cause of the problem or grievance. If it is genuine, apologise and try and put it right. If it is the result of a misunderstanding, take control of the conversation and calmly explain when and how the misunderstanding may have arisen. Try to avoid getting involved in an argument.

If the person is not satisfied with your attempts to make amends or explain the reason for the problems or grievance, then offer to transfer the call to a team leader or manager to solve.

There are no guaranteed ways of dealing with difficult callers; you will usually need to see what works best for you. You may find that your organisation publishes guidelines for you to follow when dealing with difficult callers. If so you should follow these.

Check it out

- ◆ Does your organisation have guidelines for dealing with difficult callers?
- ◆ What are these? Make a note of them to keep as evidence.

How to remain calm when faced with a difficult situation

Whatever type of difficult caller you are required to deal with, the most important point is always to remain calm. If the situation you are dealing with becomes aggressive or abusive, if you remain calm there is a likely possibility that the other person will calm down and let you talk to them. It is also imperative that you remain calm whenever the call is full of tension, such as when someone is summoning help to an accident, fire, or a vehicle breakdown.

A caller may be very distressed and need your help. Always remain calm

How do you remain calm in difficult situations?

Most of this will come with experience. However, at first you are likely to feel the adrenalin flowing whenever such an occasion arises; this is not a bad thing, but you cannot survive on adrenalin all the time. Some situations will be emotionally draining, but you must continue as though nothing is affecting you. After it is all over you can release your emotions and show that you have been affected.

The following are useful hints on how to remain calm:

- ◆ take a deep breath
- ◆ remain dispassionate

- remain emotionally aloof
- avoid confrontations.

Where the other person is aggressive and/or abusive, you must ignore any insults and threats whether they are directed at you or in general. If you react, the other person has won and he or she will be encouraged to continue, but if you remain calm then he or she will see that it is not going to be easy to draw you into the argument, and will hopefully give up.

There may also be situations that will be very emotionally charged, such as road traffic accidents where children are involved or where there are life-threatening illnesses. It is essential that you remain dispassionate and emotionally aloof in order to be able to operate efficiently and effectively.

Possible further actions when dealing with difficult callers

Imagine that you have tried all possible ways to handle a call from a difficult caller – all to no avail. You have tried listening and reasoning, and you have remained calm throughout, but you are still having difficulty. What other actions are available to you?

You can:

- seek advice
- transfer the call to your supervisor or another suitable person
- arrange for the relevant person to return the call
- terminate the call.

Whichever option you select, you should always advise the caller of your intentions before taking the action. This should avoid the caller becoming even more difficult.

Seek advice

When seeking advice about how to handle difficult callers, it is appropriate to go to your supervisor or some other person in authority. This may save you problems in future if any other action is taken with regards to the difficult caller. Advice from colleagues may be inappropriate if the matter gets out of hand.

You must be prepared to summarise the call so far and explain what actions you have already taken. If the person you go to gives you advice, you should follow it, or else be prepared to justify your actions and explain the reason for ignoring it.

Transfer the call

It is very likely that the person you asked for advice will tell you to transfer the call to them. If so, you should tell the caller you are going to transfer them, you should tell them the name of the person you are transferring them to and explain the reason why you are transferring them. You should then transfer the call.

If, during your conversation with the caller, you identify a person who is more appropriate than your supervisor to take the call, then you should contact this person and ask if they are prepared to talk to the caller. Again you should be prepared to summarise the call so far and explain what actions you have already taken.

Arrange for the relevant person to return a call

If after a conversation with a difficult caller you are unable to help, but you have identified an appropriate person who may be able to help, you should attempt to contact the person. But if that is not possible you should advise the caller that you will arrange for the person to call them back.

In such cases you should discuss with the caller what might be an appropriate time for the person to ring back, but on no account make any firm promises.

When making arrangements with the person to ring the caller back, it is advisable to give the person as much information as possible about the conversation, and the actions and advice you have already given the caller. This may be in the form of an email, note or voice bank.

Terminate the call

Terminating a call should only be undertaken as a last resort when everything else has been tried. The caller should be advised that he or she has left you no other option but to terminate the call.

Keys to good practice

✓ Build empathy; try to put the caller at ease.

✓ Address the caller by their name when appropriate.

✓ Develop and maintain a supportive atmosphere.

✓ At all times remain calm.

✓ Maintain effective control and take responsibility for the problem.

✓ Try to manage the expectations of the caller wherever possible.

Check your knowledge

1 List four things you need to do to prepare for handling calls.
2 Use the Phonetic Alphabet to spell EXAMPLE.
3 Why is it important to finish a call on a positive note?
4 What do the initials RNID stand for?
5 Why is it important to address a caller by their name?
6 When would you use an open question?
7 Closed questions normally only receive one-word responses – what can they be used for?
8 How can the different types of questions be combined to gain the most information?
9 When is the most appropriate time to ask a probing question?
10 List three of the most important stages of transferring a call.
11 For what two purposes can a business legitimately monitor calls without seeking authority?
12 Why is it important to maintain the confidentiality of information given to you during a call?
13 List eight pieces of advice that may be helpful when dealing with difficult callers.

UNIT 25 Contribute to an effective and safe working environment

This mandatory unit is all about the contributions that you can make to an effective and safe working environment through the manner in which you work. It covers the abilities required to ensure that your work meets your organisation's requirements in terms of service levels and quality standards. It also includes: aspects of health and safety; safe working practices; how to get on with your colleagues; and how to work as part of a team.

This unit has four elements:

♦ work to agreed performance and quality standards
♦ improve your own performance
♦ monitor and maintain health and safety in the workplace
♦ create and maintain effective working relationships with colleagues.

After you have completed this unit, you will be able to:

♦ identify and work towards your organisation's quality standards and agreed levels of service
♦ rate your own abilities
♦ focus on and deal with any shortfalls in your own performance
♦ recognise and minimise any risks to health and safety that you may encounter in the workplace
♦ work as an effective member of a team.

The case studies in this chapter have been based on a fictitious company – 'Fancy Goods Direct' a mail order supplier of luxury goods. Examples from other sectors such as banking, insurance, telemarketing and office supplies are covered in other chapters.

Did you know?

It is estimated that between 1.6 and 2 per cent of the total UK workforce is employed in call centres.

25.1 Work to agreed performance and quality standards

♦ Your organisation's service levels and quality standards and why these must be met

♦ How to identify and work to the levels of performance that apply to you personally

♦ How to monitor your own performance and identify ways of improving it

♦ How to agree a course of action with your supervisor or team leader

♦ The support that is available to help you meet agreed service levels and how to call on it.

Your organisation's service levels and quality standards and why these must be met

Case study 1 – Vikram's experiences

Here at 'Fancy Goods Direct' we have a clear set of quality standards that every employee is issued with when they start with the company. Further updates are also issued if the standards are changed or any further guidance is issued by the management.

We all call it our 'bible' as it contains everything that we need to know about how the company expects us to deal with customers. For instance, all incoming calls must be answered within two rings, and we must always greet the customer by saying, 'You are through to "Fancy Goods Direct", how may I help you?'.

It also contains information about the targets that we are expected to meet. For example, the company expects us all to process calls from customers within 90 seconds and wrap up time should be no more than 60 seconds.

1 Have you ever been briefed regarding the quality of service that you are expected to deliver?

2 How does your organisation measure quality of service?

3 Who can you turn to for advice if you have any questions about quality issues?

Your organisation should have a set of quality standards that control the way that you are expected to work. It may also have defined service levels that govern the level of service that you are expected to offer the caller.

Check it out

♦ Does your organisation have defined quality standards that you are expected to operate against? If it does then make a note of them or, if they are detailed, write down where they can be found.
♦ Does your organisation also have defined service levels that govern the quality of service offered by your organisation? If it does write them down or, if they are detailed, write down where they can be found.

The key purpose of quality management is to enhance your organisation's capacity to improve its performance and develop excellence for its customers.

It is not possible to measure the performance of a company unless you have something that you can measure it against. That is why an organisation needs to define the level of service that it intends to offer its customers. Once the level of service that your organisation intends to regularly offer its customers is set, its current level of performance can be measured against that yardstick. It is then possible to find out if your organisation is:

♦ meeting the required performance
♦ falling below that standard
♦ performing better than expected.

Check it out

♦ Find out if your organisation sets and monitors company performance targets.
♦ Are you ever given any feedback on your company's performance? If you are: when did this last happen? How well was your company performing?

The commitment of everyone is needed for your organisation to perform to its own pre-determined service levels, as the contributions made by its employees are dependent upon one another. For example, if there has to be a chain of events for a successful outcome to be achieved, then failure to complete any one of the events in the chain on time could mean that a successful outcome is not achieved.

Case study 2 – Carmel's experiences

At 'Fancy Goods Direct' we tell our customers that they will always receive their goods within 24 hours of placing their order. For that to happen:

♦ our call centre has to take the details of their order
♦ the warehousing department has to be notified of the details of the order
♦ the goods need to be in stock in the warehouse
♦ an order processing team has to retrieve each of the items in the order and package the goods ready for dispatch
♦ the goods then have to be loaded onto one of our vans and delivered direct to the customer's door.

In order for the target of delivery within 24 hours to be met, all the people involved in the chain above must perform their job roles to the best of their abilities. We therefore make sure that all our staff:

♦ know exactly what is expected of them
♦ understand the importance of their part in the chain
♦ appreciate why they must meet the levels of service that they have been set.

1 Are you clear about what your organisation expects you to do?
2 Are you aware of the standard to which you must perform?
3 How important is your role within your organisation?
4 If you were unable to perform your job role to the standard required, who else in your organisation could that affect?
5 Could you take any action to minimise any knock-on effect?

All employees share the responsibilities for meeting customers' requirements and promoting continuous improvement in the quality of your organisation's products and services, therefore it is important that you understand what is expected of you.

You will also need to know exactly what is expected of you if you are going to be able to perform consistently and identify any opportunities for improvement. What would you do if you could think of a better way of doing your job?

Think about it

♦ If you had some ideas for improvements in your job, who could you approach with your suggestions?
♦ Do you think that your organisation would give your suggestions due consideration?
♦ Have you ever made any suggestions in the past? If so, what happened?

How to identify and work to the levels of performance that apply to you personally

On page 57, you found out if your organisation sets itself performance targets and monitors its performance against those targets. We will now look in more detail at the level of performance monitoring that may take place within your organisation.

It is an almost universal working practice for the productivity of most call handlers to be assessed by some form of electronic performance monitoring. Monitoring is used as a basis for training, improving customer service and determining performance related pay.

Quantitative monitoring

This is the minute-by-minute gathering of quantitative data, which is done automatically by the computer system. It includes such statistics as:

♦ the percentage of a specified period that a call handler is on the telephone
♦ the average duration of a call handler's calls
♦ the average time spent wrapping up a call
♦ the length of time that call handlers are logged off on breaks.

The printout below shows an example of quantitative monitoring. It shows the performance of one of Fancy Goods Direct's agents, Jenny Green, as monitored automatically by the system during a week in April. The data gathered in this way can be analysed to provide statistical information about individuals, teams or the call centre as a whole.

Targets are normally set for each of the statistics that are monitored and call centres often have an overhead display that shows figures like the number of calls waiting and the longest time waited.

Weekly team performance from Jenny Green on Team 16

Date	Planned Staff Time	Actual Staff Time exc add time	Additional time O/T, Flexi, etc	Efficiency	Forecast no of calls based on planned using AHT 2:12	Actual calls taken	Prod inc staff avail	Staff avail	Forecast no of calls exc staff avail using AHT 2:12	Prod exc staff avail using AHT 2:12	Forecast no of calls exc staff avail using team AHT	Prod exc staff avail using team AHT of :-	
Monday 22april	44 hrs 45 mins	44 hrs 42 mins	1 hrs 59 mins	99.89%	1220	834	68.34%	9:03:27	1026	81.29%	1034	2.11	80.66%
Tuesday 23april	40 hrs 30 mins	40 hrs 29 mins	1 hrs 6 mins	99.96%	1105	569	51.51%	16:48:34	676	84.17%	713	2.05	79.80%
Wednesday 24 April	43 hrs 55 mins	43 hrs 52 mins	0 hrs 59 mins	99.89%	1198	574	47.92%	19:58:40	678	84.66%	684	2.11	83.92%
Thursday 25april	41 hrs 50 mins	41 hrs 39 mins	0 hrs 29 mins	99.56%	1141	592	51.89%	16:48:25	691	85.67%	670	2.16	88.36%
Friday 26 April	37 hrs 50 mins	37 hrs 49 mins	0 hrs 45 mins	99.96%	1032	575	55.73%	12:19:01	716	80.31%	670	2.21	85.82%
Saturday	0 hrs 0 mins	0 hrs 0 mins	0 hrs 0 mins	#DIV/0!	0	0	#DIV/0!	0:0:0	0	#DIV/0!	#DIV/0!	.0	#DIV/0!
Average	41 hrs 46 mins	41 hrs 42 mins	1 hrs 4 mins	99.85%	1139	629	55.20%	14:59:37	757	83.06%	753	2.13	83.51%

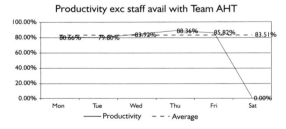

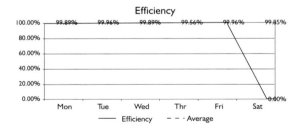

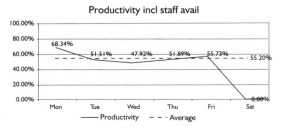

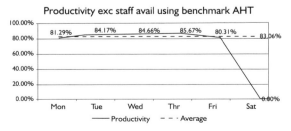

Figure 25.1 An example of quantitative monitoring

Qualitative monitoring

Some form of qualitative monitoring also normally takes place, such as team leaders listening in when call handlers are on the telephone – this may happen in real time or may be through the use of recordings.

This type of monitoring is carried out so that the organisation can check that call handlers are giving customers the correct information and that they are handling calls well and in accordance with company procedure.

Check it out

Find out if your organisation sets individual targets and monitors the performance of individuals.

♦ Are targets set for all members of staff? If targets are only set for some staff members, which members of staff are they?

♦ Have you been set any individual performance targets?

♦ Does your organisation monitor your performance against the targets you have been set? If it does, then write down how your performance is monitored.

♦ Are you given feedback on your performance or how well you are meeting your targets? If you are: when were you last given any feedback? Are you meeting your targets? Is there any room for improvement?

Happy staff can lead to improvements in service

If an organisation is going to be able to improve the level of service that it offers, then all its employees will need to perform better for improvement to be possible.

How to monitor your own performance and identify ways of improving it

There is now so much competition between companies, and customers require such high levels of customer service, that organisations will only retain staff who:

- are highly motivated
- are good at their job
- strive to improve their performance whenever possible.

No one can afford to be complacent and assume that their performance must be good enough if no one has yet complained. You need to take an active approach and assume responsibility both for your current level of performance and also for seeking ways in which that performance can be improved. It is not a difficult thing to do – you just need to put some careful thought into what you do and how well you do it. You also need to make a commitment to be honest with yourself. To start you off, have a go at the 'Try it out' exercise below.

Try it out

Copy out and complete the table below by thinking about what you do and how well you do it. You can print out a copy of this table from the CD-ROM.

List here the tasks that you perform as part of your job role	How often do you do this?			How well do you think you do it?				Do you think you could do it any better? (Yes/No)
	Regularly	Often	Not very often	Not very well	OK	Well	Very Well	

You now need to consider the content of the above table in detail.

Think about it

First, think about the activities that you have indicated that you do well or very well.

- Write down why you think you are good at doing these things.
- Have you identified any activities that you do not do well? If you have, write down why you think you do not currently do them well.
- Are the tasks that you do not do well things that you do not do often? If so, do you think that you could do them better if you had more practice at them?
- Did you identify any activities that you thought you could do better? If so, write down what you think you could do to improve your performance.
- Do you need any help or support, such as further training, for you to be able to bring about an improvement? If you do, write down what sort of support you think you need.
- Do you have any special needs that are not currently being recognised? If you have, write down what they are.

An earlier exercise, on page 57, gave you the opportunity to find out the full extent of any performance monitoring that goes on within your organisation.

If your organisation:

♦ sets you individual targets
♦ monitors your performance against those targets
♦ gives you any feedback regarding your performance

then you can compare that feedback with the results of your own performance review. Hopefully, if you have been honest with yourself, the two should tally.

However, the two views could turn out to be different. This could be because:

♦ you have not been honest with yourself and you have rated your own performance higher than it really is
♦ you have been too hard on yourself and you have rated your own performance lower than it really is.

It would not be unusual if you have done either of these! Try to use any feedback obtained from company monitoring systems to improve your own ability to rate yourself. Although the information obtained from company monitoring can give you a valuable insight into the level of your performance, it cannot tell you why you have achieved that level of performance. Only you will know why you may be performing well or badly, which is valuable information in itself.

If your organisation does not monitor the performance of individuals against targets, you will have to rely on any feedback that you can obtain from other members of your organisation, such as your supervisor or team leader. This will be covered later in the unit on page 66.

How to agree a course of action with your supervisor or team leader

In the last two sections, you have:

♦ looked in detail at what you do and how well you think you do it
♦ thought about any further training or support that you think you may need
♦ considered any other ways you think you may be able to improve your performance.

You should now be able to put all this information together into a self-development plan to help improve your performance. Make sure that you are not over ambitious about what you can achieve. Your plan must be both realistic and achievable.

Once you have drawn up your self-development plan, you should arrange to meet with your supervisor or team leader so that you can discuss your plan with them and gain their agreement to support your further development. You will now be able to undertake the developmental activities that you have identified.

Remember to review your performance again a little while after you have completed your further development so that you can decide if your performance has improved.

Line manager and employee in consultation

The support that is available to help you meet agreed service levels and how to call on it

The support that you can call on if you need help to meet agreed service levels will vary from one organisation to another, depending on the size and culture of your organisation. You will need to find out for yourself what level of support is available within your own organisation and how you can call on it should the need arise.

Check it out

♦ What support is available to you within your organisation to help you to achieve agreed service levels and quality standards?

♦ How can you call on this support?

Keys to good practice

✓ Make sure that you are familiar with any quality standards set by your organisation. You should be clear about why they have been set and why they must be met.

✓ If you are not clear about what your organisation expects you to do and how well they expect you to do it, ask your manager.

✓ If your manager has never given you any feedback about your performance ask for some.

✓ Do not assume that your performance must be good enough just because nobody has complained about it.

✓ Take an active approach and periodically review your own performance.

✓ Look at ways in which you can improve your performance and draw up a self-development plan.

✓ Gain your supervisor or team leader's support and agreement for your development plan.

✓ Undertake suitable developmental activities.

✓ Continue to review your performance at regular intervals.

25.2 Improve your own performance

- ◆ How to identify the skills and knowledge you require to perform your duties to the agreed standard
- ◆ How to assess your competence and identify any developmental needs
- ◆ How to obtain and use feedback constructively to improve your performance
- ◆ Who to approach about your developmental needs and agreeing a way forward.

Case study 3 – Jenny's experiences

Our company 'bible' tells us all about the quality standards that we are expected to work to and also gives details of the targets that we are all required to meet.

It is easy for us to find out whether or not we are meeting our performance targets as the company uses electronic performance monitoring to capture information about how well we are doing in relation to our targets. Weekly printouts are produced which contain statistics that show how we have performed against the targets. Two types of printout are produced: one which shows overall company performance; and one which is broken down into a sheet for each agent which shows our individual performances. Our team leader then normally goes through the individual performance figures with each agent on a Friday morning and lets us know how the company has performed overall at the same time. My team leader has always been very supportive on the odd occasion when I haven't met my targets. She normally discusses the figures with me to try and find out why it has happened and helps me to decide what I need to do to make sure I am on target next time. Her suggestions are usually very constructive.

1 Does your organisation use any form of electronic performance monitoring?
2 Do you get any feedback regarding your performance?
3 Are you able to discuss your level of performance with anyone?
4 Are you offered any form of support to help you improve your level of performance?
5 Who can you talk to if you have any concerns regarding your self-development?

An example of a weekly printout which shows the performance of one of Fancy Goods Direct's Agents, Jenny Green, was given on page 59. An example of a weekly printout showing the overall company performance is shown in Figure 25.2 on page 66.

How to identify the skills and knowledge you require to perform your duties to the agreed standard

You may already have a detailed job description which defines the level of skills and knowledge that you are expected to have to perform your job role. However, if not, the exercises that you have done in this unit should have provided enough information for you to identify accurately the skills and knowledge that you need.

To recap, you have looked at:

♦ the service and quality standards set by your organisation
♦ any company performance targets or individual targets set by your organisation
♦ if – and how – your organisation monitors both its own performance and the performance of individuals
♦ the tasks that you perform as part of your job role and how well you do them.

Now put all of that information together and try to complete the exercise below. You may, for example, think that you need to understand your organisation's policies and procedures or you need to be able to use and manage information effectively.

Weekly team performance - Week Ending : 27th April

Team	Planned Staff Time	Actual Staff Time exc add time	Additional time O/T, Flexi, etc	Efficiency	Forecast no of calls based on planned using target AHT	Actual calls taken	Prod inc staff avail	Total time worked	Staff avail	Forecast no of calls exc staff avail using target AHT	Prod exc staff avail using target AHT	Forecast no of calls exc staff avail using team AHT	Prod exc staff avail using team AHT of :-	
	A	B	C	B/A	D=(A/aht)*100%	E	E/D	B+C	F	G=(((B+C)-F)/aht)*100%	E/G	H=(((B+C)-F)/J)*100%	J	E/H
CED	2564 hrs 39 mins	2539 hrs 02 mins	131 hrs 56 mins	99.00%	71,572	55,908	78.11%	2670 hrs 58 mins	321:46:25	65,559	85.28%	64,558	2.11	86.60%
CEV	3163 hrs 19 mins	3127 hrs 06 mins	158 hrs 40 mins	98.86%	86,272	47,971	55.60%	3285 hrs 46 mins	1207:28:52	56,681	84.63%	55,421	2.15	86.56%
CEG Total	5727 hrs 58 mins	5666 hrs 08 mins	290 hrs 36 mins	98.92%	157,844	103,879	65.81%	5956 hrs 44 mins	1529:15:17	122,240	84.98%	119,979	2.13	86.58%
CEG Average	2863 hrs 59 mins	2833 hrs 04 mins	145 hrs 18 mins	98.92%	78,922	51,940	65.81%	2978 hrs 22 mins	764:37:39	61,120	84.98%	59,990	2.13	86.58%

Target AHT: CED - 2:09   CEV - 2:12

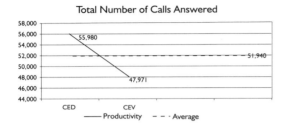

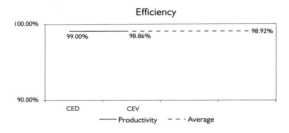

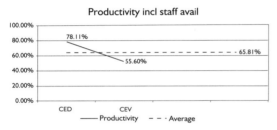

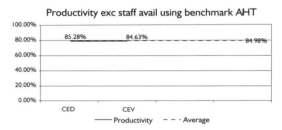

Figure 25.2 An example of a weekly printout which shows the overall performance of Fancy Goods Direct

Try it out

Print out a copy from the CD-ROM and try to complete the first two columns of the table below by defining the skills and knowledge that you think you need to perform your job role to the standard set by your organisation. Forget about the last two columns at the moment, we will be considering these in the next section.

Skill/knowledge area	Level of skill/knowledge required	Do I currently possess this? (Yes/No)	Do I require further training? (Yes/No)

How to assess your competence and identify any developmental needs

In the exercise above, you identified the skills and knowledge that you thought were necessary to perform your job role to the required standard. You now need to decide if you already possess *all* the skills and knowledge that you identified or if you require any further personal development.

Go back and re-visit the exercise above. Try to complete the last two columns. When you have finished, use this information to complete the exercise that follows.

Think about it

♦ Do you think that you currently possess all the skills and knowledge that you identified as being required?

♦ Do you think that you need any further training? What sort of training might this be? If you do not think that you need any further training, how do you think you could gain the skills and knowledge that you have identified that you need?

♦ Do you think that you have any skills or knowledge that you do not use within your current job role? What are they?

How to obtain and use feedback constructively to improve your performance

Team leaders usually provide feedback to call handlers on the information collected by the performance monitoring carried out by an organisation. This is usually done immediately when the team leader has been actively listening to a call or it may be done later in a one-to-one session.

You can use any feedback that you are given as a result of on-going electronic performance monitoring to improve your performance, as it will highlight any instances of poor performance as well as identifying areas of good practice. This will help you to focus on any areas of weakness that you may need to tackle, so that you can begin to build a suitable self-development plan.

If you are never given any feedback as a result of electronic performance monitoring then you will need to elicit feedback from the people that you work with. You could try asking:

♦ the person responsible for your training
♦ your supervisor or team leader
♦ your colleagues.

Whoever you choose to approach for feedback, remember that the person may not feel able to give you feedback there and then but will probably prefer to go away and think about it. You will then receive considered feedback which will probably tell you much more about your performance overall. If it is possible, try to arrange to meet the person away from both your desks so that you can get the feedback without interruption.

Always bear in mind that the feedback you receive may not always be what you may want to hear! If there are views that you do not agree with, or that you feel are unfair, always remember that everyone is entitled to their opinion and that they are only telling you what they think.

Try not to contradict the person giving you feedback or argue if you do not agree with what is said. Make sure to say thank you for the feedback.

If you do not agree with the feedback that you receive, there are several options:

♦ take the feedback graciously and then go away and think about it for a while; if you give it careful consideration, you may find there is some truth in what was said and that you may have been trying to ignore the fact yourself

♦ ask other people for feedback and see if the same theme re-occurs – if other people have the same opinion it may be more valid than you care to admit

♦ if you end up admitting that the feedback is valid, you may wish to ask for suggestions about how you could deal with the issues. You will probably find that the people who gave you the feedback are more than willing to help. It will also let them know that you have taken their feedback in good faith with no hard feelings.

Who to approach about your developmental needs and agreeing a way forward

On page 63, we looked at drawing up a self-development plan. You should now be able to re-visit this and update it to take account of any further development needs that you may have identified. You can also use any feedback that you have elicited so far to further refine your self-development plan.

Once you have reviewed your plan to take account of all the information now available, you should discuss your revised plan with your supervisor or team leader and gain their support for your further development.

Keys to good practice

✓ You should look at the level of skills and knowledge that are required for you to be able to perform your duties to the agreed standard and then carry out a skills audit on yourself to identify if any further development is required.

✓ Make sure that you obtain feedback from others and use this constructively to help you review your abilities.

✓ Always take any feedback offered graciously and thank the other person for giving it – even if it is not what you wanted to hear.

✓ Update your self-development plan to take account of any further development that has been identified and approach and gain your supervisor or team leader's support.

✓ Always continue to review your abilities periodically and identify any further development that may be required.

25.3 Monitor and maintain health and safety in the workplace

- ◆ The impact of relevant health and safety legislation
- ◆ The nature of possible hazards and how to deal with them
- ◆ Reporting hazards: who to and how
- ◆ Setting up your work area to minimise risks and why it is important to do so
- ◆ Other health and safety issues that you need to be aware of
- ◆ Your organisation's working practices and how to report any non conformances
- ◆ How to deal with, report and record emergencies in the workplace.

Did you know?

There are currently between 3000 and 5000 call centres in the UK.

Case study 4 – Carolyn's experiences

When I joined 'Fancy Goods Direct', I was given a health and safety briefing as part of my induction training. There were several other people who started at the same time and we were all sent on a half-day briefing that was given by the company's health and safety representative.

She went through a range of general health and safety issues and then focused on the issues that related to our particular job roles. As all the attendees were call centre agents, this involved how to work at the computer safely and how we should adjust our workstations to meet our individual needs, like adjusting our chairs and headsets so that we are always comfortable when we work. It was stressed that we needed to do this to make sure that we avoid any risk of RSI (repetitive strain injury, or upper limb disorders as I think they tend to call it these days).

We get the odd circular now and again if there are any health and safety issues that we need to be made aware of.

If there is anything really urgent then our team leader discusses it with each of us individually. If any one has any individual concerns then we can speak to our team leader about it or go and see the company's health and safety representative.

1 Have you ever received any health and safety training with regard to your current job role?
2 Have you been kept up-to-date since then regarding health and safety issues?

3   Do you think you are fully aware of any risks that may be associated with your working environment?
4   Do you know what you should be doing to minimise any risks?
5   Do you feel you are currently minimising any risks to your well-being?
6   Who could you contact if you have any questions or worries regarding health and safety issues?

The impact of relevant health and safety legislation

You should be aware that there are a number of regulations that govern the condition of your working environment. Relevant health and safety legislation includes:

- The Workplace (Health, Safety and Welfare) Regulations 1992
- The Management of Health and Safety at Work Regulations 1999
- The Provision and Use of Work Equipment Regulations 1998
- The Health and Safety (Display Screen Equipment) Regulations 1992
- The Safety Representatives and Safety Committees Regulations 1977
- The Health and Safety (Consultation with Employees) Regulations 1996.

We will now look at the effect of some of this legislation in more detail.

The Workplace (Health, Safety and Welfare) Regulations 1992

These regulations govern the condition of the working environment that you are expected to operate within. They contain strict guidance that your organisation must follow to make sure that you are provided with a suitable working environment that does not endanger your health or safety.

The table below shows the requirements of some of the regulations that are part of the Workplace (Health, Safety and Welfare) Regulations 1992.

Regulation	The effect of this regulation
Regulation 5	Requires all workstation equipment to be maintained in good repair. There should also be a simple procedure for employees to report defective equipment and all reports should be investigated promptly. Faulty equipment should be removed from service immediately for repair or to be discarded – this includes chairs with adjustment mechanisms that do not work, as they are a risk to health.
Regulation 6	Requires all workplaces, including offices, to be ventilated with either fresh air from outside or re-circulated air that has been adequately filtered and purified. This is to ensure that stale, contaminated, hot or humid air is removed so that workers do not suffer ill health effects such as tiredness, lethargy, headaches, dry or itchy skin or eye irritation. Adequate ventilation is particularly important in call centres, as the high concentration of employees and high level of occupation increases the risk of airborne pollutants and irritants. These, in turn, increase the risk of sickness absence, as bacteria and viruses can cause colds and dust can irritate the throat and lungs, which may contribute to voice problems or trigger asthma.

Regulation	The effect of this regulation
Regulation 7	Requires the temperature in all workplaces inside buildings to be reasonable during working hours. A reasonable temperature for a call centre is around 19°C.
Regulation 8	Requires every workplace to have suitable and sufficient lighting, which (if it is reasonably practicable) should be natural light.
Regulation 9	Requires workplaces to be kept clean.
Regulation 10	Requires call centres to have enough free space to allow people to get to and from workstations and to move around within the call centre with ease.
Regulation 11	Requires workstations to be suitable for both the users and for the work to be done, so that all operations can be performed safely. Where work can be done sitting down, a seat must be provided, together with a footrest where necessary.

A good working environment will safeguard everyone's health and safety

The Management of Health and Safety at Work Regulations 1999

These regulations exist to ensure that your organisation manages health and safety within the workplace and maximises the well-being of all its employees. To comply with these regulations, your organisation is required to:

◆ assess risks to health and safety
◆ plan, organise, control, monitor and review measures
◆ provide health surveillance
◆ appoint a **competent person** to advise on health and safety

- set up emergency procedures
- provide information and training to employees.

This legislation includes your employer's duty to ensure, so far as is reasonably practicable, the health of its employees at work. The risk of ill health from work-related stress must also be assessed and regularly reviewed by your employer, in consultation with employees or their representatives and action taken to prevent or reduce it.

The Provision and Use of Work Equipment Regulations 1998

These regulations exist to ensure that your organisation makes sure that any equipment it expects you to use as part of job role is suitable, safe and properly maintained. To comply with these regulations, your organisation must:

- select equipment which is safe for the working conditions
- ensure that work equipment is suitable and properly maintained
- provide employees with information about the equipment and instruction and training regarding its operation.

The Health and Safety (Display Screen Equipment) Regulations 1992

These regulations help to make display screen work safer and more comfortable. They set out the six main obligations that employers have towards users of display screen equipment. Employers must:

- assess the risks arising from the use of display screen workstations and take steps to reduce them to the **lowest extent reasonably practicable**
- ensure that new workstations meet the minimum ergonomic standards set out in the regulations
- inform users about the results of the assessments, any actions that the employer is taking and the users' entitlements under the regulations
- plan display screen work so that users are provided with regular breaks or changes of activity
- offer eye tests before display screen use, at regular intervals and if the user is experiencing visual problems. If the eye test shows that they are necessary, and normal reading glasses are unsuitable, the employer must pay for basic prescription glasses for display screen work
- provide appropriate health and safety training for users before display screen use or whenever a workstation is **suitably modified**.

As the main work activity of most call handlers is responding to telephone calls whilst simultaneously using a computer to provide information and enter data, call handlers are classed as display screen equipment users as they use display screen equipment for most of their working day.

However, in comparison to typical office workers, call handlers may be at an even higher risk from display screen equipment related hazards because they do not usually have the same opportunities as typical office workers to take breaks away from display screen activities.

It is important to understand the possible health implications that may be associated with working with a computer all day long and that you actively take precautions to minimise any possible risks to your well being. (See page 74.)

Think about it

Do you habitually use display screen equipment as a significant part of your normal work? If so, you should now consider the following questions:

♦ Has your employer ever given you training on how to use display screen equipment safely?
♦ Has your employer ever offered you an eye test?
♦ Are you given the opportunity to take regular breaks from using the display screen equipment?

If you have answered **No** to any of these questions, you should bring this to your manager's attention or consult your health and safety representative for advice.

The Safety Representatives and Safety Committees Regulations 1977

These regulations allow recognised trade unions to appoint employee safety representatives, who then have rights to:

♦ be consulted about health and safety issues
♦ inspect the premises
♦ investigate reportable accidents, occupational diseases and dangerous occurrences
♦ attend safety committee meetings
♦ request a safety committee be formed
♦ contact enforcing authority inspectors.

The Health and Safety (Consultation with Employees) Regulations 1996

Under these regulations, your employer has a duty to consult employees in good time on a range of matters affecting their health and safety at work, including in particular:

♦ the introduction of any measure at the workplace which may substantially affect the health and safety of employees
♦ any health and safety information the employer is required to provide to employees
♦ the planning and organisation of any health and safety training the employer is required to provide
♦ the health and safety consequences for those employees of the introduction of new technologies into the workplace.

Such consultation can be with the employees directly or through elected **representatives of employee safety**. This elected representative of safety is not the same person as the **competent person** referred to in the Management of Health and Safety at Work Regulations 1999; the elected representative **represents** the views of employees and should be separate from management.

Your employer must listen to the views of employees and consider them before making any decisions or taking any action.

Check it out

- Find out how your organisation consults its employees regarding health and safety issues.
- What approach does your organisation use?
- Do you have an appointed health and safety representative? If so, who is it and how would you contact this person if you needed to speak to them?

The nature of possible hazards and how to deal with them

A **hazard** is anything that can cause harm, such as chemicals, electricity or working from ladders.

Think about it

What hazards do you think there may be within a call centre environment?

In most firms in the commercial and service sectors, hazards are few and simple. They are usually easily identified by applying common sense. You probably already know if you have any equipment that could cause harm or if there is an awkward entrance or stairwell where someone could be hurt.

Look for the hazards in your workplace, such as trailing cables. Walk around your workplace and look afresh at anything that could have the potential to cause harm. Manufacturer's instructions or data sheets can also help you to spot potential hazards, as can accident and ill-health records.

Now think about who could be harmed by any of these potential hazards and how it could happen. Don't forget to include:

- young workers, trainees and expectant mothers, etc. who may be at particular risk
- cleaners, visitors, contractors or maintenance workers who may not be in the workplace all the time
- members of the public or people you share your workplace with if there is a chance that they could be hurt by your activities.

Finally, consider each of the hazards in turn and ask yourself two questions:

1 Can I get rid of the hazard altogether?
2 If not, how can I control the risks so that harm is unlikely?

A **risk** is the chance, high or low, that somebody will be harmed by a **hazard**. For those hazards that you cannot get rid of, you must decide how likely it is that they could cause harm. When you have evaluated the risks, you should then be able to decide whether existing precautions are adequate or if more needs to be done to reduce the risk.

Even after all possible precautions have been taken, some risk may still remain. You then have to decide whether this remaining risk is as low as it can be.

It is possible that you could identify hazards that are outside your area of responsibility. If you do, you will probably be unable to remove these hazards or put suitable control measures in place yourself. You then need to make sure that you report any such hazards to a higher authority.

Reporting hazards: who to and how

Your organisation should have a set of procedures that you are expected to follow when you have identified a hazard in the workplace and need to report it to a higher authority.

Check it out

♦ Does your organisation have a set of procedures that you are expected to follow when you need to report an existing or potential hazard in the workplace that is outside your authority?

Setting up your work area to minimise risks and why it is important to do so

Think about it

♦ What risks to your health and well-being do you think there may be within a call centre environment?
♦ Are you currently doing anything to minimise these risks?

The main health and safety risks associated with working in a call centre are work-related upper limb disorders (also sometimes referred to as repetitive strain injury or RSI), voice loss, eye strain, stress and a feeling of being cooped up (a bit like battery animals).

Did you know?

Last year 5.4 million days were lost in sick leave due to RSI.

It is the duty of your employer to make sure that any potential risks to your health are minimised. This can be done by controlling and optimising your working environment. There are several things that your organisation can do to provide you with a suitable working environment, such as:

- *maintaining comfortable temperature levels* – optimal environmental conditions are essential for your comfort, as you are required to sit for long periods of time at your workstation without a break. Sitting in a draught could cause muscular tension which has the potential to become a musculo-skeletal disorder
- *maintaining a suitable level of humidity* – the risk of low relative humidity is high in call centres because the large number of computers (which may be generating heat 24 hours a day, seven days a week) can dry the air. Low relative humidity can make you dehydrated, which may leave you suffering from sore eyes, voice loss, headaches and skin rashes
- *optimising the positioning of a call centre within a building* – if a call centre is sited within the middle of a floor with no access to natural light or windows, it can lead to a feeling of isolation and depression unless great care is taken with the lighting and décor
- *providing adequate, good quality lighting* – eye strain and headaches can be caused by screen glare and bad lighting.

However, you are also personally responsible for minimising the risks to your health or well-being wherever possible. There are a number of actions that you can take, such as:

- making sure that your working environment is suitably tailored to your personal needs, by adjusting things like your chair and footrest, the position of your microphone and the volume control on your headset
- drinking plenty of water or caffeine-free soft drinks – tea and coffee are diuretics and they can increase the risk of dehydration
- taking breaks away from your workstation whenever possible – do not spend your lunch break surfing the Internet or emailing friends as you will not get the proper break away from the computer that you need.

It is particularly important that you make sure your working environment is suitably tailored to your personal needs if your organisation uses **hot-desking**. This is where workstations are not assigned to individuals, so people may end up sitting at a different workstation each day.

If you are required to work in this way, you must ensure that you adjust your workstation to meet your physical needs each time that you are allocated to a new workstation.

Did you know?

Every day last year six workers left their jobs forever because of RSI.

How can I make sure that my workstation is set up properly to meet my needs?

Your keyboard and your monitor should be directly in front of you with your mouse next to it. Make sure that your mouse is within easy reach so that your elbow can remain next to your side when you are using it.

Place the materials on your desk in accordance with how frequently you use them

Adjust the height of your chair so that your keyboard and mouse are at or below elbow height and make sure that your feet are well supported and that your shoulders are relaxed.

Place the materials on your desk in accordance with how frequently you use them, so:

♦ the things that you use most frequently are closest to you
♦ materials that you use occasionally are no further than an arm's length away
♦ things that you use infrequently can be placed further away.

Place any documents that you need while typing close to the monitor to reduce frequent head turning and changing of eye focus. Using a document holder is a good idea.

What is repetitive strain injury and what causes it?

A repetitive strain injury (RSI) is a soft tissue injury in which muscles, nerves or tendons become irritated or inflamed. Repetitive strain injuries can occur when repeated physical movements cause damage to tendons, nerves, muscles and other soft body tissues. You should note that it is far easier to prevent the condition than it is to cure it once it is contracted.

RSI can be a serious and painful condition that can occur even in young, physically fit individuals and it can leave people permanently disabled and unable to perform certain tasks such as driving or dressing themselves.

Did you know?

About a third of workers with RSI are under 45 and just over half
(55 per cent – 276,000) are women.

The rise of computer use and flat, light-touch keyboards that permit high
speed typing have resulted in an epidemic of injuries to the hands, arms
and shoulders. Use of pointing devices such as mice are also a cause, if not
more so. The thousands of repeated keystrokes and long periods of
clutching and dragging with mice slowly accumulates damage to the body.

Damage is more likely to occur if poor body posture is adopted as this
places unnecessary stress on the tendons and nerves in the hand, wrist,
arms and even the shoulders and neck. Lack of adequate rest and breaks
and using excessive force will compound this and further increase the risk
of injury. As more and more work and recreation involves the use of
computers, everyone needs to be aware of the danger of RSI.

Did you know?

Repetitive Strain Injury is not new. In 1713 Bernardino Ramazzini, the father
of occupational medicine, described pain in the hands of scribes.

Studies have shown that you can be at risk of suffering from repetitive
strain injury if you use a keyboard and/or mouse. Some research suggests
that the following may be associated with physical discomfort and injury to
nerves, tendons and muscles:

♦ static muscle loading
♦ long periods of repetitive motion
♦ using an improperly set up work space
♦ incorrect body posture
♦ poor work habits.

Static muscle loading is muscular activity that involves holding an object or
maintaining a certain posture or position – it involves little or no
movement. For muscles to be able to contract, they require energy, which
is delivered to them via the blood stream. When muscles contract they
effectively compress the blood vessels that feed them so, if a contraction is
maintained for any length of time – as happens during static activity – the
blood supply to the muscles is reduced and a build-up of waste products
can accumulate. This can result in muscle fatigue, which is usually
experienced as an ache or discomfort.

Computer work can cause static muscle loading in a variety of body areas
unless you take regular breaks or are given the opportunity to vary your
activities. When you use a keyboard, static muscle work is required to hold
your arms and hands in place. If your back is not well supported, static
muscle activity also takes place there and in the muscles of your neck.
Over time, this can lead to localised muscle tightness and postural

imbalances which can compromise the blood supply and the nerve function in your arms and hands.

Long periods of continuous repetitive motion can lead to the over-use of specific muscles and risks straining the tissues beyond their normal capacity. Initially fatigue will occur and, if demands increase or a break is not taken, it can lead to aches and pains or even injury.

The most commonly reported symptons of discomfort are:

1 Fatigue

2 Neck discomfort

3 Shoulder discomfort

4 Focusing difficulties

5 Discomfort in the hands or fingers

However, the risk of possible injury can be reduced if you take some sensible precautions. The way in which an activity is performed can affect the likelihood of a problem occurring. For example, if we look at the angle of your wrist while you are typing or using a mouse. If your wrist is in a neutral position (it is relaxed and straight) the risk of a problem occurring due to overuse is greatly reduced compared to typing or using a mouse with your wrist stretched or bent. This is because your muscles are using the minimum amount of effort.

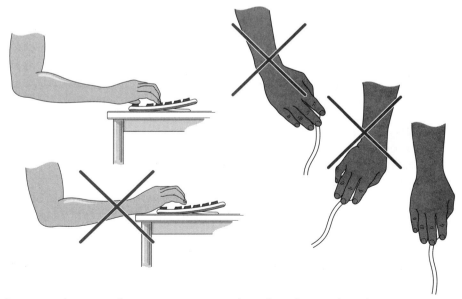

Always make sure that your wrist is relaxed and straight when using a keyboard or mouse

Stress can also play an important part in the onset of RSI, as it causes increased muscle tension. Stress also generally sensitises the nervous system which increases your ability to perceive pain. (See page 83.)

What are the symptoms of RSI?

These include:

- tightness, discomfort, stiffness, soreness or burning in the hands, wrists, fingers, forearms or elbows
- tingling, coldness or numbness in the hands
- clumsiness or loss of strength and co-ordination in the hands
- pain that wakes you up at night
- feeling a need to massage your hands, wrists and arms.

Problems commonly start in the dominant wrist, hand or arm (although the neck and shoulders can also be involved at this stage). Initial signs of RSI may be fatigue, numbness and general aching of the affected part of the body.

At first, it is usual for symptoms to only occur after prolonged activity and for them to cease when the activity stops. However, as damage progresses, the pain may not go away even after rest. The area becomes more sensitive and easily damaged, and unrelated activities may cause pain. In extreme cases, the pain can become severe and debilitating.

Did you know?

Figures released by the TUC show that one in every 50 workers (506,000) is suffering from the symptoms of RSI.

If, at any time, you believe that you may be suffering from a repetitive strain injury, you should always seek advice from a qualified medical practitioner at the earliest opportunity.

What can I do to prevent RSI?

If it is possible within the constraints of your job role, you should:

- *take frequent short breaks* – get up and walk around at least a couple of times every hour
- *vary your tasks throughout the day* – do something different with your hands and arms for a while
- *adjust your chair and keyboard* so that your wrists are straight. Also position your keyboard and mouse so that you do not have to stretch to reach them
- *use a light touch on your keyboard*
- *keep your shoulders, arms, wrists and hands relaxed and comfortable as you work* – to keep your shoulders, arms, wrists and hands relaxed as you work, let them hang loosely at your sides for a moment. Allow them to dangle toward the floor and to become relaxed. Now try to maintain this relaxed feeling while you work
- *avoid placing or supporting your wrists on sharp edges or on your desktop* – if you use a wrist or palm rest, do not use it whilst typing as

this may increase pressure against the hand and could increase the chance of injury

♦ *make sure that your elbows are next to your sides.*

Always be alert for any signs of discomfort. If at any time during or after typing, or using a mouse, you feel pain, weakness, numbness or tingling in your hands, wrists, elbows, shoulders, neck or back then you should consult a qualified medical practitioner.

Ten tips for comfortable working

1 Adjust the height of your chair until your forearms are parallel to the keyboard when typing and your wrists are in a neutral position.

2 Ensure that your eyes are at the same height as the top of the screen. When your eyes are relaxed, your viewing angle is a downward gaze of about 15° below the horizontal. Therefore, if you position the monitor so that your eyes are level with the top of it, providing that you are about 400mm away (the recommended distance) you will naturally focus on the middle of the screen.

3 Make sure that your thighs are parallel to the floor and that your feet rest firmly on the ground or on a footrest.

4 Locate the keyboard and mouse close to you so that you do not stretch to reach them.

5 Leave a space in front of the keyboard so that you have somewhere to rest your hands when you are not using the keyboard.

6 Position the screen and keyboard in the best position for your task. This may be directly in front of you or slightly to one side.

7 Ensure that the seat of your chair is short enough from front to back to enable you to make contact with the backrest. Adjust the height of the backrest so that it provides adequate support for your back and make sure that you make full use of the seat back at all times.

8 Remove any clutter from under your desk so that you have sufficient leg room.

9 If you copy type, use a document holder, as it reduces the amount of bending you have to do to constantly look between the document and the screen.

10 Try to take breaks away from the computer, ideally every 45–60 minutes, and regularly refocus your eyes by looking at a distant object for a few minutes to avoid visual fatigue.

Do I need to take any additional precautions if I am pregnant?

One of the most emotive occupational health issues in recent years has been the suggestion that prolonged display screen work may have an adverse impact on pregnancy. The main impetus for this suggestion was the reporting of clusters of adverse outcomes. Several studies have since demonstrated that statistical chance is quite sufficient to explain the reported clusters.

Many studies have now been conducted world-wide on long term display screen workers and these have failed to find any link between miscarriages or birth defects and display screens. If you are pregnant, or planning to have children, and you are worried about working with a display screen then you should discuss your concerns with someone who is adequately informed about the issues and the scientific evidence.

Pregnancy leads to a variety of bodily changes, which can lead to a number of physical problems from lower back pain to swollen ankles. Some of the common conditions that are suffered by pregnant women are:

◆ a tingling and numbness in the wrists and hands
◆ back problems
◆ varicose veins.

The fluid levels in the body change during pregnancy – this can lead to an increase in pressure in the carpal tunnel area of the wrist. This is the narrow channel through which many of the nerves, tendons and blood vessels pass into the hand. If the pressure in this tunnel is increased, it can cause compression of the nerves, which may lead to a tingling and numbness in the hand. It is most common in the morning and can be relieved by raising your hands above your head or by rolling your shoulders.

It is quite common for pregnant women to experience back pain. This is because the shape of the spine changes during the course of pregnancy – the lumbar curve tends to become more pronounced as the baby gets bigger. This increased curvature causes the joints of the spine to take more strain, which can lead to back pain.

During pregnancy, the connective tissue throughout the body also undergoes changes. In the back, this can affect the ligaments. The relaxing of the ligaments of the spine can, in turn, lead to an increase in muscle tension in the lumbar area as the muscles try to compensate.

Good posture is therefore essential if you want to reduce the risk of back problems during pregnancy. You not only need to understand how to sit and stand but also how to perform everyday movements in a way that reduces strain on the lower back.

The softening of the connective tissue during pregnancy can also affect the walls of the blood vessels, making them less rigid. This can lead to the valves that help to direct the flow of blood through the veins of the legs and back to the heart becoming unable to propel the increased volume of blood back through the legs. Pumping your feet up and down while you are sitting can help the movement of blood through your legs and any position that could constrict the flow of the blood through your legs further, such as sitting with your legs crossed, should be avoided.

Six ways to minimise aches and pains if you are pregnant

1 Do not rest your wrists on your desk while you are typing as this can put even more pressure on the carpal tunnel area. Use a soft foam or gel wrist rest instead, as this will reduce the risk of compression.

2 If the backrest of your chair does not provide sufficient lumbar support, use a lumbar roll or cushion. Make sure that using this additional support does not result in the rest of your back losing contact with the backrest – you may need to change the angle of the backrest or the seat to achieve this. Wearing flat shoes can also reduce strain on the lumbar area.

3 Use a footrest to keep the hip and knees joints at 90° when sitting as this will reduce the pressure placed on the back of the thighs by the edge of the chair seat.

4 Increase the size of the font that you normally use on the screen to avoid eye strain, as increases in the fluid levels in the body during pregnancy can change your visual ability.

5 Keep the mouse and keyboard as close to you as possible – as the size of your 'bump' grows this will become more difficult, so you may notice tension in your shoulder muscles by the end of the day.

6 If possible, take more frequent breaks away from your computer, as the risks of muscular and visual fatigue are greater during pregnancy.

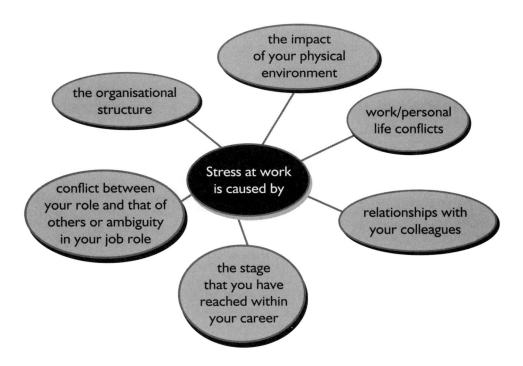

Figure 25.3 Some major sources of stress at work

How can I recognise and manage stress?

Work-related stress is defined by the Health and Safety Executive as: *'the adverse reaction people have to excessive pressures or other types of demand placed on them'*.

Stress is not a disease, but if the stress reaction is intense and it goes on for some time, it can lead to mental and/or physical ill health such as depression, a nervous breakdown or heart disease.

Researchers believe that there are six major sources of stress at work. These are shown in Figure 25.3.

Think about it

Consider your own job role and working environment.
- What do you think the typical sources of stress could be?
- Do you currently feel stressed?
- Why do you think this is?
- What could you do about stress at work?

The table below shows some of the typical sources of stress that may be present within a call handling working environment.

Typical stress factors	Indicators
Company culture	A positive culture reduces the risk of stress through: - regular and open two-way communication between call handlers and managers - managers consulting call handling staff and allowing them to participate in decisions that may affect them - staff welfare being a priority – organisations with positive cultures have a clear sickness or absence policy and encourage call handlers to recover fully before returning to work from sick leave.
Work overload	You are at risk from work-related stress if you are given too much work to do in the time allocated. Productivity is often assessed by electronic performance monitoring, which has been reported to cause stress because it can make people feel under pressure. New call handlers should be set lower targets than experienced call handlers, with the number of calls being increased over a suitable period of time. If targets are set too high, you may consistently receive negative feedback about not achieving your targets, which can be stressful. A supportive line manager has been shown to be associated with lower levels of stress in a monitored workplace.
Lack of training	You are at risk from work-related stress when you are not adequately trained to do your work. Your organisation should make sure that you are capable of doing your job by making sure that you have the necessary skills and knowledge to be able to meet the demands of your job role.
The repetitive nature of your work	You may experience work-related stress if you feel that your work is repetitive and boring and it does not make the most of your skills or challenge you.

Typical stress factors	Indicators
The nature of your physical environment	Working in a poor physical environment, such as one that is draughty, overcrowded or badly lit can be stressful to endure. If you have no control over your working environment because the temperature or humidity, etc. are all controlled centrally and you are not able to open a window to let in fresh air, this is likely to cause stress. A thorough cleaning and maintenance regime reduces the risk of work-related stress arising from unhygienic or inoperable workstation equipment.
Shift work	If you work shifts and your shifts are constantly being changed (especially at short notice) it can become stressful, as it may be difficult to alter your domestic or social arrangements.
Lack of control over your work	You probably have little control over when you take calls, as calls are usually distributed automatically. How long you spend on a call may well be controlled by your targets and what you actually say during a call may even be controlled by the use of a script. This can all lead to you feeling that you have little or no control over your work.
Organisational change	The call handling sector is a rapidly changing industry, which in itself can be unsettling for some people. Frequent business restructuring may mean that teams are re-organised and that business objectives, procedures and performance targets regularly change. Technology is also changing rapidly and automation may be a threat to job security. All of these factors can be stressful.
The nature of your job role	Your job role itself may be stressful if you are not clear about what is expected of you. Constraints placed on your job role may not allow you to offer the quality of service that is required because it is being compromised by call volume targets.
Level of support offered by management and colleagues	Practical and emotional support from your line manager or your peers can help to protect you from work-related stress. However, if you are required to hot-desk, you may not always be sitting with other members of your team so you may feel isolated from their support. Constant pressure to meet targets may also mean that your peers do not have time to support you.
The balance between life and work	Work-related stress may be reduced by ensuring that work does not dominate your life to the detriment of out-of-work activities and interests – keep a balance between your work and home life.

A recent study undertaken by the Health and Safety Laboratory on working practices in UK call centres has identified that the physical environment and hot-desking are regarded as major sources of stress for many call handlers. Some call handlers are also frustrated by the lack of opportunities to break the monotony of answering calls by doing other tasks, whilst others are stressed by the verbal abuse coming from callers and the constant pressure from their team leaders to answer calls.

Did you know?

One in five workers feel stressed by their work. This equates to about 5 million workers in the UK.

We can all be vulnerable to suffering from stress – it just depends on how much pressure we may be under at any given time. Even people who are normally very hardy can succumb to stress. Recognising the signs of stress is the first step to managing the stresses that you can be exposed to in life.

There can be a number of outward signs of stress, such as:

♦ changes in your mood or behaviour which can lead to deteriorating relationships with colleagues
♦ irritability
♦ not being able to make up your mind
♦ absenteeism
♦ reduced performance.

People who suffer from stress may also complain about their health. They may, for example, suffer from frequent headaches. It is also not uncommon for people who are suffering from stress to smoke or drink alcohol more than usual or even turn to using drugs.

Did you know?

About 91 million working days per year – a third of all sick leave – are lost because of stress.

If your organisation is forward thinking then you may be provided with stress management training, which teaches people to cope better with the pressures that they may come across, or it is possible that there may be a counselling service.

Check it out

♦ Does your organisation offer any form of stress management training or a stress counselling service? If so, make a note of what you need to do to get appropriate training and who you need to speak to if you think you may be suffering from stress.

If your organisation does not have a formal mechanism for recognising and dealing with stress, and you suspect that you may be suffering from work-related stress then you should approach your manager and explain how you are feeling. If you feel unable to approach your manager then consult your doctor.

How can I reduce the risk of visual fatigue?

If you spend a lot of time using a Visual Display Unit (VDU), you are at risk from visual fatigue. This is because your blink rate drops when you use a VDU, so your eyes become less well lubricated which can lead to tired and sore eyes. The risk is highest for contact lens wearers as contact lenses stop blinks from lubricating the eye properly. However, you can reduce the risk of suffering from visual fatigue by taking certain precautions as shown below.

> **Nine ways to avoid visual fatigue**
>
> 1 Take advantage of the eye tests that your employer is obliged to offer you.
>
> 2 Adjust the brightness and contrast settings on your VDU.
>
> 3 Keep the screen of your VDU clean and smear-free.
>
> 4 Position your screen to avoid reflections – if this is not possible, a filter can be fitted to your screen to eliminate reflections.
>
> 5 Do not use software fonts that are smaller than size 12.
>
> 6 Use a document holder when referring to both the screen and documentation.
>
> 7 Exercise and stretch your eye-movement muscles from time to time by rolling your eyes.
>
> 8 Look away from your screen from time to time and focus on a distant object as this relaxes the eye muscles.
>
> 9 Take regular breaks away from the screen.

Other health and safety issues that you need to be aware of

Undertaking shift work

Shift work is a common practice in many call centres, so you need to consider the risks involved. Arriving for work or leaving work either late at night or early in the morning makes you particularly vulnerable to physical attack. If public transport is not available to you at these times, walking to or from work could expose you to further risk.

Working shifts also increases your risk of suffering from dietary problems as working irregular or unsociable hours often leads to irregular meal times and snacking.

You should be aware that you are entitled to a medical assessment to ensure that you are fit to undertake night work.

Dealing with verbal abuse

You may be exposed to more verbal abuse than a typical office worker as you spend more time on the telephone. Your employer should therefore offer you training so that you know how to deal with callers who make insulting or aggressive comments, shout or swear. You should bear in mind the advice given below.

> **Ten tips for dealing with abusive callers**
>
> 1 Try not to panic or put the receiver down.
>
> 2 Be patient, as the abuse may stop.
>
> 3 Try not to lose your temper or be tempted to react with a similar response.

4 Try not to take the remarks personally or become upset.

5 If the caller is not satisfied with the answers you give, offer to pass the caller to a colleague or a supervisor, or offer to take the person's number and call them back when further investigations have been made.

6 If the caller does not calm down, clearly state that unless they are able to continue the call in a civil manner the call will be terminated.

7 If, despite a warning, the caller's behaviour does not improve then you may terminate the call.

8 You should notify your team leader or supervisor if you receive a call of an abusive nature.

9 After you have dealt with an abusive call, take a short break or speak to your team leader or supervisor if you think it will help you to recover.

10 If the call has been recorded, listen to it again with your team leader or supervisor as this may help you to identify alternative ways of dealing with similar calls in the future.

Keeping your headset clean

If you wear a headset throughout your working day, it needs to be fully adjustable so that you can make it fit comfortably – this is particularly important if the ear pieces sit at the entrance to your ear canal rather than resting on the outside of your ears.

When you wear a headset for any length of time, you may find that there is an increased risk of your ears becoming irritated or that you contract an ear infection. The voice tube on the headset can also become blocked, which compromises the effectiveness of the microphone. You therefore need to clean the ear pads and voice tube regularly to reduce the risk of ear infections and voice strain.

  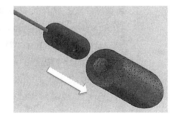

To clean the earpad, remove it by holding the receiver with your left hand and pulling the edge of the earpad with your right hand.

To replace earpad, hold the receiver and the partially replaced earpad in your left hand and fit it over the earpiece with your right hand.

To clean or replace the foam cover, simply remove the cover over the microphone.

Your organisation's working practices and how to report any non conformances

Your organisation may well have documented procedures that give you guidance regarding the working practices it expects you to adopt.

Check it out

Does your organisation have a set of documented working practices that you are expected to operate against?

Your organisation's working practices should take account of the rights that you are afforded under the Working Time Regulations, 1998. These regulations came into force on the 1 October 1998 and they protect workers from being forced to work excessive hours. They also make the provision of paid annual leave mandatory and include rights to rest breaks and uninterrupted periods of rest.

The rights laid out within the Working Time Regulations, 1998 apply to most workers, although there are some exceptions for transport workers, people working at sea, doctors in training and the police and armed forces.

The Working Time Regulations, 1998

Working hours
- a worker's working time, including overtime, must not exceed an average of 48 hours in each 7 days

- if a worker claims this right to not exceed 48 hours, then he or she must not suffer any detriment because of it, such as a reduced chance of promotion

- employers are obliged to keep records of the hours worked.

Night work
- the normal hours of work for night workers will not exceed an average of 8 hours for each 24 hours (the average is measured over a reference period of 17 weeks)

- if the night work involves any 'special hazards' or heavy physical or mental strain, then this limit is reduced to 8 hours worked in any 24-hour period.

Daily rest periods
- adult workers are entitled to a rest period of not less than 11 consecutive hours in each 24-hour period worked

- this rest period may be interrupted for certain types of work where the activities are split up over the day or are of short duration

---

- where an adult worker's daily working time is more than 6 hours, then he or she is entitled to a rest break of at least 20 minutes.

Weekly rest periods
- adult workers are entitled to at least 24 hours uninterrupted rest in each 7 day working period
- as an alternative, the employer may choose to provide either: two rest periods of 24 hours in each 14 day period worked *or* one 48 hour rest period in each 14 day period.

Annual leave
- workers are entitled to at least four weeks leave per year
- they shall be paid at the rate of a week's pay for each week of leave.

Think about it

What do you think you should do if:

- any of the rights that you are afforded under the Working Time Regulations, 1998 are being ignored?
- you are asked to work in a manner that is not consistent with your company's documented working practices?

Who should you speak to in your organisation if you need advice or guidance about working practices?

Your organisation should also have a set procedure that you are expected to follow if:

- you are faced with an instance where the working practices that you have seen taking place do not conform with your organisation's documented working practices *or*
- you are asked to work in a manner that is not consistent with your organisation's documented working practices.

For example, your organisation's documented working practices may state that when you log on at the start of your shift, before you receive your first call, you should make sure that any necessary adjustments have been made to your workstation equipment. This is to ensure that you will be comfortable when you are working and to make sure that you have taken adequate precautions to avoid the risk of RSI. Your organisation may even have provided you with a checklist that you are expected to work through to make sure you do not overlook anything. In this instance, if you were to log on to the system without working through your checklist or making any necessary adjustments, then that would be classed as a non-conformance with your organisation's working practices.

All staff are expected to conform with set working practices for a good reason – it could be to safeguard your health and safety, or the health and safety of others, or it may be to ensure the smooth and efficient running of your department. Either way, it is important that all staff do what is expected of them. Therefore, if you become aware of any instances where set working practices are not being followed it is important that you report this.

Going back to the example above, it could be that your colleague often arrives late for their shift and you are aware that this person frequently just logs straight onto the system and starts taking calls without making the stipulated checks or any adjustments that may be necessary. Or it could be that you are not given sufficient time to carry out your own checks and make any necessary adjustments to your workstation before you are fed calls by the system.

Non-conformances like those above should always be reported because if they were to continue long term they constitute a risk to the health and well-being of staff.

Check it out

♦ Find out if your organisation has a set procedure to follow if you become aware of any instances of non-conformance of company working practices.

How to deal with, report and record emergencies in the workplace

Your organisation should have a set procedure that you are expected to follow when you are faced with dealing with an emergency in the workplace, recording it and reporting it to a higher authority.

Check it out

♦ Who is your appointed First Aider? Make a note of their name and contact details.
♦ Does your organisation have a set procedure that you are expected to follow when you are faced with dealing with, reporting and recording an emergency in the workplace and reporting it to a higher authority?
♦ Does your organisation have its own accident report form that you are expected to complete when you are faced with an emergency in the workplace? If it does, get a copy of the form and familiarise yourself with it.

Dealing with emergencies

This book provides a summary of some of the basic first aid procedures. Please remember that reading this section is **not** a substitute for completing a first aid course. In an emergency situation you will always need to call your company's qualified First Aider to help. If you ever have to deal with an emergency in the workplace, there are four key things to remember (see below).

Four key priorities when faced with an emergency situation

1 Assess the situation – do *not* put yourself in danger.

2 Make the area safe.

3 Assess all casualties and attend first to any *unconscious* casualties.

4 Send for help – *do not delay*.

If there is no response to gentle shaking of the shoulders of the casualty and shouting, the casualty may be unconscious. The priority will now be to check the person's:

♦ **Airway**
♦ **Breathing**
♦ **Circulation**.

This is the **ABC** of resuscitation – in most cases the ABC procedure could save a life.

A person's airway is made up of their windpipe and air passages. If an unconscious casualty is not breathing, it could be because their airway is blocked. The most common cause of a blocked airway is the tongue falling to the back of the throat (see below). It is essential to open the airway for anyone who is not breathing – this can save the person's life.

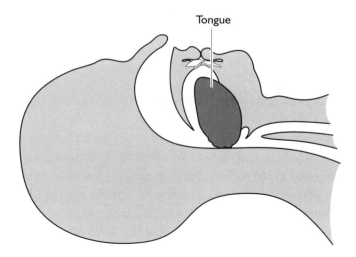

Tongue

If the airway is blocked by the tongue a person cannot breathe

To open the airway:

- place one hand on the casualty's forehead and gently tilt the head back
- remove any obvious obstruction from the casualty's mouth
- lift the chin with two fingertips.

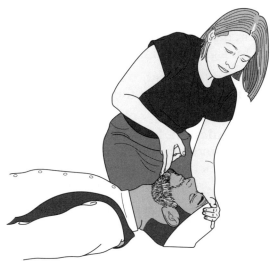

Opening the airway

Look along the chest, listen and feel at the mouth for signs of normal breathing. If the casualty is breathing:

- place the casualty in the recovery position (shown below) and ensure that their airway remains open
- send for help and monitor the casualty until help arrives.

The recovery position

If the casualty is **not** breathing:

- send for help
- keep the airway open by maintaining the head tilt and chin lift
- pinch the casualty's nose closed and allow the mouth to open

- take a full breath and place your mouth around the casualty's mouth, making a good seal
- blow slowly into their mouth until their chest rises
- remove your mouth from the casualty and let the chest fall
- give the casualty a second slow breath and then look for signs of a circulation.

If signs of a circulation are present, continue breathing for the casualty and recheck for signs of a circulation about every 10 breaths.

If the casualty starts to breathe, but remains unconscious, put them in the recovery position. Ensure that their airway remains open and monitor them until help arrives.

To check for **circulation**: look, listen and feel for normal breathing, coughing or movement in the casualty. You should also check for a pulse in the casualty (either in the wrist or neck). If there are no signs of a circulation, or you are at all unsure, immediately start chest compressions.

To find the right place to give chest compressions, put the heel of your hand three-quarters of the way down the breastbone – the diagram below shows the correct point. You should be able to feel where the lower ribs join the breastbone, two finger-breadths above this point is where the heel of your hand should go.

The correct position to give chest compressions

To give chest compressions:

- lean over the casualty, place the heel of your other hand on top of the hand that you have already placed in the correct position on the breastbone and interlock your fingers (see diagram on page 94)
- with your arms straight and held vertical press the breastbone down by about 4 to 5cm (for an average adult) and then release the pressure
- give 15 rapid chest compressions (at a rate of about 100 per minute) followed by two breaths
- continue alternating 15 chest compressions with two breaths until help arrives or the casualty shows signs of recovery.

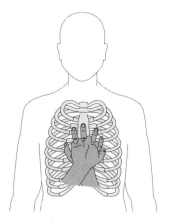

Use the heel of your hand to give chest compressions

Basic first aid

If the casualty is bleeding severely:

- apply direct pressure to the wound
- raise and support the injured part (unless it is broken)
- apply a dressing and bandage firmly in place.

If a broken bone or spinal injury is suspected, get expert help at once. **Do not** move casualties unless they are in immediate danger.

If the casualty has suffered burns, cool that part of the body with cold water until pain is relieved – this could take 10 minutes or more. Burns can be serious, so if you are in any doubt, seek medical help.

If the casualty has something in the eye, wash out the eye with clean water, or sterile fluid from a sealed container to remove any loose material. **Do not** attempt to remove anything that is embedded in the eye.

Try it out

Look at the scene below: Judith has just received an electric shock when she went to tighten one of the connections on her computer. If you were faced with this situation, what would you do?

Reporting work-related accidents, diseases and dangerous occurrences

Try it out

Using the accident report form you obtained earlier, try filling it in based on the emergency that occurred in the previous exercise when Judith received an electric shock.

You need to be aware that, as well as your own organisational requirements, there is also a legal requirement for you to report accidents and ill health at work. The Reporting of Injuries, Diseases and Dangerous Occurrences Regulations 1995 (RIDDOR '95) set out what is required by law. If your organisation has a set of procedures that you are expected to follow for dealing with and recording an emergency in the workplace and reporting it to a higher authority, they should take account of this piece of legislation.

RIDDOR '95 requires the reporting of work-related accidents, diseases and dangerous occurrences. It applies to all work activities but does not apply to all incidents. The information gathered as a result of this piece of legislation allows the enforcing authorities to identify where and how risks arise and enables them to investigate serious accidents. They are then able to help and advise people on preventative action that can be taken to reduce injury, ill health and accidental loss.

If there is an accident connected with work and:

♦ an employee
♦ a self-employed person working on your organisation's premises
♦ a member of the public

is killed or suffers a major injury and is taken to hospital, then the enforcing authority must be notified without delay. This must then be followed up within ten days by sending them a completed accident report form (see page 96).

In general, if you work in an office-based environment then the enforcing authority that needs to be contacted is the environmental health department of your local authority. Their address and telephone number will be in the telephone book under the authority's name.

Keeping records

Records must be kept of any reportable injury, disease or dangerous occurrence. They can be kept in any form but they must include:

♦ the date and method of reporting
♦ the date, time and place of the event
♦ personal details of those involved
♦ a brief description of the nature of the event or disease.

Health & Safety at Work etc Act 1974.
The Reporting of Injuries, Diseases and Dangerous Occurrences Regulations 1995

HSE
Health & Safety Executive

Report of an injury or dangerous occurrence

Filling in this form
This form must be filled in by an employer or other responsible person

Part A

About you
1 What is your full name?

2 What is your job title?

3 What is your telephone number?

About your organisation
4 What is the name of your organisation?

5 What is its address and postcode?

6 What type of work does the organisation do?

Part B

About the incident
1 On what date did the incident happen?

2 At what time did the incident happen?
   (Please use the 24-hour clock eg 0600}

3 Did the incident happen at the above
address?
   Yes ☐ Go to question 4
   No ☐ Where did the incident happen?
        ☐ elsewhere in your organisation - give
        the name, address and postcode
        ☐ at someone else's premises - give
        the name, address and postcode
        ☐ in a public place - give details of
        where it happened

If you do not know the postcode, what is the
name of the local authority?

4 In which department, or where on the
premises, did the incident happen?

Part C

About the injured person
If you are reporting a dangerous occurrence, go
to Part F.
If more than one person was injured in the same
incident, please attach the details asked for in
Part C and Part D for each injured person.

1 What is their full name?

2 What is their home address and postcode?

3 What is their home phone number?

4 How old are they?

5 Are they
   ☐ male ?
   ☐ female ?
6 What is their job title?

7 was the injured person (place x in one box}
   ☐ one of your employees?
   ☐ on a training scheme? Give details:

   ☐ on work experience?
   ☐ employed by someone else? Give details
     of the employer:

   ☐ self-employed and at work?
   ☐ a member of the public?

Part D

About the injury
1 What was the injury?
   (eg fracture, laceration)

2 What part of the body was injured?

A copy of the Accident Report Form

3 Was the injury (place x in one box that applies)
- ☐ a fatality
- ☐ a major injury or condition?
  (see accompanying notes)
- ☐ an injury to an employee or self-employed person which prevented them doing their normal work for more than 3 days?
- ☐ an injury to a member of the public which meant they had to be taken from the scene of the accident to a hospital for treatment?

4 Did the injured person (place x in all the boxes that apply)
- ☐ become unconscious?
- ☐ need resuscitation?
- ☐ remain in hospital for more than 24 hours?
- ☐ none of the above?

Part E

About the kind of accident
Please place an x in one box that best describes what happened, then go to part G

- ☐ Contact with moving machinery or material being machined
- ☐ Hit by a moving, flying or falling object
- ☐ Hit by a moving vehicle
- ☐ Hit something fixed or stationary

- ☐ Injured while handling, lifting or carrying
- ☐ Slipped, tripped or fell on the same level
- ☐ Fell from a height
  How high was the fall in metres?
  [
- ☐ Trapped by something collapsing

- ☐ Drowned or asphyxiated
- ☐ Exposed to, or in contact with, a harmful substance
- ☐ Exposed to fire
- ☐ Exposed to an explosion

- ☐ Contact with electricity or an electrical discharge
- ☐ Injured by an animal
- ☐ Physically assaulted by a person

- ☐ Another kind of accident(describe it in PartG)

Part F

Dangerous occurrences
Enter the number of the dangerous occurrence you are reporting. (The numbers are given in the Regulations and in the notes which accompany this form)

Part G

Describing what happened
Give as much detail as you can. For instance
- the name of any substance involved
- the name and type of any machine involved
- the events that led to the incident
- the part played by any people

If it was a personal injury, give details of what the person was doing. Describe any action that has since been taken to prevent a similar incident. Use a separate piece of paper if you need to.

Part H

Your signature

Date

Where to send the form
Please send it to the Enforcing Authority for the place where it happened. If you do not know the Enforcing Authority, send it to the nearest HSE office.

For official use	
Client number	Location number
Event number	
	___INV REP__Y__N

Reportable major injuries

These include:

- fractures – other than to fingers, thumbs or toes
- amputation
- dislocation of the shoulder, hip, knee or spine
- loss of sight – both temporary and permanent
- chemical or hot metal burn to the eye or any penetrating injury to the eye
- injury resulting from an electric shock or electrical burn, leading to unconsciousness or requiring resuscitation or admittance to hospital for more than 24 hours
- any other injury leading to hypothermia, heat-induced illness or unconsciousness; or requiring resuscitation or admittance to hospital for more than 24 hours
- unconsciousness caused by asphyxia or exposure to harmful substances or biological agents
- acute illness requiring medical treatment, or loss of consciousness arising from absorption of any substance by inhalation, ingestion or through the skin
- acute illness requiring medical treatment where there is reason to believe that this resulted from exposure to a biological agent or its toxins or infected material.

Reportable dangerous occurrences

These are:

- collapse, overturning or failure of load-bearing parts of lifts and lifting equipment
- explosion, collapse or bursting of any closed vessel or associated pipework
- failure of any freight container or any of its load-bearing parts
- plant or equipment coming into contact with overhead power lines
- electrical short circuit or overload causing fire or explosion
- any unintentional explosion, misfire, failure of demolition to cause the intended collapse, projection of material beyond a site boundary, injury caused by an explosion
- accidental release of a biological agent likely to cause severe human illness
- failure of industrial radiography or irradiation equipment to de-energise or return to its safe position after the intended exposure period
- malfunction of breathing apparatus while in use or during testing immediately before use
- failure or endangering of diving equipment, the trapping of a diver, an explosion near a diver, or an uncontrolled ascent
- collapse or partial collapse of a scaffold over 5 m high, or erected near water where there could be a risk of drowning after a fall
- unintended collision of a train with any vehicle
- dangerous occurrence at a well (other than a water well)
- dangerous occurrence at a pipeline

- failure of any load-bearing fairground equipment, or derailment or unintended collision of cars or trains
- if a road tanker carrying a dangerous substance overturns, suffers serious damage, catches fire or the substance is released
- if a dangerous substance being conveyed by road is involved in a fire or released.

The following dangerous occurrences are reportable except in relation to offshore workplaces:

- unintended collapse of any building or structure under construction, alteration or demolition where over 5 tonnes of material falls; a wall or floor in a place of work
- explosion or fire causing suspension of normal work for over 24 hours
- sudden, uncontrolled release in a building of: 100 kg or more of flammable liquid; 10 kg of flammable liquid above its boiling point
- 10 kg or more of flammable gas; or of 500 kg of these substances if the release is in the open air
- accidental release of any substance which may damage health.

Reportable diseases
These include:

- certain poisonings
- some skin diseases, such as dermatitis, skin cancer, chrome ulcer, oil folliculitis/acne
- lung diseases including: occupational asthma, farner's lung, pneumoconiosis, asbestosis, mesothelioma
- infections such as: leptospirosis, hepatitis, tuberculosis, anthrax, legionellosis and tetanus
- other conditions such as occupational cancer, certain musculoskeletal disorders, decompression illness and hand-arm vibration syndrome.

Think about it

- Have you ever been faced with any of the situations listed in the categories of reportable major injuries, dangerous occurrences or diseases?

Keys to good practice

✓ Make sure that you know who your Health and Safety Representative is and how to contact this person should you ever need advice regarding health and safety matters.

✓ Ensure that you are aware of any hazards that may exist within your workplace and that you have taken adequate precautions to minimise any risks they pose.

✓ If you encounter any hazards that you are unable to deal with yourself, make sure that they have been reported to a higher authority.

✓ Always ensure that you have set up your workstation to minimise any risks to your health and maximise your comfort.

✓ Make sure that you take adequate precautions when working with display screen equipment.

✓ Always try to manage the level of stress that you may be exposed to.

✓ Make sure that you are familiar with and that you follow your organisation's working practices. If you spot any non-conformances you should ensure that they are reported to the relevant authority.

✓ Make sure that you know who your appointed First Aider is and that you know their contact details.

✓ Ensure that you know what to do in the event of an emergency as it could save lives.

✓ Make sure that you are familiar with any recording documents that you may need to complete in the event of an emergency.

25.4 Create and maintain effective working relationships with colleagues

WHAT YOU NEED TO KNOW OR LEARN

♦ How to relate to and respect other people and the importance of honouring commitments

♦ How to work effectively as part of a team

♦ The information that colleagues may require and how to provide it

♦ How to deal with requests from colleagues in a willing, timely and effective manner

♦ How to ask for help from colleagues in a polite manner that takes into account their workloads

♦ How to report any difficulties in working relationships.

Did you know?

It is estimated that by the year 2010 approximately 3 per cent of the working population will be working in a call centre.

Case study 5 – Peter's experiences

I work in the Order Processing Department, as part of Number 3 Order Processing Team. There are three different Order Processing Teams that are each made up of four people. I work with Francis, Denzel and Robert.

We get on really well together as we always help each other out and know that we can rely on each other. We nearly always manage to meet our team targets and earn our bonus payments, unlike the other teams. I am sure that it must be because we work so well together.

We usually have a good laugh but we always still manage to get things done. We often go out for a drink together after work and always have a great time.

1 Why do you think that Number 3 Order Processing Team is so successful?
2 Do you work as part of a team within your job role?
3 How well do you get on with your team members or colleagues?
4 Do you think there is anything that you can do to improve your working relationships?

How to relate to and respect other people and the importance of honouring commitments

Wherever you work, you will probably be dealing with both external and internal customers. Your external customers are the people who buy the products or use the services offered by your organisation.

Your internal customers are the people who work for your organisation that you regularly deal with – your colleagues. These people may work in the same office as yourself or they may work in another part of your organisation. They are your customers because what you do has an effect on them – it can either help or hinder them when they are trying to carry out their own job role.

All your internal customers rely on you to provide them with good customer service so that they, in turn, can provide good customer service to their internal and external customers.

Think about it

♦ Who are your internal customers?

Good customer service is the responsibility of everyone within your organisation. If any member of staff fails to co-operate with colleagues, it could ultimately affect the quality of service offered to external customers. All employees must therefore work together as a team. Any personal differences or selfish motivations must be put aside for the good of the team and ultimately the benefit of the external customer.

There are many ways in which you can contribute to good working relationships with others, such as:

♦ working co-operatively with your colleagues

- looking for opportunities to improve your working relationships with your colleagues
- offering help to your colleagues when they are under pressure
- exchanging information with your colleagues so that you can all continually update your knowledge of your organisation's products and services.

If you try to get on with your colleagues, you will be contributing towards a happy and effective working environment. Even the smallest of gestures can have a positive effect.

Think about it

Have you ever been in a situation where you did not get on well with your colleagues and it was affecting your ability to work together?

- What did you do about it?
- Did the situation ever improve?
- How did this happen? If it did not improve, what do you think you could have done to create a positive working atmosphere with your colleagues?

There are a number of positive things that you can do, such as:

- *providing your colleagues with accurate information, on time* – if you are asked for information, do not keep people waiting and make sure the information that you provide is accurate, up to date and complete
- *sharing new information with your colleagues* – if important information like price changes or problems with suppliers comes to your attention, make sure that you let other people know the details
- *considering how your actions may affect other people* – if you leave jobs unfinished or forget to do things, this could have a detrimental effect on others
- *being open and honest* – always be truthful and explain if you have made a mistake. People can only help you when things go wrong if they know what is happening
- *being a reliable member of the team* – if you say you are going to do something, then make sure that you do it. People need to know that they can rely on you
- *doing a good job* – always do your job to the best of your ability
- *doing your fair share of the work* – never try to get out of doing things
- *lending a helping hand* – always be ready and willing to help people
- *respecting other people for the knowledge and experience they may have* – you can draw on this to improve your own knowledge so that you are better able to do your job
- *listening to what others have to say* – if a colleague makes a suggestion about how you could improve the level of service that you offer, then pay attention to them and take their suggestions seriously.

You should constantly look out for positive things that you can do to improve your working relationships with your colleagues.

Think about it

- Have you ever helped a colleague or has a colleague ever helped you?
- What were the circumstances?
- What effect did it have on your working relationship?
- What did you learn from the experience?

Working co-operatively with your colleagues can have long term benefits, as you will generally find that the people you have helped in the past will be willing to help you when you need it.

If things go wrong, never:

- blame your colleagues
- complain about colleagues to customers.

It is much more professional to apologise and then concentrate on what can be done to put the matter right.

How to work effectively as part of a team

Good teamwork is very important to organisations. Every day we are all surrounded by teams working together to achieve a common objective, such as:

- staff in a restaurant providing meals
- fire fighters working together to put out fires
- pop groups making music.

Think about it

- How would you describe a team? Complete the following sentence.
  I think that a team is a group of people who . . .

Being able to work as a member of a team is an important part of many jobs. It is essential to remember that:

- everyone in a team has an important role to play
- everyone in a team relies on everyone else to do their job to the best of their ability
- everyone in the team needs to have the same understanding about what the team wants to achieve.

Think about it

♦ What qualities and skills do you think that your team members need to have? Make a note of them.

♦ Do you have all these qualities and skills yourself.

If you are required to work as part of a team in your job role, you can use the list of qualities and skills that you feel you need but do not yet have as part of your personal development plan. You can then look to address these developmental needs as discussed on page 65.

How can you become a valuable team member?

There are certain things that you can do to make a worthwhile contribution to your team, such as:

♦ trusting, respecting and supporting your colleagues
♦ communicating openly and honestly with other team members
♦ co-operating and working together with your colleagues
♦ sharing responsibility for getting the job done
♦ facing up to problems and dealing with them.

We will now look at each of these things in turn in more detail.

If a team is to be effective, then the members of the team must learn to **trust** each other. They must also respect and value the contribution that each person can make to the team. Each team member contributes their own skills and abilities which, when pooled together, can make a strong team. The strength of every team is that it is composed of different people with different skills, abilities and experiences.

Team members must also **listen** to one another and **share** their opinions and ideas. All members of the team should feel able to make suggestions without being laughed at or shouted down. No team member should gossip, spread rumours or withhold information from other team members.

Co-operation and willingness to help each other are the hallmark of an effective team. As team members realise that the purpose of the team is to achieve a common goal, everyone is willing to go out of their way to help one another. One of the advantages of being a member of a team is knowing that when you need help your colleagues will be there for you – in return for you being there for them.

Team members do whatever needs to be done, because it needs doing. In an effective team people share **responsibility** for getting the job done. They know that if they do a bit extra today for a team member then that same team member will do a bit extra for them another day.

If a problem occurs, team members face facts and work together to find a sensible solution to the problem. No one panics or starts blaming someone else. Instead, they put their heads together calmly to work out what needs to be done.

How can you make a positive contribution to the effectiveness of your team?

There are some things that you can do personally to help your team to work more co-operatively and therefore be more effective. These include:

♦ *proving yourself to be a reliable team member* – always keep your word. Do not make promises unless you know that you can keep them

♦ *considering how what you say and do can affect the team*, for example always make sure that you meet any personal deadlines

♦ *communicating and sharing information*, for example always take time to listen to people and make sure that you explain things properly

♦ *supporting team decisions* – even if you disagree with something, if the team has made a decision to go ahead then your contribution will be required to make it work

♦ *including everyone* – always remember that you are all on the same team and are therefore all working towards the same objective

♦ *encouraging and praising other team members* – do not resent other people's skills or abilities as every success for a team member is also a success for the team and therefore ultimately a success for you

♦ *accepting some responsibility for creating good teamwork* – always do your bit.

What are the advantages of working as part of a team?

The main advantage of working as a member of a team is that you do not have to struggle along on your own when problems arise. There is often someone in the team who has the knowledge, skills or experience to give you a helping hand when you need it most.

Failing that, you can all pool your knowledge, skills and experience to solve the problem.

The information that colleagues may require and how to provide it

It is possible that colleagues will ask you for information that is a 'one-off', in which case you will have to try to provide them with what they need when they ask for it. However, look out for any patterns in the requests that colleagues make and try to anticipate their needs whenever possible.

For example, if a certain colleague always asks for the same type of information on a certain day, try to be ready for them. If you have any spare time available and it is possible to do so, try to prepare this information in advance so that you can have it ready for them when they ask for it.

Think about it

♦ What sort of information do you think that your colleagues might want from you?

♦ Are you likely to be asked for the same information more than once?

If important information (like price changes or problems with suppliers) comes to your attention, make sure that you let your colleagues know the details if they need to know this information too. Never withhold vital information from colleagues.

Think about it

♦ Do you sometimes get to hear important information before some of your colleagues do? If so, do you always make sure that you pass this vital information on to your colleagues?

♦ If you have not always passed vital information on, why have you not done so?

Always make sure the information that you give to others is:

♦ accurate
♦ on time
♦ presented in an appropriate format
♦ clear and legible.

How to deal with requests from colleagues

If a colleague asks for your assistance, always make sure that you do your utmost to help them – even if you are busy yourself. You never know just when you may need them to help you in return.

If you really feel that you cannot help because of your other commitments then tell them *why* you are unable to help them in that way but also offer them whatever help you think you may be able to provide. For example: if a colleague wants you to provide them with some information immediately and you cannot because you are already dealing with a customer; explain that but offer to get the information as soon as you can and say when that is likely to be.

Think about it

♦ Have you ever been in the situation where a colleague was especially helpful despite being very busy with their own work? If you have, how did it make you feel?

Your colleagues realise that you have your own responsibilities to deal with and they will appreciate the effort you make to try your best to satisfy their needs. So always treat your colleagues as you would want them to treat you:

♦ always be courteous and friendly
♦ try your best to be helpful
♦ always keep them informed.

How to ask for help from colleagues

If you need a colleague to help you, then you should always:

♦ be polite and friendly
♦ make allowances for their own workload
♦ appreciate that they may not be able to offer you exactly the help you want within the timescale that you may be hoping for.

Always check your colleagues workload

The same rule applies again: always treat your colleagues as you would want them to treat you.

When you do ask for help from colleagues, make sure that you are clear about what you expect the other person to do for you and check that they understand what you want.

Think about it

♦ Have you ever been in the situation where you have been asked to do something and you have spent all day doing it – only to be told when you have finished that you have wasted your time because it was not what was wanted? If you have, how did it make you feel?

How to report any difficulties in working relationships

Your organisation should have some guidance material or a set of procedures that you are expected to follow if you encounter difficulties in your working relationships with colleagues that you are unable to resolve yourself.

Keys to good practice

✓ Your colleagues are important people, who should be dealt with using courtesy, care and common sense.

✓ You can provide good customer service to your colleagues by: taking responsibility for your own work; finishing tasks on time; keeping your promises and being helpful, courteous and pleasant.

✓ Try to get on with your colleagues, as it contributes towards a happy and effective working environment.

✓ Improve your working relationships with colleagues by helping them and working co-operatively with them.

✓ You should constantly look out for positive things that you can do to improve your working relationships with your colleagues – even the smallest of gestures can have a positive effect.

✓ If a team is to be effective, all the members of the team must trust each other.

✓ The strength of every team lies in the fact that it is composed of different people with varying skills, abilities and experiences.

✓ Everyone in a team has an important part to play – make sure that you respect and value the contribution that each person can make.

✓ Co-operation and willingness to help each other are the hallmarks of effective team members.

✓ Always treat your colleagues as you would want them to treat you.

Check your knowledge

1 Why do organisations set service levels and quality standards?
2 What is the key purpose of quality management?
3 Why do you need to understand what your organisation expects of you?
4 Why should you monitor your own performance?
5 What is a self-development plan?
6 What are the six pieces of health and safety legislation that have an effect on your working environment and what effect do they have?
7 What is a hazard?
8 What is a risk?
9 Why do you need to set up your workstation to suit your personal needs?
10 What is RSI?
11 List six things that you can do to ensure your comfort at work.
12 List three symptoms of stress.
13 Why were the Working Time Regulations, 1998 brought in?
14 What are the four key priorities if you are faced with an emergency situation?
15 What is RIDDOR '95?
16 Who are your internal customers?
17 List four ways in which you can improve your working relationships with colleagues.

UNIT Contribute to improving the
26 quality of service provision

This mandatory unit is all about looking at how you do your job and seeing if you could improve the way you work. It also includes looking at the organisation and how it works and recommending improvements to the services it provides; this could include recommending changes to policies and procedures or the way people work. You would only be expected to do this in the areas of the organisation where you work.

This unit has two elements:

♦ evaluate the effectiveness of service provision
♦ make recommendations for improving service provision.

There are very strong links between this unit and mandatory Unit 25, especially where it covers contributing to an effective working environment.

After you have completed this unit, you will be able to:

♦ look at how you work and interact with your organisation
♦ identify the key aspects of your job role, including your limits of responsibility
♦ look at your organisation objectively to see how it is performing
♦ identify the key areas of service provision within your organisation
♦ use techniques to evaluate, analyse and assess information collected within your organisation
♦ recommend improvements within your organisation.

The case studies in this chapter have been based on a fictitious company – 'First Line Banking', a bank with no high street branches which only operates through its call centres either by customers calling in or using on-line internet banking facilities. Examples from other sectors such as insurance, telemarketing, telecommunications and office supplies are covered in other chapters.

Contributing to the quality of service provision within your organisation is not a one-off activity. It is something you should be doing constantly as part of your job; this is why it is one of the mandatory units within the qualification. It is an excellent work ethic that we should constantly strive to improve our own performance, and the performance of the organisation that we work in. You often find that an effective high quality organisation has a happy and contented workforce.

Several organisations have a suggestions box and members of staff are encouraged to 'post' into it good ideas they have had. Other organisations have a formal system based on a standard template, usually on the IT system, where you can complete the ideas section and submit it to your team leader or line manager for consideration. Many organisations have a reward scheme – if the recommendation you have made is taken up by the organisation they could pay you a bonus for the idea you have had.

Sadly some organisations don't want their agents to recommend any improvements at all.

Check it out

♦ Do you have a suggestions box in your organisation? If so where is it located?
♦ Is there a formal ideas/recommendations scheme?
♦ Have you made any recommendations in the past?

Did you know?

When it comes to evaluating and analysing, you are already doing it quite often. When you go to the travel agents to pick up holiday brochures and take them home to see where you might want to go on holiday, you sit down and start to compare what is in the brochures to see which is the best suited to you. How do you do this? You probably have a holiday specification in your head that you want to match, which might look something like this:

♦ must be the airport that is one hour away, and the flight should not be more than 4 hours long
♦ guaranteed sunshine with temperatures between 25–30°C
♦ hotel 5–10 minutes from the beach, also a pool at the hotel
♦ good children's events for families or good nightlife for singles.

The list could go on. The important thing is that once you have your list you start to evaluate what is in the brochures to find what best matches your specification. You analyse the data until you have limited the choices available, and then from your shortlist you choose the one that you think is going to be the best.

How do you choose a new mobile phone? You compare, analyse and evaluate.

How do you choose a new car? The list could go on.

So don't think that this is something new, you will find that it is something you are already quite good at, we are just going to apply it to something you might not have thought about before, that is – how you work.

Case study 1 – Hari's solution

When you actually thought about it – the solution was quite simple really. In our call centre we only deal with general current account queries but we used to get customers who would call with queries relating to their mortgage and we don't deal with those here, they have to ring the centre in Lowestoft, which is a different freephone number. The problem was you couldn't tell them that until they had got through and asked a question about their mortgage. People would get very angry, with comments like, 'Seven minutes I waited in the queue and now you tell me I have to go and join another queue?' You would then have to try and do damage limitation and pacify the customer without letting them get to you.

We had just launched a marketing campaign where we were offering free mortgage checkups to see if we could reduce the cost of monthly repayments for existing borrowers and the calls were up 20 per cent. This increased the length of the queues and made the callers even angrier when we told them the number they then needed to ring.

Our standard front end electronic introduction is: 'Thank you for calling First Line Banking, unfortunately all of our agents are busy, please hold the line and we will connect you to the first available agent', and then every 20 seconds it says, 'We apologise for the delay, your call is valuable to us, please continue to hold'.

I suggested to my team leader that we should amend the front end introduction to say: 'Thank you for calling First Line Banking, unfortunately all of our agents are busy, if you are calling regarding your mortgage, please call First Line Mortgages on 0800 123 4567, otherwise please hold the line and we will connect you to the first available agent.'
Problem sorted.

Hari's solution reduced the number of calls received by the call centre, reduced the number of angry callers and streamlined the queuing process. It is usually the simple things like this that make the difference. Anything that makes your organisation more efficient or improves the way that you work will contribute to improving the quality of service provision in some way.

26.1   Evaluate the effectiveness of service provision

WHAT YOU NEED TO KNOW OR LEARN

- ◆ How to evaluate information on the operation of the organisation
- ◆ The different methods for the analysis of information
- ◆ How to evaluate the quality of the services you supply

- How to identify areas where potential improvements could be made
- How to evaluate the impact on the organisation if the potential improvements are implemented
- How to record and document the potential improvements you have identified
- Who to pass information on potential improvements to.

How to evaluate information on the operation of the organisation

The first thing to consider is whether any information is relevant to how the organisation is operating. If it is not relevant then discard it; if it is relevant you will then have to decide on the best methods of evaluation. Evaluation is the process of comparing, ranking, and grading information by the use of specific **qualitative** or **quantitative** factors, such as mental and physical skills, degrees of responsibility and working conditions. This can be linked to job evaluation to identify individual skills, although it is important to remember that it is the job – and not the person performing it – that is evaluated.

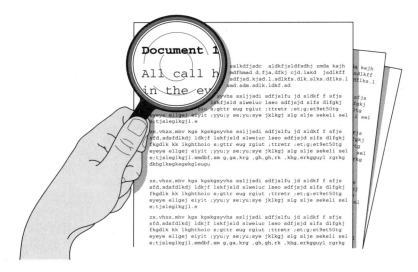

It is important to evaluate all information carefully

We would want to evaluate how the organisation is performing in order to identify strengths and weaknesses within its operations, and then build on these by recommending improvements to the way the organisation operates.

You will need to consider:

- what aspect of the organisation you want to look at
- what information you need
- who can provide the information
- how the information can be collected
- how the information can be evaluated

- what to do with the results of the evaluation
- how the information evaluated can be presented.

The different methods for the analysis of information

We mentioned above **qualitative** and **quantitative** factors and how these can be applied to measuring how well the organisation is doing. We will now look at these in a little more detail (they are also covered in Unit 25).

Qualitative information is an individual measurement of how well each agent is doing within the organisation, normally based on call monitoring against a planned schedule so that each agent is listened to by their team leader at least once per month. From this the team leader can gather information about the agent and use this information either to support the agent's appraisal or for one-to-one sessions. When this is then applied to the whole team a bigger picture begins to emerge and it is possible to look at the quality of the team. When all of the teams are added together we can look at how well the whole call centre is performing relating to the quality of service provided to all of the customers.

Some organisations record conversations so that they can be listened to at a later date for call monitoring. Some organisations record every conversation, such as the emergency services. Some organisations do not record any conversations at all.

Quantitative information is likely to come from the call centre applications such as the Automated Call Distribution system (ACD). This can be used as a statistical tool to analyse several different types of information that will assist in evaluating how well individuals and the organisation are performing. This information can be collected for any time of the day or any day of the week or multiples of both.

Listed below are some of the types of information that can be gathered and analysed:

- number of agents logged on and available to take calls
- amount of time agents log out for whilst on shift
- total number of calls taken during the period specified (normally measured in the total number of calls taken per hour or day, either collectively or by individual agents)
- total number of missed or lost calls
- average waiting times for calls to be connected to an agent
- average call time
- how many calls are referred for further action or escalated to a higher level
- types of calls received (usually listed by product or service required)
- number of inbound calls taken by individual agents
- number of outbound calls made by individual agents
- amount of time agents take completing administration between calls (wrap time).

Quantitative information can be valuable but must not be taken out of context. For example, from your analysis you might see that John takes an average of 24 calls per hour and Michael only takes 11. Your immediate impression might be that John is a better agent because he takes more calls, what you cannot get from this data is the quality of the call. Michael may take fewer calls but it could be that he is far more thorough and has a higher customer satisfaction rating because he is taking the time to address all of their needs and presenting the organisation in a positive, caring manner.

How to evaluate the quality of the services you supply

Your organisation will have set itself targets against which it wants to measure itself and this will be a balance of qualitative and quantitative data. It may well have a mission statement that all employees should know and be working against. You probably have a job description which states the functions you should complete to fulfil your job role.

Check it out

♦ Find out if your organisation has a mission statement. Make a note of what it is or where it can be found.

♦ Do you have a job description? If yes, write down the main job functions that you are expected to do.

♦ Does your organisation have performance targets that are set, that individuals and the call centre have to meet? If it does, make a note of them or if they are detailed, write down where they can be found.

There are many different types of improvements to consider and these can be grouped together (see Figure 26.1).

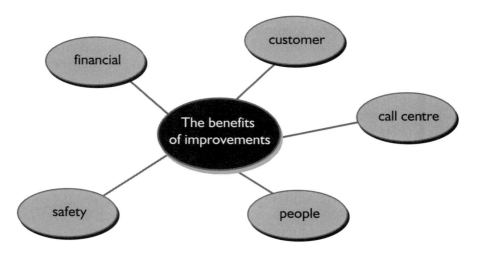

Figure 26.1 Improvements to service provision can have benefits in many areas

People benefits are based on internal working practices and how you and your team interact, including your morale and incentives to work better. They are those improvements that make the working environment better for the staff within the call centre. This can be anything from improving the refreshment facilities to identifying the need to recruit more staff to cope with promotions or increased call volumes.

Call centre benefits are likely to focus on call centre procedures, including call handling systems and applications and how these might be improved or existing problems removed. This would include anything that would improve the operational performance of the call centre.

Customer benefits will include customer care issues and how you deal with callers. Your aim will be to have a loyal customer base that wants to continue using your products and services. This will probably be linked to customer reward schemes or additional products or services that you can give to customers.

Financial benefits are likely to be in the form of bonus schemes and incentives for the staff working in the call centre, or improving the cost effectiveness of the organisation.

Health and safety issues cover the work force and the working environment. It is the responsibility of all employees to strive to work as safely as possible. Under this heading you could consider everything from 'where are the fire exits?' to 'have I changed my posture and adjusted my position in the last 20 minutes?'

How to identify areas where potential improvements could be made

The starting point for this is likely to be an existing problem within the organisation. Ask yourself:

◆ What problems occur whilst I am doing my job?
◆ How much disruption does it cause?
◆ How often does it happen?
◆ What can I do about it?

If you do not have any problems that you can use as a starting point, then look at existing systems and procedures and see if any of these can be improved upon.

SWOT analysis

One method of evaluating and analysing information is to complete a SWOT analysis. SWOT is an acronym, which stands for:

S – Strengths

W – Weaknesses

O – Opportunities

T – Threats

Strengths can relate to the organisation, to customer relations and perceptions, to market shares and to people. Other people strengths include:

♦ friendly, co-operative and supportive staff
♦ staff development and training schemes
♦ appropriate levels of staff involvement through delegation and trust.

Organisational strengths can include:

♦ customer loyalty through established customer care values
♦ organisational identity and employee loyalty, including staff development and support
♦ effective call management systems
♦ efficient systems and procedures across all aspects of the call centre.

Weaknesses should not be seen as an opportunity to 'be negative' about the organisation but an honest appraisal of the way things are. Key questions relating to organisational weaknesses could include:

♦ What obstacles prevent progress within the call centre?
♦ Which elements of the call handling operation require strengthening?
♦ Where are the complaints coming from and who is making them?
♦ Are there any real weak links in the chain?

Items to be addressed could include:

♦ lack of staff morale or motivation
♦ old product range or lack of product innovation to stimulate customer interest
♦ poor competitiveness or overpricing of the products and services offered
♦ lack of awareness of the organisation's mission statement and performance targets
♦ non-compliance or lack of awareness of legislation that affects how you operate
♦ staff absences through work pressures driven by unrealistic performance targets
♦ no method exists within the organisation to measure performance, success or failure.

It is not unusual for 'people' problems to feature among the major weaknesses. These can include poor communications, inadequate leadership, lack of motivation, too little delegation or no trust in the work force and poor staff development.

Opportunities can be very diverse and can have implications both within and outside the organisation. They are likely to be linked to increasing the profitability of the organisation, depending mainly on how much disposable income your customers have within your customer base. Opportunities can include some of the following:

♦ new markets or product ranges that you could target or offer
♦ changes in call handling technology and call centre applications
♦ new government or call sector initiatives

- new programmes for monitoring quality and training staff
- changes in financial circumstances, such as an increase or decrease in interest rates
- targeting different age profiles, especially with an ageing population as people continue to live longer
- looking at the strengths and weaknesses of your competitors
- the timescales involved and how long the opportunities might last in order to take the most advantage from them.

Threats are the opposite of opportunities; all of the factors listed above under opportunities could have an adverse effect if turned around and looked at from a different perspective or change of emphasis.

Think about it

- Look at all of the items listed above under **opportunities** and change the statements so that they become threats. Then look at the potential impact on your organisation.

Check it out

Look at your organisation.

- Do you have any threats within your organisation that have not been covered?

Once you have completed the SWOT analysis you should have four lists. You must then evaluate each item or idea and decide if it is important enough for you to take it forward as a potential improvement within your organisation.

How to evaluate the impact on the organisation if the potential improvements are implemented

You would only consider ideas that had a positive impact on the organisation; any ideas that would have a negative impact should be discarded. For example, a recommendation could be that shifts are extended by one hour to allow a more flexible shift changeover period. This could be a positive benefit for people coming on shift, but the impact on staff morale for those having to stay on shift could have a very detrimental effect and could affect customer satisfaction.

A good way to approach the evaluation is to ask yourself two questions at each stage of the evaluation: *What if?* and *So what?* From this you will get *'if I did this what would the impact be?'* and *'So what are the implications for the agents and the organisation?'*

Case study 2 – Sanjiv and the morning break

We work on a three shift rotation: 08.00 to 16.00, 16.00 to midnight and midnight to 08.00, so we work on a 3 × 8 hour cycle. We have some part-time agents who work around school hours and do 09.30 to 14.30. We also have some agents who do part-time evenings, 18.00 to 22.00.

We are allowed a 5-minute break each hour or we can stay on shift and add these together. We also have a 10 minute break after the first 2 hours on shift, 30 minutes after 4 hours, and 10 minutes after 6 hours. We all appreciate that this is very generous, but it does help to keep the stress levels down.

We used to have a shortage of agents available to take calls between 10.00 and 10.30 during the morning. I decided to see if I could find out what the problem was and my team leader let me have the call statistics 08.00 to 12.00 for the last month. I noticed immediately that no-one was taking the 5 minute break at the end of the first hour and that 62 per cent of agents were saving their 5 minute breaks to add to the 10 minute break and having 20 minutes at 10.00; 8 per cent were taking 25 minutes at 11.00 and 30 per cent worked straight through to the main break and took 1 hour.

So what? If we could reduce the number of agents taking a 20-minute break at 10.00 we would have more agents on the phones and reduce the queue times.

What if? We tried to encourage some agents to take the 5 minutes at the end of the first hour and then take 20 minutes between 10.30 and 11.00 by bringing the next 5 minutes forward a little. This would then encourage them to take the lunch break slightly later so that the problem did not repeat itself later in the shift.

I put together a simple questionnaire to get the team's opinions, based on 50 per cent taking the 5 minute break at 1 hour and the 20 minute break at 10.30. The responses were great, especially with those that had needed a comfort break after the first hour but held over because they wanted the full 20 minutes – not just 15. We now have half of the team rotating around this scheme and alternating on a weekly basis and everybody seems to be happy. The other teams have also looked at this on the other shifts and it seems to be working there also.

1 Do you think this could work in your organisation?
2 Do you have periods when you are short of agents during your shift?
3 How long are the breaks you are allowed during your shift?
4 Can you think of another way this problem could have been solved?

How to record and document the potential improvements you have identified

If you have a formal recommendation system then you will use this format to record and document your ideas on how things can be improved. If you do not have a formal system it would be logical to list the potential improvements in an order of priority as to which you think is the best and then the second best and so on. For each potential improvement you would want to include the following information:

♦ what the potential improvement is
♦ why you think the existing system needs improving
♦ why you think this is an improvement over the existing systems
♦ the benefits, advantages and disadvantages of the potential improvement
♦ the impact on the organisation
♦ the achievability of the potential improvement.

If you have no formal system for evaluating and recommending improvements within your organisation the following format may help you.

Over the next full working week (or longer if required) look at how you work and try to identify areas where you feel work could be improved if your employer adopted your ideas. Keep a record of all the things you have evaluated and the dates on which you have been looking at them. Make sure that you look at both qualitative and quantitative data as you complete the exercise. Then as a separate list write down the things you would like to recommend as improvements.

You can see from this that it is not a difficult process to look at what you do and try to see if you can improve how you work. The motto 'Work smarter not harder' is often a good starting point, especially if it is an information technology or call centre application that can be improved upon to make your work easier.

The simple exercise listed above is included on the CD ROM in the form of a blank template that you can use or customise for your own use.

Who to pass information on potential improvements to

Your team leader would be the first place to start, or you may have another person within the organisation who has been nominated to deal with suggestions made by yourself or other agents. The operations manager would then look at the benefits of the potential improvements to see if they are necessary or practical to implement and that the benefits outweigh any potential disadvantages. It may be that your call centre is so small that you only have one manager to deal with all of the day-to-day running of the call centre.

It is possible that different people within your organisation would look at different aspects of how the organisation works. The health and safety officer would deal with anything to do with work safety, the human resources department might deal with people/agent issues and the operations department might look at how the call centre is operating.

Check it out

- Look at your organisation. Is there a person nominated to deal with suggestions from staff? If not, to whom would you give your ideas and potential improvements?
- Have you ever made any suggested improvements in the past?
- Were these implemented by your organisation? Even if they were not taken up by your organisation, make a list them for your portfolio.

Keys to good practice

✓ It's often the simplest ideas that can make the difference.

✓ Always discuss your ideas at an early stage so that if they are not going to be practical you do not spend too much time researching something that will not be adopted.

✓ Consider the impact of your suggestions on individuals as well as the organisation.

✓ Try to use SWOT or some other form of analytical tool to evaluate your ideas.

✓ Remember: *So what?* and *What if?*

✓ Find out whom you should contact within your organisation with your ideas and suggestions.

 Make recommendations for improving service provision

WHAT YOU NEED TO KNOW OR LEARN

- How to identify which would be the best improvements to recommend
- How to establish the feasibility of the potential improvements
- How to present information on potential improvements to the correct people
- How to state the benefits of the potential improvement.

How to identify which would be the best improvements to recommend

The work you have done in the last section should have left you with a series of lists based on what you have identified as Strengths, Weaknesses, Opportunities and Threats with areas where improvements can be implemented.

We now need to prioritise from these lists which are the most important elements. You may find that what you think is very important is of little concern to the organisation or something that you think is of little consequence is vital to the organisation – so it is important to get a balanced view. This may involve asking colleagues and others about what they think is or is not important and then grading the list.

The grading criteria are therefore important and it is useful to have a standard list of things to consider and what the effect would be if the recommendation were to go forward. These could include the impact on:

♦ the customer
♦ the quality of call handling
♦ the quantity of calls handled
♦ operational efficiency
♦ individuals within the call centre.

This could then be put into a table format, with a scale of one to five, where one is low impact and five is high impact so the higher the score the higher the impact. If you can think of anything that is a specific consideration within your organisation you could add it to the table below.

My idea:					
My ideas impact on what?	**1**	**2**	**3**	**4**	**5**
Impact on customers?					
Impact on the quality of call handling?					
Impact on the quantity of calls handed?					
Impact on operational efficiency?					
Impact on individuals within the call centre?					

From this you may find that something has very little impact and it can be rejected at this point. What you should look for is medium to high impact across several of the areas.

How to establish the feasibility of the potential improvements

You may have had a brilliant idea – but it is completely unachievable.

You have to consider whether your ideas and suggestions are feasible.

The most obvious consideration is the cost to the organisation; if it is going to cost a lot of money with little immediate benefit it is most likely that the organisation would discard the idea immediately. Other factors to consider could also include:

♦ Time scale to implementation? Is it going to be out of date before we can get it in place?

You may have a brilliant idea!

It is just completely unachievable

- Will our existing technology cope with it? Will current call centre applications allow this to be implemented using our existing systems?
- Will it be accessible to all or limited? Who are the improvements targeted at and will it lead to discrimination or affect staff morale?
- Is there going to be a balance between the benefits to customers, call centre agents and call centre operations?
- Will it have an impact on our competitors and how do we think they will respond?

How to present information on potential improvements to the correct people

Is there an existing format for you to use for recommending improvements laid down by your organisation? If not, there are different formats ranging from informal discussions with your supervisor or at team meetings, to full blown presentations to the call centre management team using multimedia presentation formats. These different formats could include:

- handwritten notes
- word-processed notes
- tape recordings to illustrate voice procedures
- video recordings
- role-plays using agents
- acetates for use with an overhead projector
- lists or points for discussion on white boards, chalk boards or flip charts
- PowerPoint presentations or other IT applications using slide shows
- existing lists, tables and statistics extracted and printed from the call management systems, normally in the form of queries or reports.

Tape recordings, videos and role-plays are good ways of presenting qualitative data. Tables, lists and statistics are good for presenting quantitative data.

You will have to ask yourself 'which is the most appropriate for my idea.' If it is a low impact idea or suggestion you would probably hand write a memo to your team leader or perhaps send an internal email. If it is a high impact idea or suggestion for improvement you will need to spend more time in preparing how you want to present the information that you have analysed and evaluated.

Making presentations

The basic structure for a presentation has three parts: the beginning, the middle and the end.

The **beginning** would cover:

- an introduction to the presentation, how long it is going to take and what you aim to achieve by the end
- the area of the call handling operation that you have evaluated
- the reason why you felt your evaluation was necessary, including the background to the problem or why you think improvement is necessary
- how you would like to deal with questions from your audience.

The **middle** would cover:

♦ the methodology you applied to the area that you looked at, including qualitative and quantitative concerns
♦ how you conducted your research and the different methods you used to analyse and evaluate the data
♦ the benefits and disadvantages to the organisation, including the 'impact' questions
♦ the rationale that led to the improvement that you wish to make.

It is best to keep your presentation as simple as possible

The **end** would cover:

♦ your conclusions and the outcome of the analysis you have made
♦ your recommendations for improvements
♦ a summary of the benefits to the organisation or individuals
♦ a way forward should the organisation adopt the recommendations.

The CD-ROM has a simple presentation with the headings from the list above already included that you can customise for your own use.

If you are not giving a presentation and you wish to produce a written report, the headings listed above may still be used so that your report can follow a structure that will lead you through all of the areas and topics you wish to cover. The CD-ROM has a blank Word template with the headings from the list above already included that you can customise for your own use.

Case study 3 – Mandy's presentation

I had been working on a hyperlink so that when you put the customer's account number into the system and their main account screen appears, the last set of text notes entered on their file would be linked so that you could call them up straight away in case they were referring back to the last conversation they had with the call centre. My team leader, Julie, thought it was an excellent idea and that I should put together a formal presentation using PowerPoint that I could give to the team at the next meeting.

I was very nervous, but once I got started it just seemed to come out in the way that I had planned, the slides made me keep to the order in which I wanted to cover things.

Julie has put my idea forward for the next management meeting and thinks it will speed up calls from regular callers, which will have a positive impact on the quantity of calls handled, operational efficiency and customer satisfaction – not to mention entry into the call centre's rewards scheme for good ideas!

1 Do you know how to make a hyperlink?
2 Do you have a system for linking to notes about customers on your system?
3 Have you ever used PowerPoint or been at a PowerPoint presentation?
4 Do you ever have formal presentations at your team meetings?
5 Do you have a reward scheme for ideas in your organisation?

How to state the benefits of the potential improvements

Most ideas are likely to have advantages and disadvantages; we need to look at how we state the benefits of the potential improvements which we have identified as outweighing any potential disadvantages. The person who can identify a problem and then take the problem to the correct person with a good sound practical solution effectively removes the problem. It is likely to be your team leader or line manager within the call centre that you would go to first.

Did you know?

Most of the best ideas come from the call centre agents who complete the job and expect no incentive other than recognition that they are trying to make the call centre work better.

Again we would want to use the questions we have asked earlier in this section but now looking at the **benefits** of what we want to recommend, i.e. benefits to:

◆ the customer
◆ the quality of call handling
◆ the quantity of calls handled

- ◆ operational efficiency
- ◆ individuals within the call centre
- ◆ finances
- ◆ health and safety benefits.

You must be honest and state all of the advantages and disadvantages to the organisation. If you are presenting a balanced view, looking at all aspects of the potential improvements you have considered, and you have done your analysis properly, then the benefits will outweigh the disadvantages.

Keys to good practice

✓ Use the lists you have compiled from the evaluation exercise as the starting point for your analysis and evaluation – SWOT.

✓ Use your lists to choose which is the best idea or potential improvement to recommend.

✓ Consider the feasibility of your ideas at an early stage so that those likely to be unachievable can be discarded without too much time and effort being spent on them.

✓ Complete the *impact on* exercises and score your findings.

✓ Do not spend a lot of time considering low impact ideas unless they are likely to be implemented with little effort on your part.

✓ When making a presentation, keep it as simple as possible whilst achieving your aim.

✓ When stating the benefits of your recommendations, ensure the positive aspects outweigh the negative.

Check your knowledge

1 How do you evaluate information on how well the organisation is operating?

2 What are the different methods for the analysis of information that can be used within your organisation?

3 How do you evaluate the quality of the services you supply both individually and as an organisation?

4 How do you identify areas where potential improvements could be made?

5 How do you evaluate the impact on the organisation if the potential improvements you have identified are implemented?

6 Is there a standard recording process used within your organisation for documenting ideas and potential improvements?

7 If there is not a standard recording process within your organisation, how would you record and document the potential improvements you have identified?

8 Who within the organisation would you pass information on potential improvements to for consideration or approval?

9 From all of the potential improvements you have identified, how would you identify which would be the best improvements to recommend?

10 How would you establish the feasibility of the potential improvements you have identified?

11 What are the different formats available within your organisation for presenting information on potential improvements?

12 How would you state the benefits of the potential improvements to the correct people within your organisation?

13 List the names of the people within your organisation that you would present your ideas or potential improvements to.

UNIT 2 Address the needs of callers

This option unit is all about establishing the needs of callers, by telephone and, where appropriate, by email. It is also about taking the correct steps to meet those needs within your levels of responsibility. Callers may be from within your organisation or they could be from outside.

This unit has two elements:

♦ identify the needs of the caller
♦ meet the needs of callers.

This unit will provide you with an understanding of customer service. It will also help you to develop the listening, questioning and communication skills you will need to ensure that you offer sensitive, respectful and responsive service to customers requesting assistance over the telephone.

After you have completed this unit, you will be able to:

♦ understand the difference between 'excellent' and 'acceptable' customer service
♦ question customers, using encouragement and summarising techniques to meet the caller's needs
♦ use appropriate language to demonstrate caring, gain trust and arrive at quality solutions to the issues in hand.

Your ability to meet the needs of the customer can have a crucial effect on the customer's perception of your organisation.

Did you know?

90 per cent of individuals who lodge a complaint will return or speak well of the company if their complaint was well handled.

If a customer receives bad service, it is likely that they would not want to use the products or services of your organisation again. Also, if they were upset by the experience, they will probably mention what happened to other people.

Did you know?

Dissatisfied customers will tell 9 to 20 other people about their dissatisfaction.

When they hear about the problems or difficulties encountered by the original customer, these other people may well decide not to use your organisation's products or services either. It is therefore possible that just one experience of bad customer service could create a ripple effect that results in your organisation losing many customers.

Today's customers expect good service at all times.

The table below shows how customers generally react to different types of service.

Type of service	Nature of customer's reaction
The customer service is poor.	The customer is very disappointed and may be unwilling to use the products or services offered by your organisation again.
The customer service is acceptable.	The customer is neither impressed nor disappointed. However, the customer is unlikely to show any commitment to your organisation and may want to try other organisations in order to compare the level of service.
The customer service is good.	The customer feels that the service received was good but it will not necessarily influence them to continue to use your organisation. The customer may use your organisation again to see if your level of service improves.
The customer service is very good.	The customer is pleasantly surprised by the level of customer service received and if all the other influencing factors, such as the price of your products or services, are favourable, will continue to use your organisation.
The customer service is excellent.	The customer is delighted with the quality of the service received. The customer is impressed enough to tell friends about how good your organisation is and is very likely to continue to use your organisation even if other factors like price and convenience are not as favourable. Some customers are happy to pay more in order to get top quality customer service.

The case studies in this chapter have been based on a fictitious company – 'Globe Trotters Direct', a travel agency. Examples from other sectors such as banking, insurance, telemarketing and office supplies will be covered in other chapters.

Globe Trotters Direct

Case Study 1 – Tracy's experiences

The caller wanted to find out if we had any last minute cheap holidays available to Spain. As we always have short notice deals available to several Spanish resorts, I needed to find out whether any of them would be suitable for her. To do this, I had to find out what her exact requirements were.

I started by telling the customer that we always have a number of last minute holidays available at good prices. I then asked her where in Spain she would like to go. She said that she did not mind where, as long as it was hot and sunny. This was useful to know as we only have cheap deals to three Spanish resorts, so we cannot offer much choice. However, at this time of year all three resorts are hot and sunny so I now knew that any of them should be suitable for her.

I then asked the customer if she knew when she would like to go; how long she would like to go for; and how many people would be in her party, as I needed to know this in order to search our database for a suitable holiday. She said that she could get time off work any time in the next month, that she would like to go for a week and that she would be travelling alone.

I now had enough information about the customer's requirements to be able to make a basic search of our database to see if we had any vacancies that might suit her. The computer system brought up several possibilities, so I now just had to determine which of these most appealed to the customer. However, I wanted to check first that I had fully understood the customer's requirements, so I told her that there were a number of possibilities open to her and asked if I could just confirm that I had understood her requirements correctly. She was happy for me to this, so I summarised the search I had made on the computer. I told her that I had brought up all the holidays that were available to hot and sunny Spanish resorts with a departure date within the next three weeks and a duration of 10 days or less. I explained that I had extended the search to up to 10 days for her as you can often get 10 day breaks for very little extra cost. She said that sounded great.

I then asked her if she would like me to sort them by price as I remembered that she had asked for a cheap deal when she initially enquired and that she did not seem to mind where she went. She seemed pleased that I had noted her requirements so well. I brought up the holidays that fitted her criteria in order of price and went through the three cheapest options with her.

She was pleased with the selection and reserved the most expensive one of the three offered – it was a ten day break to Benidorm and was only £25 dearer than the others, which were only seven day breaks. She said that she would go back and check that she would be able to get eight days off work instead of a week before she confirmed the booking but that she didn't think it would be a problem. She then thanked me for being so helpful.

I was pleased that I had been able to find her exactly what she wanted, as she was obviously very happy with what we had agreed. I was also conscious that I would earn more commission because I had let her consider a longer holiday.

1 How did Tracy find out if Globe Trotters Direct had any holidays available that would be of interest to the customer?
2 How did Tracy confirm that she had understood the caller's requirements?
3 How did she persuade the customer to consider a more expensive holiday?
4 How did she help the customer to decide which holiday she would like to book?
5 Do you think that Tracy met the customer's requirements?
6 Do you think that Tracy built a good rapport with the customer?
7 Do you think that the customer went away feeling that her needs had been met?

2.1 Identify the needs of the caller

- ◆ Your organisation's procedures for greeting customers and confirming their identity
- ◆ How to build a rapport with the customer
- ◆ How to find out what the customer wants from your organisation through the use of appropriate questioning techniques
- ◆ How to confirm with the customer your understanding of their needs
- ◆ The importance of maintaining the confidentiality and security of information
- ◆ How to ensure the accuracy and reliability of data
- ◆ Your obligations under the Data Protection Act.

Your organisation's procedures for greeting customers and confirming their identity

Greeting customers

Your introduction may be the first contact that the caller has ever had with your organisation. Your greeting should be warm and friendly (let the customer 'hear' your smile) whilst still being professional – this balance is not always easy, but you can perfect it with practice.

It is all about first impressions – telephone greetings are critical. Prospective customers are deciding whether or not to do business with you, whilst irate customers are deciding how helpful and competent you are.

Think about it

Can you think of an occasion when you contacted a company by telephone only to find that they did not treat you like a valued customer? Maybe they were rude and impatient or perhaps they seemed disinterested.

◆ How did it make you feel?

As customers cannot see you when you communicate over the telephone, they cannot read your body language. They will therefore form judgements about you, and your organisation, which are based on:

- ◆ what you say – the words that you use
- ◆ how you say it – your tone, clarity of voice and the speed at which you speak.

Did you know?

About 80 per cent of respondents indicate that the way the telephone is answered influences their opinion of the service they are calling.

You should always try to answer the telephone as swiftly as you can. Many companies aim to answer incoming calls within the first three rings. Pay special attention to your tone of voice, as the customer will be focusing on your voice and could detect your mood. If you are tired, bored, irritable or cannot be bothered, the caller may pick up on this.

To customers, you represent your organisation. So if you appear uninterested or unhelpful, they will automatically assume that your organisation is also uninterested and unhelpful.

Your organisation may well have a standard greeting that you are required to use. If this is the case, then you will need to find out what it is and practise using it so that it trips off the tongue and sounds natural when you use it to greet a customer.

Check it out

Find out if your organisation expects you to use a standard phrase when greeting callers. If your organisation uses more than one standard greeting, is there also guidance on which greeting to use on any particular occasion? If it does, make a note of it or, if the guidance is detailed, write down where it can be found. Keep this for your evidence. If your organisation does not use a standard greeting, think of an appropriate greeting that you could use and write it down.

Telephone greetings

The key elements that make up a telephone greeting are:

♦ the company's name
♦ your name
♦ an offer of assistance.

You should state the company's name so that customers know that they have reached the right place. Always state your name because it is a sign of authority – giving your name implies that you are accountable. It also creates a personal touch. Lastly, end with a question that expresses your desire to serve the caller.

You should also be prepared to provide the caller with your full name if this is specifically requested, as some callers like to make a note of your full name if they think that they may need to contact your organisation again regarding the same subject.

Your greeting needs to feel natural, as it makes it easier for you to sound pleasant consistently. Your delivery should always be courteous, articulate, friendly, unrushed and enthusiastic.

If you are having difficulty thinking up a suitable greeting, a commonly used greeting that you could tailor is:

'Thank you for calling Globe Trotters Direct, Matt speaking, how may I help you?'

Also make sure that you have a pen and paper ready, so that you can take down the caller's name as early in the conversation as possible.

Confirming the customer's identity

If the customer wants you to do something on their behalf, such as change or cancel their order or amend the details of their account, you will normally need to confirm the identity of the caller before you carry out their request. This helps to ensure that the caller is someone who is permitted to make such a request.

It may be as simple as asking the customer for their address or date of birth so that you can check it against the details held on file. You may also ask for their account number or order number, depending on the nature of the request, and it is also possible, especially if the request is in connection with a credit card account, that you may need to ask the caller for a pre-agreed password.

Your organisation's procedures should tell you what type of confirmation you will need to carry out.

Check it out

Does your organisation have a set of procedures for confirming the identity of the caller that you are expected to follow?

How to build a rapport with the customer

It is your responsibility to put callers at ease at all times by helping them to feel that they are free to talk. This is often called a *permissive environment*. Show the caller that you want to listen – sound interested by using encouraging, affirmative expressions such as *'uh-huh'*, *'I see'* or *'yes'*.

You should try to make the customer feel important by:

♦ always being patient and giving the caller as much time as he or she needs
♦ not rushing the caller and trying not to interrupt
♦ giving them your undivided attention – do not doodle or shuffle papers
♦ not sounding monotonous or irritated.

You need to think about how your caller is feeling. Try to establish a two-way relationship as soon as possible, particularly if you are likely to be talking to them at some length. To do this, you need to establish an empathy between yourself and the caller. Empathy is about being able to put yourself in the caller's position so that you are better able to understand them. It will enable you to gain an accurate understanding of the message that they are trying to get across and the feeling behind that message.

Listening skills

Most people think about speaking when they think about communication skills. They think about forming sentences effectively, perhaps being funny or using expressive phrases. They may also think about how they are able to come to the point quickly and clearly. All this is important. However, the best path toward being a good communicator is to be *quick to listen and slow to speak*. Listening skills are more important than most people realise. Those who do realise it are probably the best communicators.

Try it out

See how good a listener you really are.

In pairs, listen to a short conversation, about 10 minutes long, on the radio or the television. Now summarise the conversation you have just heard.

Compare notes to see how much you both remembered.

If you found this exercise easy, you listened well. If you did not find it easy to remember what was said and summarise it yourself, it was probably because you were not listening effectively. Think about how well you were really listening – could you have done anything differently that would have improved your ability to listen, such as concentrating harder? You may wish to repeat the exercise until you find that you can do it easily.

It is important to concentrate on what is being said

If you are a good listener you can accomplish more in a shorter period of time because you get the right information to begin with. You reduce the margin for error because you are focused on what the customer is saying instead of on what you are going to be saying next. When you listen well, the conversation stays on track and, even more valuable, the customer may like you more. It helps to build a rapport with the customer that is based on genuine interest and caring.

Tone, volume and speed

In order to react appropriately to your customers, you must be able to gauge how they are feeling. The tone and volume of their voice, and the speed at which they are speaking, can all give you an indication about how the caller is feeling.

Speaking loudly could indicate that someone is angry. However, it is also something that some people do when they speak on the telephone. It could also indicate that the caller has some hearing loss and they are not aware that they are shouting. You should therefore not assume that they are angry.

Speaking slowly or quietly, with words that trail off at the end of the sentence, could mean that the person is feeling anxious, insecure, confused or even frightened. However, it could also be that this person always speaks slowly and hesitantly.

Speaking very fast, with words that tumble out and get mixed up, may mean that the person is feeling upset, irritated, confused or unsure. Or it could mean that the caller is just in a hurry and desperate to get away.

Being able to judge accurately how a customer is feeling, and knowing how to respond appropriately, are important aspects of providing good customer service. If someone is anxious, upset, confused or angry then you need to be able to:

◆ recognise how they are feeling
◆ behave in a way that shows the customer that you understand their feelings and that you want to offer them reassurance, assistance or whatever else is most appropriate at that time.

You will not begin to pick up on the subtle clues from a person's verbal communication, such as their rate of speech, the tone of their voice, or their choice of words, if you are not concentrating. The most important part of learning to listen effectively is making sure that you are paying attention.

There are five reasons why we sometimes have trouble paying attention to customers. If you understand these factors, you will be better able to avoid them. The five factors that can prevent us from listening are described in the table below.

Factor	How this can stop you listening effectively
Environmental distractions	A call handling facility can often be a beehive of activity. You might be on the telephone with a customer when a colleague waves a piece of paper in front of your face or a red light may begin flashing because there are so many customers in the queue. All kinds of distractions and interruptions can take place. However, in the midst of it all, you need to pay attention and remain focused.

Factor	How this can stop you listening effectively
The third ear syndrome	Many customer contact agents develop a 'third ear'. While you are on the telephone listening to the customer with two ears, you might have a 'third ear' tuned in to what is going on in the background. If this happens, it might be because you care about your colleagues or customers. You might suddenly overhear another agent attempting to solve a tricky problem that you spent a lot of time solving the previous day. Or conversely, you might hear someone solving a tricky problem that you could not solve. While this distraction is based upon good intentions, it detracts from your ability to focus on the task at hand – resolving your current call.
Jumping ahead	Another factor that prevents us from listening is that we sometimes focus on what we are going to say next. Sometimes we mentally jump ahead in the conversation. This has to do with two factors. First, we are expected to solve problems as quickly as possible and, second, we can listen at a faster rate than we can speak.
Emotional filters	Some organisations serve the same customer base all the time. If this is the case, you could get to know some of your customers and develop an emotional response to them. These are called emotional filters. For example, you might think that a particular customer is always angry. In response to this, you might 'brace yourself' whenever that customer calls, which could unfairly influence the transaction. Good listeners are careful to make sure that they are not unduly influenced by past experiences. You need to keep an open mind from the beginning of every conversation.
Day dreaming	Another reason why we do not always pay attention is because of day dreaming. For example, imagine that it is late morning and you get the type of call that you have been handling all morning. You know what the customer is going to say, as you have handled a number of these calls already. Now you are wondering, 'what shall I have for lunch?' You re-engage yourself in the conversation and find that you have not missed much. The customer continues to talk and you work together to define the problem. Then maybe you think you know what the customer is going to say next again, so you decide you are going to get a sandwich from the shop down the road and that you could buy a magazine to read while you are in there. You start thinking about what else you could do while you are out, and so on. Now you are day dreaming. When you come back to the conversation, you have lost the thread – your day dreaming has gone on for too long. You have wasted time, and you have to back track in the conversation by asking the customer to repeat what was said. This can happen because we think much more quickly than we can talk. Just being aware of this tendency will help you to stay with the conversation and focus on what the customer is saying.

When you speak to the caller, you need to concentrate on what you say and how you say it, as the words that you use can influence the mood of the conversation. How you phrase things can also affect the customer's reaction to you and what you are saying.

Use positive words and phrasing at all times. The table below shows examples of how to phrase things positively.

Phrases to avoid	It is better to say
Bear with me *or* Just a sec	May I put you on hold for a moment?
Hang on *or* hold on	May I put you on hold for a moment?
I can't	I am unable
I'll try	Certainly
I'm afraid	I am sorry
I might be able to	I should be able to
This problem	This situation *or* this issue
OK *or* Yeah	Yes
Thanks	Thank you
Bye	Goodbye and thank you for calling

You must also be careful not to use sentences or phrases that may sound abrupt. The table below shows examples of phrases that you should avoid using.

Phrases to avoid	It is better to say
What?	Please could you repeat that for me?
What for?	Why would you want that?
Who are you?	Who am I speaking to please?
Who?	Do you know the name of the person?

Also, do not use the royal 'we', use 'I' – as it shows ownership. Do not say, '*We will sort this out for you*' it is better to say, '*I will make sure that this is sorted out for you*' as it shows the customer that you are committed to dealing with the situation on their behalf.

If you are interacting with a customer who is upset or angry, make sure that you always control your own temper – do not allow the customer to control your emotions. Do not argue with an angry customer as it will only put the person on the defensive. Instead, ask questions, as this will show that you are listening.

The following techniques and phrases can be useful when dealing with customers who are upset or angry. They can also help to stop borderline callers from becoming upset.

If the caller is upset (or on the verge of becoming upset) remember to:

♦ Empathise with the customer's concerns
  '*I can understand how that would be frustrating*'
  '*The manual can be confusing*'
♦ Apologise for the situation
  '*I am sorry that no one has called you about this*'
  '*I apologise for your inconvenience*'

♦ Let the customer know that you want to help
'I want to find a solution for this situation'
'I want to resolve this for you as quickly as possible'
♦ Probe for more information
'Please help me to understand more. . .'
'Please tell me what happened. . .'
♦ Repeat the customer's concerns to make sure that you have a clear understanding
'Let me see if I have understood this clearly. . .'
'Before proceeding, I would like to make sure that I have understood all the facts. . .'
♦ Show the caller that you value their business
'We value your business and want to fix this promptly for you'
'You are an important customer so we want to resolve this quickly for you'
♦ Give the customer several options, or ask the customer what they would like your company to do
'There are three actions that I could take to resolve this. Which one would you prefer?'
'Can you think of a fair way of resolving this?'
♦ Summarise any actions that need to be taken – both yours and the customer's
'Mrs Jones, as we agreed, you will fax me a copy of the letter that you received and I will forward it immediately to my manager for a resolution'
♦ End pleasantly and always thank the caller for the complaint.

How to find out what the customer wants from your organisation through the use of appropriate questioning techniques

You should encourage and allow the caller to state their requirements in full, whilst maintaining control of the call. If a customer is being particularly talkative, it is your responsibility to control the call in a professional way – without making the caller feel that you are trying to rush the call.

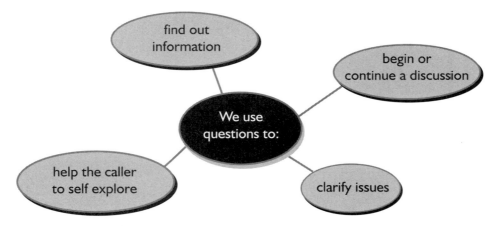

Figure 2.1 Why do we use questions?

In order to balance quality and call handling time, when a caller is being vague in their request, you should use appropriate questioning techniques to obtain more information. We use questions every day – most of our daily conversations involve either asking or answering questions.

You will need to become skilled at asking the right kinds of questions and at being able to interpret the answers. Watch good interviewers on the television – what makes them so powerful? On the other hand, what makes other interviewers so bad?

Check it out

Watch some interviews being conducted on the television. What makes an interviewer good or bad?

There are several different types of questions that you can use.

Closed questions are useful when you are looking for a straight '*yes*' or '*no*' answer. A closed question can be easily recognised, as it starts with such words as those in Figure 2.2.

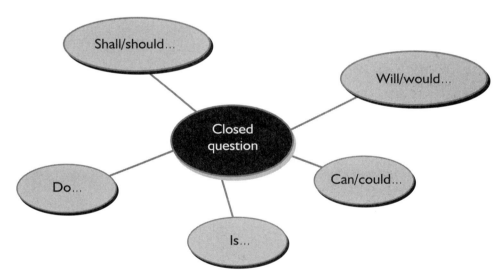

Figure 2.2 Asking a closed question

Some examples of closed questions are: '*Do you like to go to Spain when you go on holiday?*' or '*Will you be going to Spain next year?*'. When you ask a closed question it is very unlikely that you will get anything other than '*Yes*' or '*No*' as an answer.

However, if you need to know more than 'yes' or 'no', open questions are designed to encourage individuals to talk. Asking open questions will help you to get enough information either to solve the problem or identify the causes of the problem.

Open questions begin with words like those shown in Figure 2.3.

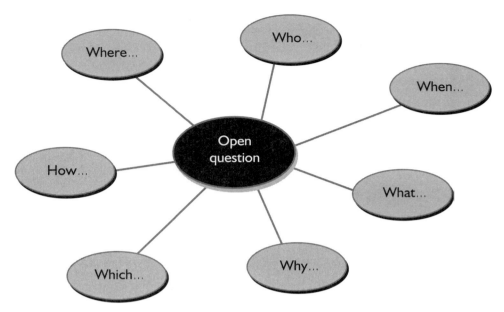

Figure 2.3 Different types of open question can start like this

Try asking a question that starts with one of these words – you will see that it is unlikely that you will get a simple *yes* or *no* answer. Therefore, if you want to gather information, asking open questions is a good way to start.

Some examples of open questions are: *'How often do you normally go on holiday?'* or *'Which holiday destination have you enjoyed the most?'*.

There are other types of questions that you can use, although they are generally specially adapted open or closed questions. A **probing question** is an open question that uses information that you have already established to narrow down the field of information further. For example, an open question could be, *'Where did you go on holiday last year?'*. The answer might be *'Spain'*. A probing question that you could use to find out more could be, *'What part of Spain did you visit?'*.

A **direct question** can be open or closed. However, all direct questions have two characteristics:

♦ you pose the question as an instruction
♦ when posing a direct question, you always use the name of the other person.

Direct questions are used when you are finding it difficult to get information out of someone and you need something that will get the other person's attention and make them give you the information that you need. A direct question would start with phrases like:

♦ *'Please tell me, Mr Patel. . .'*
♦ *'Please explain to me, Mrs Jones. . .'*
♦ *'Describe to me, Miss Brown. . .'*

By using the other person's name, you are in a good position to get their immediate attention, while phrasing the question like an instruction means that you are subconsciously giving an order. For example, an open question could be, '*How did you travel to Spain?*'. The answer might be, '*I flew*'. A direct question that you could use to find out more is, '*Tell me, Junaid, do you always fly when you go on holiday?*'

A **hypothetical question** is designed to explore possibilities. Hypothetical questions can be useful when trying to decide between a number of choices or when trying to solve a problem. For example, if we think back to Case Study 1, suppose there had not been any holidays to Spain available. Tracy might have had to say to the caller, '*I am sorry, but we do not have any cheap holidays to Spain available at the moment. Would you be interested in any other destination?*'. At this point, the caller may have said '*No thank you, I really fancied Spain*'. Tracy could then follow up with a hypothetical question to try to gain the customer's interest, '*What if I could find you a holiday to somewhere hot and sunny that would be cheaper than going to Spain?*'. In this case, the customer's response may well be that she would consider an alternative destination – asking a hypothetical question would enable Tracy to test out this possibility.

Try it out

Think back to Case Study 1. Suppose that when Tracy checked the Globe Trotters Direct database there were no holidays available to Spain that had a duration of less than 14 days. Can you think of a hypothetical question that Tracy could have asked the customer to test out the possibility of her taking a longer break?

All these types of questions can be used to filter information so that you end up with the real information that you were looking for. Figure 2.4 shows an information filter – it shows how careful use of different types of questions can enable you to find out the information that you require.

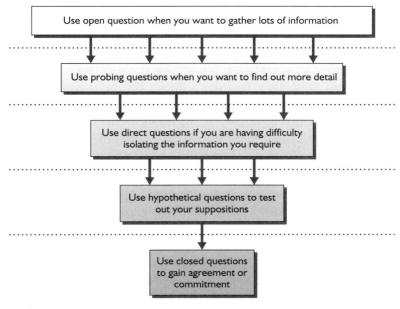

Figure 2.4 An information filter

All questions should be asked in a positive way. Avoid using accusing, sarcastic or threatening language or tone in your questions. For example, *'What exactly are you getting at? Could you please get to the point.'* should be re-phrased as *'I do not understand what you are trying to tell me. Could you please try to explain it in a different way?'*. This is an example of changing a '**you**' statement into an '**I**' statement – this re-phrasing changes the emphasis of the question and makes it more positive. A positive question is one that a caller is not afraid to answer.

Try it out

Which of the following questions are positive?

1 *'I understand that you are upset. I would like to help you, but to do so, I need you to tell me what was said that annoyed you.'*
2 *'Can you not wait a minute? I asked you to hold on for a moment. Did I not tell you that I am very busy?'*
3 *'Would you give me an example of what was done to aggravate you?'*
4 *'It seems that you are very upset. Can you tell me what happened?'*
5 *'Why didn't you say so earlier?'*

How to confirm with the customer your understanding of their needs

After you have listened to what the customer has to say, and you have asked questions to clarify things or to make sure that you have gathered sufficient information, you should summarise your understanding of what the customer has said.

Summarising involves:

♦ listening carefully to the customer and re-stating a condensed version of what has been said
♦ obtaining agreement from the customer that you have understood correctly.

Summarising your understanding of the conversation and your interpretation of the customer's needs can help you to avoid any possible confusion. It is also a good way of checking that the customer has the same understanding as you of any agreements that may have been reached during the course of the conversation.

If you are taking down any details from the customer, such as the person's name or address, you should ask the customer to spell any names or unusual words. Always use the Phonetic Alphabet to confirm what you think you have heard, especially when clarifying product details. The Phonetic Alphabet is given on page 19, Unit 1. You will need to make sure that you are extremely familiar with it and that you are able to use it spontaneously.

The importance of maintaining the confidentiality and security of information

Information processing technology is revolutionising the world of business today. The rapid development of computer technology has led to a vast quantity of information being routinely collected and used by all sectors of industry. All organisations now depend upon information for their business processes and efficiency.

Computers are an essential part of our working lives

Faster, more complex and more flexible ways of creating, using and sharing information are being developed every day. However, the risk of that information being lost, corrupted, disclosed or stolen is also increasing and the impact of such a loss on your business could be devastating.

Think about it

♦ What information does your organisation hold?
♦ How is it held? What is it used for? Who has access to it?

Whatever the nature of your organisation's business, you can be sure that it holds information that would be of interest to others.

There are two aspects of confidentiality to consider:

♦ first, if information about your organisation's business, such as its strategy documents, its marketing plans or its pricing policies, were to fall into the hands of a competitor, it could cause your company considerable damage. Any company information like this, that is of a sensitive nature, must therefore be protected
♦ second, your organisation is legally obliged to protect information that has been entrusted to it by other parties such as personnel records and any other information that falls under the scope of the Data Protection Act, such as customers' details.

Exactly how information is protected will vary from company to company, or even from department to department, but the level of protection should be the same. In order for information to remain confidential, it must be kept securely and it should only be accessible to those people who are authorised to see and handle the information.

Think about it

◆ Who is responsible for the security of information in your organisation?
◆ How does your organisation keep information secure?
◆ What are your responsibilities with regard to the security and confidentiality of information?

How to ensure the accuracy and reliability of data

It is also very important to ensure the accuracy and reliability of data. You need to know that the information you have access to can be relied upon. It must be accurate and complete. It must also be protected from unauthorised modification.

Think about it

◆ How does your organisation ensure the accuracy and reliability of data?
◆ What are your responsibilities with regard to maintaining the accuracy and reliability of information?

Your obligations under the Data Protection Act

It is extremely likely that your organisation collects and uses personal data and you may well be involved in the processing of that data. Your organisation will also probably have laid down procedures that govern the way you work. However, it is important that you have a good overall understanding of the Data Protection Act and can appreciate the constraints it places on the way your organisation can operate.

The Data Protection Act 1998 came into force on 1 March 2000. It applies to the **processing** (collecting, using, disclosing, destroying or holding data) of computerised **personal data** (data that can be associated with identifiable living individuals – it can include facts and opinions about an individual) and personal data held in structured manual files.

Organisations that process personal data are called **data controllers** and they are required to comply with the rules of good information handling, known as the **data protection principles**, which require data to be:

◆ fairly and lawfully processed
◆ processed for limited purposes
◆ adequate, relevant and not excessive
◆ accurate
◆ not kept for longer than necessary
◆ processed in accordance with individual's rights

♦ kept secure
♦ not transferred to non-EEA countries unless the data are adequately protected.

Processing may only be carried out if one of the following conditions have been met:

♦ the individual has given his or her consent to the processing
♦ the processing is necessary for the performance of a contract with the individual
♦ the processing is required under a legal obligation
♦ the processing is necessary to protect the vital interests of the individual
♦ the processing is necessary to carry out public functions
♦ the processing is necessary in order to pursue the legitimate interests of the data controller or third parties (unless it could prejudice the interests of the individual).

The Data Protection Act makes specific provision for sensitive personal data. Sensitive data include: racial or ethnic origins; religious or other beliefs; political opinions; trade union membership; health; sex life; criminal proceedings or convictions.

Sensitive data can only be processed under strict conditions, which include:

♦ having the explicit consent of the individual
♦ being required by law to process the data for employment purposes
♦ needing to process the information in order to protect the vital interests of the data subject or another
♦ dealing with the administration of justice or legal proceedings.

Data controllers must take security measures to safeguard personal data. The 1998 Act requires data controllers to take appropriate technical or organisational measures to prevent unauthorised or unlawful processing or disclosure of data.

The Act strengthens individuals' rights to:

♦ gain access to their data
♦ seek compensation.

It also creates new rights for individuals to:

♦ prevent their data from being processed in certain circumstances
♦ opt out of having their data used for direct marketing
♦ opt out of fully automated decision making about them.

An example of how the Data Protection Act could be contravened and the possible consequences of this may make it easier to understand the constraints that the Data Protection Act places on individuals and why it has been brought into force.

Thinking back to Case Study 1 on page 133 – we could suppose that Tracy happened to know the customer personally. When Tracy got home that night, she said to her flatmate Lisa, '*I bet you'll never guess who booked a holiday to Benidorm today?*'. She then told Lisa the customer's name and the details of her booking, including how much she paid and when she will be away.

This disclosure of information to Lisa contravenes the Data Protection Act, as the customer has the right for her personal information to remain confidential.

Although in this example disclosure of information of this sort may seem trivial, it could still have unforeseen consequences. For example, if Tracy were to have told Lisa this in the local pub rather than back at their flat, they could have been overheard by other people who also know the customer and where she lives. They may now know that the customer's home will be empty while she is away, which could result in Tracy's customer being burgled.

Keys to good practice

✓ Always open a call with the correct greeting.

✓ Provide the caller with your full name if it is requested.

✓ Empathise with the caller.

✓ Always listen effectively.

✓ Use positive words and phrases.

✓ Encourage the caller to state their requirements in full whilst still maintaining control of the call.

✓ Use appropriate questions to filter information and find out what the customer wants.

✓ Always phrase questions positively.

✓ Use summarising to check that you have understood the customer's needs.

✓ Make sure you know the Phonetic Alphabet and that you are able to use it fluently.

✓ Ensure that you keep data secure and information confidential.

2.2 Meet the needs of callers

WHAT YOU NEED TO KNOW OR LEARN

♦ Familiarity with the products and services offered by your organisation

♦ How to manage any possible conflicts between the needs of the caller and the requirements of your organisation

♦ How to get the customer to buy-in to a proposed solution

- Your organisation's procedures for recording agreed actions
- What to do if you are faced with a problem that you cannot resolve yourself.

Familiarity with the products and services offered by your organisation

If you are going to be able to help customers who have questions about your company's products or services, you will need to make sure that you know:

- what products and services your organisation offers
- an overview of how these products and services work
- what the possible advantages or disadvantages of each product or service are
- how much the products or services cost.

It is very unlikely that you will be able to answer every question that a customer might ask. However, if a customer has a query that you are not able to answer and you have to transfer the caller to someone else within your organisation for help, you should make sure that you try to find the answer to that query at your next possible opportunity. That way you will develop your knowledge further and you will then be better able to help the customer next time.

Check it out

What are the main products and services offered by your organisation? Make a note of them for your portfolio.

Most organisations will offer staff training and familiarisation sessions with the products or services you are expected to support. If your organisation does not automatically offer you training, and you do not feel that you are sufficiently familiar with the products or services offered by your organisation, then approach your supervisor or manager. Ask if they will help you with your self-development by suggesting ways in which you can become more familiar with your organisation's products and services.

Think about it

Imagine that you are faced with the situation of having to support products or services that you know very little about.

- Who would you approach to try to find out more about the products or services that you have been asked to support?
- What might happen if you did not try to find out more about these products or services?

Staff training will help you to offer better service

How to manage any possible conflicts between the needs of the caller and the requirements of your organisation

If you are going to be able to manage any possible conflicts that may arise, you will sometimes have to weigh up certain situations and look at them from both your customer's viewpoint and that of your organisation. You will have to look for ways in which you can balance the needs of the customer and your organisation's needs and still follow company procedures and policies; this is a key part of providing good customer service.

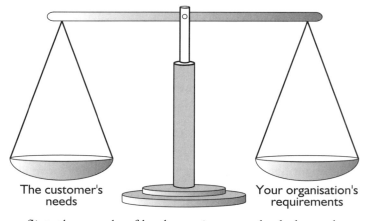

To avoid conflict, the needs of both parties must be balanced

If you are going to be able to reach a balance between the needs of your customer and the requirements of your organisation, you will need to:

♦ thoroughly understand your organisation's policies, procedures, rules and regulations
♦ know how any limitations that are imposed by these policies, procedures, rules and regulations may affect your customers
♦ be able to explain these limitations clearly to your customers
♦ be aware of the level of your autonomy and know the limits of your authority
♦ know how to deal with any situations that you cannot resolve yourself.

It is important for you to understand how much authority you may have to make decisions and for you **not** to step beyond that boundary. You will therefore need to know:

♦ whether there is any flexibility in your organisation's policies, procedures, rules or regulations which will allow you any freedom to negotiate a solution which achieves a balance between your customer's needs and your organisation's needs without causing difficulties or problems for either yourself or your organisation
♦ at what point you will need to seek assistance from a senior colleague or your manager so that you can gain authorisation for any deviations from company policy or procedures that may be necessary.

Think about it

♦ How much freedom do you have to negotiate solutions that may push the limits of your organisation's policies, procedures, rules or regulations so that you can achieve a balance between your customer's needs and your organisation's requirements?
♦ What could go wrong if you were to exceed the limits of your authority?

If you are permitted to negotiate solutions that may push the limits of your organisation's policies, procedures, rules or regulations – and it makes sense for you to do so – always make sure that any special arrangements that are made with customers are carefully recorded for future reference.

If you are unable to meet the needs of the customer because of limitations imposed by your organisation, it is important to explain to the customer why and how company policy or procedures have prevented you from meeting their needs. The more information you can provide, the better.

Customers are more likely to accept your inability to meet their needs if they are aware that you have done your best to do so and you have kept them fully informed of what has been going on.

How to get the customer to buy-in to a proposed solution

When customers have a problem, they will expect you to do something about it. Customers are not interested in hearing you say:

- *'I really don't know what to suggest, it's not my department.'*
- *'It's not my fault – I didn't take the order.'*
- *'I don't know anything about this – I was on holiday.'*
- *'There's nothing I can do about it.'*

A customer who has a problem is not interested in excuses or long-winded explanations. Customers want and expect a solution. They want you to make a sensible suggestion as to how their problem can be solved quickly, easily and efficiently.

You may not know anything at all about how or why a problem occurred, or who made a mistake in the first place. However, it is your responsibility to reassure the customer and to let them know that you will do **everything** that you possibly can to sort out the difficulty and find a solution.

From the customer's point of view, when a member of staff in an organisation makes an extra effort to meet their needs, it is likely to make that person feel like a valued customer. The customer is more likely to remain loyal to that organisation and continue to use its products or services.

Even if the solution is not perfect, the customer will still appreciate the fact that you have made a determined attempt to help. For example, we could consider Case Study 1 (page 133), where the customer wanted to go to Spain. If there were no holidays available to Spain but Tracy had suggested a sensible alternative, such as a destination that was also hot and sunny and was perhaps cheaper, then the customer would have been satisfied that Tracy had made an effort to meet her needs.

If it is possible to offer the customer more than one alternative so that the person can choose which solution they prefer, that would be even better, as it makes the customer feel in control of the situation.

You are more likely to get the customer to buy-in to any solution that you propose if you:

- explain each of the alternatives clearly to the customer
- describe the advantages and disadvantages of each option
- answer any questions that your customer may have about each option
- allow the customer time to consider the proposal.

Make sure that you do not:

- give the customer a vague description of the options
- leave out important information that the customer needs to know about, as he or she will only be even more upset and angry to find it out later
- pressurise the customer into making a snap decision
- persuade the customer to buy-in to the solution that is easiest or most convenient for you but may not be the best for that person.

Always make sure that the customer understands the proposed solution and check the person is happy with it before proceeding.

Some organisations go even further to make sure that their customers are satisfied with the actions that they take, by making courtesy calls to customers at a later date to check that they are happy that their needs have been met.

Courtesy calls may also be used to elicit feedback from customers that can be used to review the effectiveness of a company's procedures. Carrying out courtesy calls may therefore lead to further improvements in customer service.

Your organisation's procedures for recording agreed actions

Once you have established what action you are going to take on a customer's behalf, you will usually end up by recording the details of the agreed action. 'Recording' the action will mean completing a data input screen (see below) or it could be completing some paperwork.

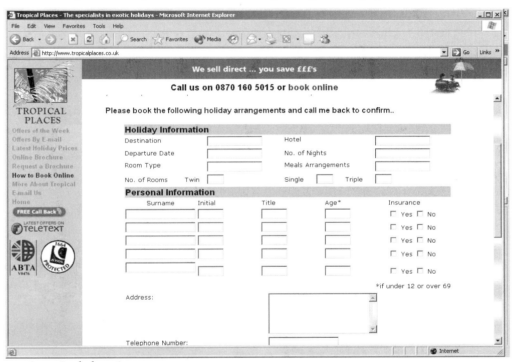

A typical data input screen

Your organisation probably has a set of procedures to explain how you should record the details of any actions that you take on behalf of customers.

Check it out

Find out if your organisation has a set of procedures that tell you how you should record any actions that you have agreed with the customer.

♦ Are you expected to complete a data input screen?
♦ Are you expected to complete any paperwork?
♦ Find a copy of each of the forms that you may need to complete and practice filling them in.

If we consider Case Study 1 (page 133) again, when the caller decided to reserve a holiday, Tracy completed a data input screen which recorded the caller's details and reserved the holiday that she chose for her.

When the customer called again later to confirm the booking, Tracy had to retrieve the details of the customer's reservation and change the reservation to a confirmed booking. Doing this ensured that tickets were issued and sent to the customer – the information that Tracy had recorded about the customer was the data that was used to issue the tickets.

What to do if you are faced with a problem that you cannot resolve yourself

Normally, you should be able to meet the needs of most callers on your own, particularly if the request is straightforward and routine. You will have dealt with these sorts of issues before and you will know where to find any information that you may need.

However, sometimes the caller's request may be:

♦ unusual
♦ extremely complex
♦ beyond the range of your authority.

When dealing with customers' requests, do not:

♦ be tempted to make rash promises to get rid of an angry caller
♦ allow yourself to be pushed into agreements which you have no authority to make
♦ agree to arrangements which you hope will be all right.

Remember: always ask for help when you need it.

If you are unable to deal with a customer's request because you do not have the authority to settle the matter, do not feel that you have failed. Your organisation would almost certainly prefer you to ask for help from a more senior person rather than let you make the wrong decision – as in the long run this could just cause more problems.

A more experienced colleague can offer help and advice

Globe Trotters Direct

Agent's Name: Justine Davies

Date:	28/4/02	Time:	10:57

Customer's Name:	Mr Stephen Fox	Reference/ Account No:	n/a

Nature of Query/Problem:	Mr Fox called to find out if we had any last minute deals available for next week to the Algarve, departing from Gatwick for a party of two adults and two children.

Summary of Action Taken:	I searched our database for Mr Fox and came up with one option that fitted his criteria, package reference number XB5736, and offered this package deal to Mr Fox. Howver the customer did not wish to proceed with a booking as he did not want to pay more than £150 pounds per person.
Referred?	No

Entered onto system:	Date: 29/4/02	Time: 15:32

An example of the type of document that you may be expected to complete

If you need to ask for help or information from another person:

♦ explain the customer's request clearly and concisely
♦ if you have already got the customer to buy in to a possible solution but you are unable to action the solution yourself, tell the other person what action the customer may be expecting your organisation to take
♦ allow the other person to ask questions to make sure that he or she understands the situation.

Your organisation may well have standard procedures that you are expected to follow if you are faced with the situation of not being able to solve a customer's request or problem yourself.

Check it out

Does your organisation have a set of procedures that you are expected to follow when you are faced with a problem that you cannot resolve yourself?

If your organisation does *not* have a set of procedures that give you clear guidance on what you are expected to do if you are unable to help a caller, then you should bear the following principles in mind.

You should always try to meet the customer's needs yourself whenever possible – try to 'own' the call, as it will help you to build your confidence. You should only transfer calls to a more senior colleague when it is absolutely necessary.

If the situation arises where a caller's request is proving difficult for you to solve, then you should place the customer on hold before you seek assistance from anyone else. If you need to do this, you should always tell the customer first that you are putting them on hold and explain why it is necessary. You should also tell the customer what will happen, for example, that they will hear music. You must then ensure that you keep the customer updated with regard to what you are doing. Always let the customer know:

♦ *what* you are going to do
♦ *how* you are going to do it
♦ *why* you are doing it.

If you do find it necessary to transfer a call to someone else, you should give the caller the name of the person you are about to transfer them to and the name of the department if you are transferring them to someone who works in a different department. You will also need to give the following information to the person to whom you are transferring the call:

♦ the customer's name
♦ the nature of the request/problem
♦ the customer's account number (if applicable)
♦ any other relevant facts.

Always thank the customer for holding prior to transferring the call.

Keys to good practice

✓ Make sure that you are familiar with the products or services offered by your organisation.

✓ If you are asked questions by a customer that you are not able to answer, make sure that you take responsibility for your own self-development by finding out the answers to those questions and further developing your knowledge.

✓ Always make determined attempts to meet your customer's needs within the limits of your own authority.

✓ Take all possible action to minimise conflict between the customer's needs and your organisation's limitations.

✓ Clearly explain any organisational limitations to your customers.

✓ When you are not able to meet the customer's needs exactly, if possible try to offer the customer more than one alternative and allow the customer to choose their own solution.

✓ Always make sure that the customer understands the proposed solution and is happy with it.

✓ Make sure that you are aware of and follow your organisation's procedures for recording details of the actions that you take.

✓ Make sure that you know what to do if you are faced with a situation that you are unable to deal with yourself.

Check your knowledge

1 What is empathy?
2 What are the five factors that can prevent us from listening?
3 Name five different types of questions that you could use to identify the needs of the caller.
4 What is summarising and why would you do it?
5 Recite the Phonetic Alphabet.
6 When did the Data Protection Act 1998 come into force?
7 What are the eight enforceable principles of good information handling?
8 What rights does the Data Protection Act afford the individual?
9 List the products or services offered by your organisation.
10 What are the limits of your authority and why should you not exceed them?
11 How can you encourage the customer to buy-in to any solutions that you propose?
12 What type of records does your organisation require you to keep regarding the actions that you take on behalf of customers?
13 What action should you take if you are faced with a problem that you are unable to deal with yourself?

UNIT 6 Make arrangements on behalf of callers

This option unit is all about making arrangements on behalf of callers to arrange for work to be done, such as; repairs, booking holidays, reserving hotel accommodation, booking tickets for events or making changes to services that you supply to callers.

This unit has two elements:

♦ consider the arrangements that will be required
♦ make arrangements for callers.

After you have completed this unit, you will be able to:

♦ prioritise arrangements for callers
♦ identify the different types of information that you will need to collect from callers so that you can make appropriate arrangements for them
♦ identify where to seek advice from within your organisation if you are having difficulty making arrangements
♦ track the progress of the arrangements you have made
♦ record the arrangements you have made within your organisation's systems
♦ appreciate the limits of your authority and responsibility
♦ balance the needs of the caller against the needs of your organisation when making arrangements.

What do we mean when we talk about making arrangements?

In the context of call handling, **making arrangements** is providing a service over the telephone that allows callers to get what they want in the easiest way possible. This can be achieved by you taking ownership of the arrangements they want made and providing the service in a polite and professional manner.

What type of arrangements do we mean?

Some examples of the type of arrangements that you could make are listed below. This list is not definitive and many more types of arrangements would also fit the criteria:

♦ booking rooms in hotels or changing bookings
♦ booking holidays or making travel arrangements – by rail, coach or air
♦ booking tickets to the theatre or the cinema
♦ taking orders for a catalogue and passing the order through to warehousing and distribution
♦ making changes to services that you may already supply, such as adding additional digital TV channels; changing mobile phone services or tariffs; or having a second telephone line installed for Internet access, etc.

- being on the reception line for an organisation and finding the correct person within the organisation that the caller needs to speak to
- taking bookings for leisure services such as squash courts or aerobics classes, etc.
- transferring money between accounts or accepting bill payments over the telephone
- arranging insurance cover or making changes to insurance cover
- arranging interviews or meetings between the caller and people within your organisation
- making arrangements for repairs to equipment that your organisation may supply such as televisions, IT systems, washing machines or telephone lines, etc.

As you can see from just these few examples, the list could go on to many more pages. The critical thing, as far as call handling is concerned, is that the arrangements are made on behalf of a caller and they are made by you using the call handling skills and techniques that you have developed.

Think about it

- Within your job role, what kind of arrangements are you likely to make on behalf of customers?

The case studies in this chapter have been based on a fictitious company – 'Hotels Inn' a nationwide, low budget hotel chain. Examples from other sectors such as banking, insurance, telemarketing and office supplies will be covered in other chapters.

'Hotels Inn' location booklet

Did you know?

Over 90 per cent of all hotel bookings are made over the telephone, either by telephoning the hotel directly, or through the hotel chain's central booking service.

 Consider the arrangements that will be required

WHAT YOU NEED TO KNOW OR LEARN

♦ How to identify the arrangements required by the caller
♦ How to determine the priority and urgency of the arrangements to be made
♦ How to identify the resources that you will need
♦ How to balance the needs of the caller against the requirements of your organisation
♦ How to obtain authority from your organisation for arrangements that exceed the level of responsibility you have been given.

How to identify the arrangements required by the caller

In most cases, this should be easy for you to do, as callers will usually know what they want and why they are calling for you to make the arrangements on their behalf.

Did you know?

Some hotel chains will not let you ring the hotel direct to book – you must ring the central booking service.

In a lot of call centres, the caller will initially go through an automated screening process which is designed to route the caller to the appropriate department within the organisation. Some callers find these type of systems annoying or stressful as it can be easy to forget which button has to be pressed.

Hotels Inn uses an automated call routing system – callers hear the following message when they call:

'Thank you for calling Hotels Inn. If you have a star key on your telephone, please press it twice now or hold for operator assistance.'

If the caller presses the star key on the telephone keypad twice, the system then knows that the caller has a touch tone telephone and can use the automated call routing system, and so continues to give further instructions. If the caller does not have a star key and continues to hold, the call will just be routed through to the next available operator.

A caller who presses the star key on the telephone keypad twice, will then hear the following instructions:

'Thank you. Please use the telephone keypad to make your selection. For further instructions on how to use this service, press 1; otherwise please hold for the main menu.

- ◆ *to obtain a copy of the Hotels Inn location booklet, please press 2*
- ◆ *to make a single reservation, please press 3*
- ◆ *to make multiple reservations, please press 4*
- ◆ *if you are a caller with special requirements or access problems, please press 5*
- ◆ *for details of special promotions or corporate discounts, please press 6*
- ◆ *for all other enquiries, please press 7*
- ◆ *To end this call, press 9 or press star to replay the menu.'*

Callers are expected to select the option that meets their requirements. Once they make their selection, the system will then route them through to an appropriate operator, who will automatically know the reason for their call.

Case study 1 – John's experiences

The caller was a regular customer and knew exactly what she wanted. She had obviously pressed 4 in response to the initial routing menu as she wanted to make a multiple reservation. She knew the format of the call and had already prepared the information needed to enter into the system: name, postcode, credit card number, etc. Some people, who do a lot of travelling, may book six to ten different hotels in one go, covering a two- to three-week period.

When I got to the '*in which town are you looking for a Hotels Inn?*' she said, '*Sheffield, Doncaster, Hull, Gateshead and Newcastle*'. From this, I assumed that it was the correct order and started with '*Hotels Inn, Sheffield – what dates are you looking for?*' and then took them one at a time from there. The system is intelligent, so when you do multiple bookings at the same time, once you have put the caller's details in from the first booking it automatically carries over their details into the remainder of the bookings. The conversation then carried on. Caller – '*Sheffield 3 December, one room for one night, non-smoking*'.

I checked availability, which showed that there were several rooms free and confirmed that this was fine. The next stage is to get their details, the sequence is surname, forename, postcode, first line of the address and to ask if the caller would like to guarantee the booking with a credit card. I then ask for their name as it appears on the card and the card number, and at this point we explain the cancellation policy. '*You can cancel up to 3 p.m. on the day of the booking, should it be later than this and the room is not let to another customer, the cost of the room will be debited from the card*'. It is very rare that this happens and we try to avoid doing it, as it upsets the caller who may then decide to go elsewhere in the future.

Once all of the details are in the system we always read back the whole booking to make sure there are no errors, '*So that's Sheffield for 3 December; one room; one person; non smoking – is that correct?*'

'*Yes*' said the caller and then I gave the booking reference and asked if written confirmation was required – most callers just want the booking reference.

We then went on to book the next reservation, '*next Hotels Inn please?*' '*Doncaster, 4 December, one person; one night; non-smoking*' said the caller. It was now easy, as all I had to do was confirm the availability and all of the caller's details were automatically transferred to the booking screen. So it got quicker and I read back the details of the booking to confirm everything was correct and gave the booking references as we went.

You can get additional bookings into the system in about 20 seconds when you have a good rapport established with the caller and they know what they are doing.

1 What would you do if there was no availability for the second booking?
2 Would you be able to take the booking if the caller refused to give you their credit card details?
3 Would you need any additional information if the caller wanted a written confirmation of the booking?
4 What would you do if the caller did not accept the cancellation policy?

Most callers will know what they want before they call. What you have to do is:

♦ capture information about the arrangements they want you to make
♦ try to meet their requirements with a minimum of fuss
♦ make the arrangements promptly on their behalf.

Think about it

♦ What key information would you need to obtain from a customer to enable you to make arrangements on their behalf?

Many organisations have recognised that in order for you to be able to make arrangements on behalf of a caller, you will need to gather a common set of information about the caller and the nature of the arrangements that they want you to make. It is therefore common for calls that require you to make arrangements on behalf of callers to be based on a script that your organisation has developed to ensure that you do not fail to gather any of this vital information.

The purpose of the script is to ensure that you collect the relevant information from the caller in the most efficient way. It allows you to identify quickly what it is that the caller wants you to do. Even in cases where the caller may be confused or not sure about what they want, the script will be structured in such a way that it allows you to offer choices to the caller so that you can narrow down their requirements.

Check it out

Find out if your organisation expects you to follow a set or standard script when dealing with callers who expect you to make arrangements on their behalf.

♦ If it does, then make a note of it or, if detailed, write down where the script can be found.
♦ If there is more than one standard script, does your organisation also provide guidance on which script should be used on any particular occasion?

How to determine the priority and urgency of the arrangements to be made

It will be tempting for you to give all your arrangements either top-priority or low-priority status, as there is a natural tendency for people to do this. So how do you actually decide what should be given the highest priority?

First, you have to understand the difference between something that is important and something that is urgent. If something is important, it means that it *needs to be done*. If something is urgent, it means that it must be done *immediately*.

All the arrangements that you are asked to make on behalf of callers *need to be made* – you do not, therefore, need to focus on the importance of the arrangements. What you need to consider is their degree of urgency so that you can decide which arrangements need to be given the *highest priority*. You will then need to make sure that you start with the arrangements which you have given the highest priority.

Try it out

As an example, let's consider the gas industry. Imagine that you are responsible for making arrangements on behalf of the people who call the 'Gas Care Line'. It is the middle of winter and let's assume that you have received three calls so far this morning in quick succession:

1 The manager of a residential home for the elderly has reported that the home's central heating has failed and they are without any form of heating.
2 A caller has rung to report that one of the rings on her gas cooker is not working and has asked for it to be fixed under her 'Gas Care Policy'.

3 A caller can smell gas and believes there may be a gas leak.

♦ Write down the priority that you would give to each of these three calls, giving your reasons.

Your organisation may well have guidance or a set of procedures that you are expected to follow that will help you to determine the priority and urgency of any arrangements that need to be made.

Check it out

Does your organisation have guidance material or a set of procedures that you are expected to follow when trying to decide the priority and urgency of the arrangements that you are required to make?

An example of a set of procedures for determining priorities is shown below.

The following is a rough guide only as an example; each organisation will set its own priorities. These procedures are based on service repair engineers.

Priority One – Immediate response.	Engineer to be sent within 1 hour to deal with the problem, supersedes all other priorities, engineers to be diverted from other jobs to deal with priority one.
Priority Two – Within four hours.	Next available engineer to deal with these problems (including diverting engineer from routine jobs) and must be completed during that day if reported before midday.
Priority Three – Within eight hours.	Next available engineer to deal with these problems (including diverting engineer from routine jobs) and must be completed by the end of the next day.
Priority Four – Next day.	Engineer to be despatched to deal with this problem when available
Priority Five – Routine repair.	Next available engineer.

Different warranty obligations could also affect response priorities.

Another set of priorities might be:

Priority One	Same Day.
Priority Two	Next Day.
Priority Three	Within One Week.

If your organisation does not provide you with such guidance, working through the following exercise will allow you to look at the sort of questions that you should ask yourself when you are trying to determine the priority and urgency of the particular arrangements that you are required to make.

Think about it

Look back at the **'Try it out'** exercise on page 166 when you considered the priority of three different incoming calls to the 'Gas Care Line'. In order to decide how urgent each of the calls were, you probably asked yourself the following questions.

1 How soon does the caller expect the arrangements to be made?
   (a) With regard to the residential home for the elderly, the manager would be expecting a response *as soon as humanly possible*.
   (b) With regard to the caller whose cooker needed fixing, she expects a response *within the timescale quoted under her 'Gas Care Policy'* which is within 48 hours.
   (c) With regard to the caller who could smell gas, *an immediate response is expected*.

2 What is the worst thing that could happen if the arrangements are not completed immediately?
   (a) *For the residential home for the elderly, the residents' health could be at risk if they are left for any length of time without heating.*
   (b) *For the caller whose cooker needed fixing, it will merely be an inconvenience. As long as the repairs are made within the timscale quoted within their 'Gas Care Policy' (48 hours), the customer should be satisfied.*
   (c) *For the caller who could smell gas, if there is a gas leak people are in immediate danger and could be killed.*

Other questions you should also ask yourself are:

1 Will postponing one set of arrangements have an affect on any other arrangements that you may need to make?
   Remember the domino effect. If you make one set of arrangements, but fail to make another, you may have wasted effort on the first task. For example, if you schedule a date for one of your installation teams to install some equipment in a client's premises but wait until the last minute to order the parts required for the installation, the whole thing could fall apart if the parts needed are out of stock.
2 Have you focused on quantity instead of quality?
   It can give you a sense of accomplishment to cross several tasks off your list. However, this can be short lived if your urgent tasks remain on your list, uncompleted.

How to identify the resources that you will need

Resources are valuable commodities for an organisation – they can be human, physical, financial or time based.

If we consider Case Study 1 again, let's look at the resources that John can call upon within his job role to enable him to make arrangements for his callers.

The most important resource available to John, without which he is unlikely to be able to make the arrangements that his callers require, is vacant hotel rooms dotted around the country in any of the hotels owned by Hotels Inn. If there are no hotel rooms available, then John will not be able to help his callers.

Another important resource that John uses is his computerised booking system. The system lets him find out where any vacant hotel rooms may be and allows him to claim any of those resources (book rooms) on behalf of his customers.

John could still do his job without the computerised booking system, as he could take bookings manually and would need to check the availability of rooms by telephoning each of the Hotels Inn hotels directly and speaking to the hotel manager. This is part of the Hotels Inn back-up procedure that enables John to carry out his job if the computerised system fails. However, this is only done when it is absolutely necessary, as it is quicker and therefore a far more efficient use of time for John to use his computer system. This leads us on to another valuable resource – John's time.

Vacant hotel rooms; John's time; and his computerised booking system are therefore the most critical resources that John needs. Other resources that are available to John that enable him to make arrangements for callers are the consumables that he uses every day, like Hotels Inn headed paper for writing confirmation letters, etc.

Think about it

♦ What resources do you need to enable you to perform your job role?
♦ What resources are you usually able to call upon when you are required to make arrangements for callers?
♦ How would you go about obtaining any additional resources that you may require?
♦ Would you need to gain approval from a more senior member of staff to be able to obtain certain resources? If you need approval, how would you gain it?

Remember that the use of any resource has a cost attached to it, so you must always ensure that you use all the resources available to you in the most efficient way possible.

If we think back again to John at Hotels Inn, we have seen that it is possible for John to take bookings manually if he telephones each of the

Hotels Inn hotels directly to check the availability of rooms. However, bookings are only done this way when it is absolutely necessary. This is because it is so time consuming and John's time is an expensive resource that must not be wasted.

Think about it

How do you try to ensure that any actions you take to satisfy the needs of customers:

a use as few resources as possible?
b use your time effectively?

How to balance the needs of the caller against the requirements of your organisation

In order to do this you will need to:

♦ gather sufficient information about the needs of the caller
♦ be very familiar with the requirements and limitations of your organisation
♦ understand any legal rights the caller may have
♦ be able to systematically weigh up all the options so that you can choose a solution that is best for both parties
♦ be aware of the limits of your own authority and ability to make decisions.

Establishing the needs of the caller

This topic has already been covered in depth in Chapter 2, in section 2.1 entitled '**Identify the needs of the caller**', see page 135.

Your organisation's requirements and limitations

Your organisation should have a set of service standards that govern the level of service that you are expected to offer the caller and may even have a code of practice that you are expected to work to.

You will need to refer to both of these when you are trying to balance the needs of the caller against the requirements of your organisation.

Check it out

Find out if your organisation has a defined set of service standards or a code of practice that you are expected to work to. If so, find out what they are called and make a note of them.

♦ Does your organisation have a code of practice that covers the sector that you operate in?
♦ If it does, write it down for your evidence. If it is detailed, then write down where it can be found.

It is possible that you may not always be able to meet the needs of the customer precisely because of limitations placed on you by your organisation. If this is the case, it is important that you explain to the caller why you have been unable to meet his or her needs exactly. For example, it could be that the caller wants an item of equipment repaired immediately, but the earliest date that you can schedule it is in a week's time because that is the first date that a repair person is available. In this instance, you would not be able to meet the needs of the caller, so you would need to explain politely to the caller why you cannot arrange for the repair to be done any sooner.

You need to make sure that you are fully aware of any organisational limitations that your company expects you to work to. For example, perhaps you are only allowed to send things out to customers via second-class mail in order to keep costs down.

Check it out

♦ Are you expected to work within any organisational limitations?
♦ How would you explain these limitations to your customers?

Remember: One thing that you must never do is promise the caller things that you cannot deliver.

If you make a promise that you know you will not be able to keep, you could be starting a process that could have a significant impact on you, the caller and your organisation. What may have been a difficult situation to start with could become a complete disaster if you make a promise that you cannot keep.

It is far better to be completely honest – explain the situation to the caller and ask if what you are able to do is acceptable. Usually, when you explain the situation correctly, most people are quite reasonable.

You must also *not* withhold important information from the customer. Even things you may consider harmless, such as being a little vague about timescales or not actually telling the caller that what they want is out of stock and that it could take a couple of weeks to arrive, can damage the reputation of your organisation.

Never say it's not your fault, or blame a different part of the organisation, '*Oh, they always make mistakes in the distribution warehouse*' does not present your organisation as being very efficient.

The customer's rights

As well as knowing about your organisation's requirements and limitations, you also need to be aware of the law you must work within. This includes knowing about your customers' legal rights.

For example, if your organisation supplies goods, the Supply of Goods and Services Act 1996 gives your customers certain basic rights. The Act states that any goods that a consumer buys from a business must meet three basic requirements. They must be:

- **of satisfactory quality** – this means that the goods must be of a standard that a reasonable person would consider satisfactory with regard to fitness for purpose, appearance and finish, freedom from defects, safety and durability. The goods should therefore do what a customer would reasonably expect them to do. For example, a fridge should keep things cold
- **as described** – this means that the goods must fit the description given by the retailer verbally or by any label attached to them. Therefore, if you say things about a product, then the product supplied must match what you have said about it. For example, a 'feather' pillow cannot be filled with polyester stuffing
- **fit for purpose** – this means that the goods must be fit for any particular purpose made known either expressly, or by implication, to the seller. Therefore the goods should do the job they are supposed to do. For example, if the customer asks for a video recorder that is capable of playing back NTSC version video tapes, then the product you recommend must be able to do this.

If your organisation supplies services, then the same Act still applies. It defines the level of expectation the customer is entitled to. When work is carried out by a trader, the customer can expect it to be done:

- **with reasonable care and skill** – this means that any work carried out must be done by someone who has at least the skill level of an 'average practitioner in that field'. For example, the customer would expect a gas boiler to be serviced by a person who is CORGI registered as that is the industry standard
- **within a reasonable time scale** if no specific time frame has been agreed
- **for a reasonable charge** if no price was agreed.

Depending on the nature of its business, your organisation may well be governed by other specific legislation, such as:

- **The Consumer Credit Act 1974** – this law governs personal loans and other credit agreements. It demands that full written details of the true interest rate (i.e. annual percentage rate) be quoted; a 'cooling-off' period be allowed during which borrowers may change their minds and cancel agreements and that all agreements are in writing.
- **The Financial Services Act 1986** – this Act lays down clear rules and regulations governing the activities of those involved in the investment business. All potential investors must be warned that investment in new business carries high risks as well as the possibility of high rewards and they should also be encouraged to take advice from a person authorised under the Act who is specialised in advising on investment.
- **The Trade Description Act 1968** – this Act makes it a criminal offence for a person, in the course of business, to apply false or misleading trade descriptions to goods. The term 'trade description' includes, amongst others, an indication, however given, of the 'place of manufacture, production, processing or reconditioning' of the goods.

- **The Data Protection Act 1998** – this particular Act is covered in section 2.1, see page 148 for further information.
- **The Consumer Protection (Distance Selling) Regulations 2000** – these regulations say that you should be given clear information about the order and the company, along with a cooling-off period, and protection against credit card fraud and the menace of unsolicited goods.

You will need to find out about the legislation that relates to your job role within your particular organisation, as you should be aware of the effect it may have on how you deal with callers. You should also be aware of any rights that the applicable legislation may afford your customers.

Check it out

Find out about the legislation that governs your job role.
- What legislation applies?
- What is the effect of this legislation?
- What rights does it give your customers?

Weighing up all the options

When there is more than one possible course of action open to you, you will need to consider each of the options in turn. You will need to look at them from both your organisation's viewpoint and that of your customer so that you can select the option which is most favourable for both of them.

Try to balance the needs of both parties

The limits of your authority within the organisation

If you cannot balance the needs of the caller and your organisation, you may have to move the call on to the next level; i.e. to escalate it to someone with greater authority than yourself, who can make higher level decisions.

When you are trying to satisfy a customer, you need to know when you can use your own initiative to come up with a solution and when you need to seek assistance from others. For example, if one of your customers were to demand a discount, would you be able to tell them 'yes' or 'no' yourself or would you need to refer them to someone else?

It is also possible that you will sometimes need to call on additional resources that may not normally be available to you. To help you decide if any additional resources are required, you may find it useful to ask yourself the questions in the 'Think about it' exercise below.

Think about it

1 Will I be able to make the required arrangements myself, without the assistance of anyone else?
   If the answer to this question is **no**, *then you will need to decide whose assistance is required and make sure that you enlist their help in accordance with your organisation's procedures.*

2 Will the use of any non-standard items (such as unusual tools and equipment) or consumables (such as spare parts) be needed to achieve the required task?
   If the answer to this question is **yes**, *then you will need to make sure that the non-standard items or consumables are sourced and made available as required.*

3 Are there any additional costs associated with the required arrangements?
   If the answer to this question is **yes**, *then you will need to ask yourself an additional question:*
   Do you need to gain approval for the additional costs involved?
   If the answer to this question is **yes**, *then you will need to make sure that you seek the appropriate approval in accordance with your organisation's procedures before making the necessary arrangements.*

4 How long will it take to make the arrangements – do you have sufficient time available to complete the arrangements yourself within the timescales agreed with the client?
   If the answer to this question is **no**, *then you have two options – you will need to free up some time within your own schedule if that is possible, otherwise you will need to call upon the assistance of someone else.*

How to obtain authority from your organisation for arrangements that exceed the level of responsibility you have been given

Your organisation should have a standard procedure that you are expected to follow when you need to gain authorisation for arrangements that exceed your level of responsibility.

You will need to find out if it does.

Check it out

Does your organisation have a set of procedures that you are expected to follow when you need to gain authorisation for arrangements that exceed your level of responsibility?

Keys to good practice

✓ If you are required to follow a script when making arrangements on behalf of callers, make sure that you are very familiar with the script, as it will then sound more natural when you work your way through it with the caller.

✓ Set realistic priorities.

✓ Always bear in mind the effect that one set of arrangements may have on another.

✓ Try not to underestimate what might happen.

✓ Make sure that you are familiar with your organisation's procedures for gaining any additional authorisation that may be required.

✓ Always ensure that you source any additional resources that may be required.

✓ Make sure that you are familiar with and understand your organisation's service standards and codes of practice.

✓ If you are not able to meet the needs of the customer precisely, always explain to the caller why this has not been possible.

✓ Never make promises to the caller that you can not keep or withhold important information..

6.2 Make arrangements for callers

WHAT YOU NEED TO KNOW OR LEARN

♦ How to consider your organisation's levels of service and quality against the arrangements you are making

- ◆ How to confirm details of arrangements to be made with the caller
- ◆ How to make arrangements on behalf of callers
- ◆ How to pass on information within your organisation
- ◆ How to monitor actions you have taken to make sure they have been completed
- ◆ How to maintain records of what action you have taken.

How to consider your organisation's levels of service and quality against the arrangements you are making

Customers have expectations about the level of service that they expect to receive. If you do not match up to expectations, the customer may well not give your organisation any business again.

If the customer's expectations are fulfilled, your organisation is likely to get repeat business. However, if the caller's expectations are exceeded because you provided them with *excellent* customer service, then your organisation will almost certainly get that caller's repeat business and may well draw in new business as well – as the satisfied customer spreads the word.

A customer who goes away satisfied is likely to tell their friends and family about this experience. The people they talk to may well remember this and could, in turn, tell others of the good service received by their friend or relative.

It is therefore possible that making sure the customer goes away satisfied could lead to an increase in the number of people who think positively about your organisation. All this good publicity has in itself the potential to bring about an increase in turnover for your organisation.

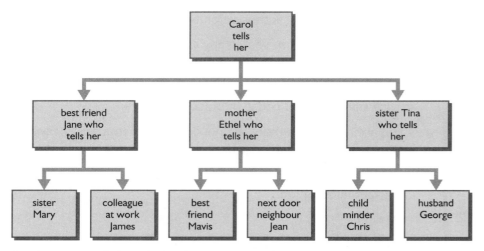

Good news travels fast – before long six people know about the wonderful service that Carol received

Figure 6.1 The benefit of good publicity

Think about it

Put yourself in the customer's shoes and ask yourself the following questions:

1 If I were the customer, how would I want to be treated?
2 What kind of service would I expect?
3 What would make me feel like I had received excellent customer service?

It is likely that you would want to do business with an organisation where the staff are pleasant, courteous and helpful. You would be even more likely to give the organisation business if the staff treat you like an individual, with individual needs, and are willing to make every effort to meet those needs.

You are very unlikely to want to do business with an organisation where the staff take your custom for granted, regard you as a nuisance or an inconvenience, and make no attempt to meet your needs.

Outstanding customer service does not happen by accident. It requires careful planning, the setting of organisational standards for customer service and a consistent focus on discovering and meeting customers' agreed needs and requirements. Everyone in the organisation needs to put extra effort into meeting those needs and requirements and should constantly strive for continuous improvement.

Earlier in this unit, in the section on how to balance the needs of the caller against the requirements of your organisation (see page 170), you checked out your own organisation's service standards and codes of practice. We will now consider further the relevance and possible impact of those standards.

Think about it

◆ How do your organisation's service standards and codes of practice help you to offer a quality service?
◆ What could go wrong when you make arrangements on behalf of customers?
◆ What are your responsibilities when things go wrong and who do you report to or inform of any problems?

How to confirm details of arrangements to be made with the caller

Always make sure that you have correctly understood what the caller wants you to do on their behalf, by checking with the customer that they are happy with the arrangements that you intend to make for them.

If you are not able to make the arrangements that are required by the caller whilst they are still on the line, then it is important that you let the customer know what you intend to do on their behalf and when you expect it to be done by. You must ensure that the intended arrangements meet the customer's needs whilst they are still on the line. You should also make sure that you take down the caller's contact details. You will then be able to call them back if there are any problems.

How to make arrangements on behalf of callers

If you are able to make the arrangements that are required by the caller whilst they are still on the line, then you should let them know the details of the arrangements that have been made as soon as they have been completed.

If we think back to Case Study 1, each time John booked a room for the customer, he read back the details of the booking to the caller so that the customer could check that the booking was correct and he also gave the booking reference number. He also asked the customer if written confirmation of the booking was required. If the caller had wanted written confirmation, then further follow up action would have been required on John's part to ensure that written confirmation was produced and sent to the caller.

If the arrangements made for the caller had involved something like a flight booking, then the flight tickets would also need to be sent along with confirmation of the booking that was made.

Think about it

♦ Are you likely to need to carry out any follow-up action after making arrangements on behalf of customers?
♦ Does the follow-up action need to be completed within a certain timescale? If it does, what is the time frame that you must work within?

How to pass on information within your organisation

Did you know?

Many service repair jobs that are reported through a call centre are then passed straight to the repair person that has responsibility for that geographical area, in many cases using some form of electronic text messaging system.

When you are making arrangements for callers, you may often have to enlist the help of colleagues. Make sure that you give your colleagues all the information they will need to complete the arrangements. If people do not have all the information they require and know exactly what arrangements are needed, errors or problems may occur.

Think about it

What key information would you need to pass on to colleagues to enable them to complete arrangements that are required?

However, it is not enough to assume that any arrangements that you have requested on a customer's behalf will be made. If you are to provide high quality customer service, you must go that step further and actually check that the arrangements have been made to the satisfaction of the customer.

How to monitor actions you have taken to make sure they have been completed

There are a number of reasons why there can be difficulty in implementing arrangements on behalf of the caller. It may be that:

◆ the arrangements were a really good idea from the customer's point of view, but not so good from your organisation's viewpoint. Perhaps they were too expensive, too time consuming or too complicated

◆ although the arrangements may have seemed reasonable, perhaps it could be difficult to get colleagues to co-operate with their implementation

◆ your colleagues may not have been supplied with all the information necessary to make the required arrangements

◆ something unexpected happened that made it impossible to complete the arrangements.

Thinking ahead may help you to ensure that any potential problems are spotted and dealt with straight away. However, you will need to be familiar with both your organisation's products or services and its procedures if you are going to be able to spot potential difficulties.

Think about it

◆ What systems and procedures exist within your organisation to ensure that arrangements made on behalf of the customer meet with their satisfaction?

◆ What part do you play in these systems and procedures?

◆ What could happen if no follow up were ever made?

If you spot any potential difficulties, never assume that someone else has noticed them and is already dealing with them. Always take appropriate action so that any potential difficulty can be sorted out before it becomes a real problem and causes inconvenience and upset for customers.

Think about it

If you were to notice a potential problem, what action would you take?

How to maintain records of what action you have taken

Once you have made suitable arrangements on behalf of the caller, you must ensure that you maintain a complete and accurate record of the details of the arrangements. Your organisation probably has a set of procedures that tell you how these details should be recorded.

Check it out

♦ Find out if your organisation has a set of procedures that tell you how you should record any actions that you have agreed with the customer.
♦ Are you expected to complete a data input screen?
♦ Are you expected to complete any paperwork?

You should find a copy of each of the forms that you may need to complete and practise filling them in.

Keys to good practice

✓ Always try to exceed the caller's expectations – if it is within your authority to do so and it is cost effective and practical to do so.

✓ If you cannot make the arrangements required by the caller while they are on the line, make sure that you let the customer know what action you intend to take on their behalf and when it will be completed by.

✓ If you are able to make the arrangements that are required by the caller whilst they are still on the line, you should let them know the details of the arrangements as soon as they have been completed.

✓ Make sure that colleagues are provided with all the information that they need when you are relying on them to complete any arrangements that are required.

✓ Do not assume that any arrangements that you initiate will be completed. Always check that they have been carried out to the satisfaction of the caller.

✓ Always think ahead and try to prevent any potential problems.

✓ Maintain complete and accurate records of the arrangements that have been made, in accordance with your organisation's procedures if they apply.

Check your knowledge

1 What key information do you need to obtain from callers?
2 How do you set realistic priorities?
3 How would you gain approval for and source any additional resources that you may need?
4 Does your organisation have a set of service standards or a code of practice?
5 What constraints do you have to work within?
6 Why should you never make promises to the caller that you cannot keep?
7 What legal rights do your customers have?
8 What are the limits of your authority?
9 Why should you try to exceed the caller's expectations?
10 Why do you need to monitor actions that you have initiated?
11 Why is it a good idea to think ahead?
12 How do you record details of the actions you take?

UNIT 7

Authorise transactions using telecommunications

This option unit is all about authorising financial transactions on behalf of callers using telecommunications. The term *authorising transactions* in this context is to gain or give permission to go ahead with the transaction. The transactions could be transfers of funds between accounts, the payments of invoices by credit or charge cards, or bank payment of accounts as a result of a telephone call.

This unit has three elements:

♦ obtain and confirm details of transactions
♦ compare transaction details with the authorisation criteria
♦ confirm the transaction.

We will look at these as they apply to the financial institutions, such as banks and building societies, organisations that accept credit or charge cards as payment for products or services they supply, and organisations that operate credit accounts for customers, such as mail order companies.

The transactions conducted by banks and building societies will probably involve:

♦ the transfer of funds from one account to another
♦ the payment of bills and invoices direct from accounts.

If yours is an organisation that accepts credit or debit cards as payments for services or products it sells, your transactions will probably involve:

♦ debiting the caller's bank account of the payment required
♦ adding the amount you require to the caller's credit card account.

If your organisation is one that operates credit accounts for its customers the transactions could include:

♦ adding the amount of the transaction to the caller's credit account
♦ deducting payments from the caller's credit account.

After you have completed this unit, you will be able to:

♦ recognise the cards used for the majority of these transactions
♦ obtain and confirm details of the transactions in a manner and at a pace suited to the callers
♦ compare the transaction details against authorisation criteria and identify discrepancies in the information provided
♦ implement approved procedures where problems are encountered in obtaining or confirming transaction details
♦ understand the reasons for imposing the authorisation criteria and only authorising transactions when the criteria have been fully met
♦ advise the caller clearly and in a manner designed to maintain goodwill that you are unable to authorise the transaction requested

- understand the necessity for completing records of the transaction accurately and completely and within agreed timescales
- understand the requirement for confidentiality in terms of the Data Protection Act.

The case studies in this chapter have been based on two fictitious organisations: 'Castle Bank' and 'Fortress Travel'. Examples from other sectors such as office supplies, insurance and telemarketing will be covered in other chapters.

7.1 Obtain and confirm details of transactions

WHAT YOU NEED TO KNOW OR LEARN

- Your organisation's requirements and procedures for confirming the caller's identity
- The details required from the caller to process the transaction
- How to confirm the details of transactions with callers
- Actions to take when problems are encountered obtaining information
- How to record details of transactions.

Your organisation's requirements and procedures for confirming the caller's identity

Your organisation's procedures for confirming the caller's identity will depend on the nature of your work and the type of transactions you are carrying out. We will consider the following types of transaction separately:

- bank transactions
- card transactions
- credit account transactions.

Bank transactions

With the emergence of telephone banking, many of the banks and building societies encouraged their customers to help combat crime and possible fraud by providing personal details known only to them, to be used as security checks whenever the customer uses the telephone to request a transaction.

The following are a few of the most common personal details that banks and building societies may ask customers to supply in order to help them confirm the customer's identity:

- mother's maiden name
- favourite place
- favourite name
- memorable number
- memorable date
- date of birth.

The list is a selection of the most commonly used details, but the list could be endless. Customers are not asked to supply all these details but to select two or three of the most appropriate ones. These details are then stored with the customer account details, so that if someone telephones requesting service, the bank or building society can confirm their identity by asking questions they have selected themselves.

This method can help to weed out unsophisticated attempts at fraud. One of its main drawbacks is that customers forget what personal details they have given. People usually remember their mother's maiden name or date of birth, but favourite names or place can easily be forgotten. This system is only as good as the caller's memory. The time between the customer first giving the details and the first time they are asked to confirm their identity may be considerable.

Banks and building societies usually have fall back arrangements if the caller provides the wrong details or cannot remember. These usually involve you asking the caller to identify one or more of the following:

♦ any regular payments into the account
♦ direct debits from the account
♦ recent transactions involving the account.

Many of the banks and financial institutions have installed automated telephone systems where calls are answered by a system which asks the callers to input their bank details, such as sort code and account number, using the telephone keypad before the call is passed to an agent. Some systems even automatically carry out the security check and ask the caller to input selected digits from the caller's memorable number or date of birth. Therefore when you answer the call the system has already identified the caller and is displaying the caller's account details. This type of system frees you to concentrate on the purpose of the call.

Other banks and financial institutions prefer to maintain the personal touch, where customers' calls are answered directly by a person who is able to deal with whatever request or transaction the caller may require. If you work for one of these organisations you will need to question the caller to gather the information you require to establish their identity. This could well include carrying out security checks using personal information provided by the customer on a previous occasion.

Card transactions

If you work for one of the many organisations that sells its products and services over the telephone, the key question you will need to ask when you have taken the order is : 'How would you like to pay?'. The caller has several possible options available: by card, by cheque or by voucher.

If the caller opts to pay by either cheque or voucher you will need to explain the process. This will involve giving the caller the following information:

♦ who to make the cheque payable to
♦ the amount to pay
♦ the address to which the payment should be sent.

You will also need to explain to the caller that the order will not be processed until the cheque or voucher has been received.

Where the caller opts for payment by card the order can usually be processed immediately.

There are many different kinds of plastic card and they can be divided simply into three basic types: pay now, pay later and pay before.

◆ Pay now

Debit cards are pay now cards, as the payment for the goods or service is deducted straight away from the customer's bank account. Payment is only made if the customer's bank account is in credit or is working within a previously agreed overdraft limit.

◆ Pay later

Credit cards and charge cards allow the customers to buy now and pay later, borrowing the money if necessary. Any purchases the customer makes are charged to his or her account as long as the borrowing does not exceed an agreed limit. Each month a statement is issued to the customer detailing all the transactions that have been made during the period and requesting payment. Depending on the type of card, the statement may require payment in full or stipulate a minimum percentage of the total outstanding. Where payment is not met in full any outstanding balance attracts an interest charge. This continues with the customer adding purchases to the account and making regular monthly payments, until all outstanding borrowing is paid off.

◆ Pay before

Pay before cards are the latest innovation in plastic card, and are in fact electronic purses that have to be loaded with money before they can be used. The early phone cards and the prepaid electricity and gas meter cards were early examples of this type of technology. With these types of cards you purchased a card with a fixed credit value, and as you used the card the credit was reduced until the credit ran out and you disposed of the card.

Although we have considered all three types of plastic cards, only the first two are likely to be used by customers who place orders over the telephone.

Did you know?

Fact 1 The world's first payment card was introduced in the USA in the 1920s. The card, known as a 'shopper's plate', was used in the retail outlet which issued it. The 'shopper's plate' was similar to the present day charge cards, with the cardholder required to settle their account in full every month.

Fact 2 Barclays was the first UK bank to launch a credit card in the UK in 1966. It was called Barclaycard and was based on the Bank Americard, now Visa.

Fact 3 Barclays issued the UK's first debit card in 1987 in co-operation with Visa, and Switch was launched in 1988.

Fact 4 In February 2002 there were more than 91 million credit and debit cards in issue in the UK.

Fact 5 Two fifths (40 per cent) of the total retail spending on the high street is by card payments and this is increasing all the time.

Fact 6 Nearly 50 per cent of the people who use credit cards pay the full amount outstanding with the next statement.

Source: Credit Card Research Group

Handling a payment using a credit or debit card face to face with the customer is usually straightforward. You ask the customer, '*How would you like to pay?*' and he or she presents the relevant debit or credit card for payment. You take the card and swipe it through the terminal that reads the card's magnetic stripe or you manually input the card number into the terminal. You then enter the details of the purchase. The machine calls the card processing service and processes the transaction, assuming everything is acceptable. The machine then prints the payment slip for the customer to sign. When signed, you compare the signature with that on the card and if they match the transaction is complete.

Throughout this process there is no requirement for you to ask for any other details as all the information you require is available on the card. If you have any doubts about the card you are offered as payment, such as whether it is valid or if it belongs to the customer, you are able to check the details or compare the signature.

You must always compare the customer's signature with that already on the card.

If, however, you are conducting the sale over the telephone the only information available to you is that which you can elicit from the caller. It is therefore essential that you are able to recognise some of the main credit and debit cards and know the key features they contain. This will not only help the transaction go smoothly and efficiently, but may also prevent fraudulent use of cards. With the ever-increasing number of people preferring to pay by credit or debit cards it is inevitable that the number of card frauds has also increased.

Credit Cards

The list of credit cards may appear to be endless, but in reality there are only two basic networks running credit cards: Visa and MasterCard. These are global organisations that support the issuing and settlement of credit card payments by a large number of banks and institutions. Banks and institutions that are members of these networks can issue credit cards that are co-branded with themselves and the network provider. For example, Abbey National issue Visa cards.

◆ Visa credit cards

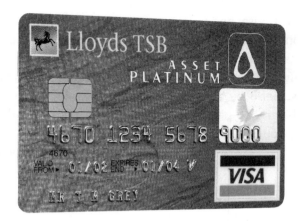

A visa credit card

1 Visa cards are identified by the Visa logo, and the dove hologram on the front of the card.
2 Visa cards have the logo of the issuing bank or financial institution on the front of the card.
3 Visa card embossed account numbers begin with a '4' and contain 16 digits.
4 The first four digits of the account number are printed below the embossed account number.
5 An embossed 'V' appears after the expiry date on the card.
6 The account number or the last four digits of the account number are printed in the signature panel on the reverse of the card followed by a three-digit number.

◆ MasterCard credit cards

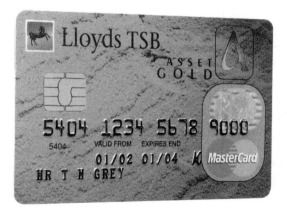

A MasterCard credit card

1 MasterCard cards are identified by the MasterCard logo, and the globe hologram on the front of the card. The globe hologram should have depth when tilted back and forth.

2 MasterCard cards have the logo of the issuing bank or financial institution on the front of the card.
3 MasterCard card embossed account numbers begin with a '5' and contain 16 digits.
4 The first four digits of the account number are printed below the embossed account number.
5 An embossed 'M' appears after the expiry date on the card.
6 The account number or the last four digits of the account number are printed in the signature panel on the reverse of the card followed by a three-digit number.

Debit Cards

Most banks and building societies issue **debit cards** for holders of their accounts. Again the list is endless, but there are only two main debit card networks in the UK: Switch and Visa.

Debit cards are linked to the customer's bank account and are often a multi-function card. This means the card can be used to pay for things at outlets displaying the appropriate logo, to withdraw money from Automatic Teller Machines (ATMs or cash machines) and as a cheque guarantee card.

♦ **Switch debit cards**

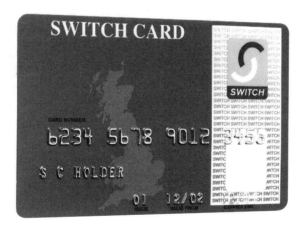

A Switch debit card

1 Switch debit cards are identified by the Switch logo, and a three-dimensional hologram depicting either the head of Shakespeare or the Switch logo. Some holograms are surrounded by the words 'Cheque Guarantee' and the amount of the guarantee, which is usually £50, £100 or £250. These holograms can be found on either the front or the back of the card.
2 Switch cards may have the logo of the issuing bank or financial institution on the front of the card.

3 All switch cards bear the Maestro and Cirrus symbols.

The Cirrus and Maestro Symbols

4 The embossed number across the centre of the card has a four digit number starting with a 6, followed by the customer's bank sort code and the customer's account number – a total of eighteen digits.

5 The main embossed number on the card is printed in the signature panel on the reverse of the card, followed by a three-digit number.

6 The card also has the customer's bank account sort code and card number embossed on the front of the card.

7 Switch cards are also embossed with an issue number and an expiry date on the front of the card.

♦ **Visa debit cards**

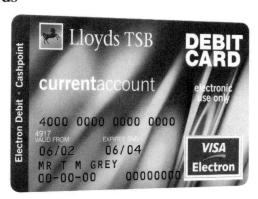

A Visa debit card (Note: this is an electronic debit card and **cannot** be accepted over the telephone)

1 Visa debit cards are identified by the Visa logo, and the dove hologram on the front of the cards.

2 Visa cards have the logo of the issuing bank or financial institution on the front of the card.

3 Visa debit cards also have a three-dimensional hologram depicting the head of Shakespeare surrounded by the words 'Cheque Guarantee' and the amount of the guarantee, which is usually £50, £100 or £250.

4 Visa card embossed account numbers begin with a '4' and contain 16 digits.

5 The first four digits of the card number are printed below the embossed card number.

6 An embossed 'V' appears after the expiry date on the card.

7 The card number followed by a three-digit number is printed in the signature panel on the reverse of the card.

8 The card also has the customer's bank account sort code and account number embossed on the card.

9 The card is also embossed with the *valid from* and *expires end* dates on the front of the card.

Above we have looked at the cards that will account for the vast majority of the transactions you will be asked to make, but there are global organisations that issue other cards such as:

◆ American Express
◆ Diner's Cards
◆ JCB.

All three of these offer charge and credit cards, but for your organisation to be able to accept any one of these it must sign an individual agreement with the issuing organisation.

Check it out

Find out what credit and debit cards your organisation can accept.

◆ Are there any that have not been covered in this section?

Confirming the card user's identity

To be able to confirm the card user's identity you will need to ask some fundamental questions:

◆ what is your name and address?
◆ what type of card is it?
◆ what is the number of your card?
◆ do you have the card in front of you?
◆ what is the name and title displayed on the card?
◆ does the card belong to you?
◆ have you a contact telephone number?
◆ what address do you want the goods sent to?

With this information you will be able to input the card number into the appropriate screen and bring up the name and address of the person the card was issued to. This is called Address Verification (AVS). If the details given by the caller agree with the name and address on the system, it is reasonable to assume the person is the same and you will be sending the goods to the address where the cardholder receives their statements. If the details do not agree you may decide to ask further questions, but you will be within your rights to refuse the transaction.

If you have any problems identifying the caller, or any of the details do not agree with information you already have, you should inform your supervisor or team leader by following your organisation's procedures.

Credit account transactions

If you work for one of the many organisations, such as mail order catalogues or bookmakers, that allow their customers to operate credit accounts you will normally confirm the caller's identity by asking the following:

- the caller's account number
- the caller's name and address
- the caller's telephone number.

By asking the caller to give his or her account number you are able to check the information given to any subsequent questions against your records and so confirm their identity. When a customer applies for an account he or she supplies all of the information before your organisation issues them with the account number. The organisation will also agree a credit limit to which the account may operate.

The details required from the caller to process the transaction

Having confirmed the identity of the caller you are now in a position to gather the information you require for processing the transaction. This information will vary depending on whether you work for a bank or financial institution, or an organisation accepting credit or debit cards, or operating credit account as payment for products or services.

Banking transactions

If you are working for a bank or financial institution you must first identify what sort of transaction the caller requires you to make. It could include:

- transferring funds between accounts belonging to the caller
- transferring funds to someone else's account
- paying bills and invoices.

Once you have confirmed the identity of the caller, the transferring of funds between accounts he or she holds with your organisation should be relatively simple. You will need to ascertain how much the caller wishes to transfer and which accounts are involved. It is likely that you will be able to access all or most of the accounts held by the caller with your organisation and assuming that there are sufficient funds available the transfer can go ahead rapidly.

Transferring funds to someone else's account may not be quite so simple. You will have to ask the caller for the amount to be transferred, the account number to be debited, the account name, branch sort code and account number of the recipient. If the recipient's account is held with your organisation you may be able to confirm that the account details of the recipient are correct, but if it is with another organisation you may have to rely on the details given by the caller.

The payment of bills and invoices using home or telephone banking is very similar to the transfer of funds to another person's account. You will need to identify the account from which the payment is to be made, the bank sort code and account number of the person or organisation whose bill or invoice is being paid, the invoice or customer account number of the bill, and the date when the caller requires the bill or invoice to be paid.

Your account number

Statement number
Q003 GP

Date
7 August 2002

If you have a query
please see reverse for
our contact details.

BT

BT Together

Statement for

Cost of calls	£ 39.05
Package benefits additional to reduced call rates	£ 0.00
Service charges	£ 47.23
VAT	£ 15.09
Total this period	£ 101.37
Brought forward	£ 83.31
Payments	- £ 72.00
Debit balance	**£ 112.68**

Make sure you're getting the
best value out of BT,
phone 150 and request your
free BT guide.

BT Together

Your package includes:
· Unlimited national evening & weekend calls (up to 1 hour per call) at no extra charge
· Unlimited local evening & weekend calls (up to 1 hour per call) at no extra charge
· Line rental (for one line)
· Friends & Family Overseas
· Low call rates per minute (inc VAT):

Time of day	local	national
Daytime	3p	4p

· Lower rates for international and mobile calls

001282

Important information
The new payment due will be
effective from 1 Oct 02

If you wish to make
alternative arrangements
please contact us. (See
reverse for our contact
details.)

Monthly Payment Plan instalment change
The balance on your Monthly Payment Plan has
exceeded your credit limit and a change is
required to your monthly payments as shown
below. We will automatically adjust the amount
of your Direct Debit and you don't need to take
any action.

Your existing payment	Your new payment	Your new credit limit
£ 24.00	£ 44.00	£ 154.00

The payment dates shown on this
statement are the dates we issue the
Direct Debit request to your bank or
building society. This is approximately
two working days earlier than the date
your bank or building society account
will be debited. The payment will not
be deducted before the agreed date.

A telephone bill

Card transactions

Having successfully confirmed the identity of the caller you will need to
gather and record the details that will enable you to process the
transaction. The details you are likely to require are as shown in
Figure 7.1.

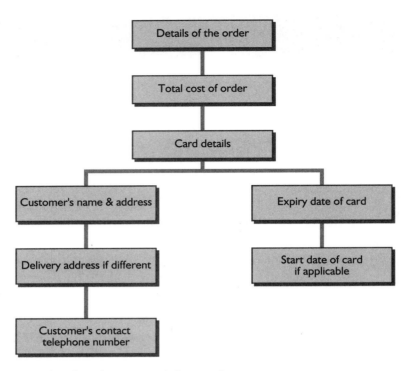

Figure 7.1 The details required for card transactions

You need to confirm the order details, inform the caller of the total cost of the transaction, confirm the delivery address and obtain a contact telephone number should there be problems processing the order or with the delivery. You should also ensure that you have sufficient details about the method of payment such as the type of card, card number and information to confirm the card is valid.

NAME	Mr / Mrs / Ms																	
ADDRESS																		
						POST CODE												

Daytime Tele No: _____   Home Tele No: _____.

Cardholder's Name (If Different): _____.

CARD NUMBER ⬚⬚⬚⬚⬚⬚⬚⬚⬚⬚⬚⬚⬚⬚⬚⬚⬚⬚⬚⬚

CARD TYPE :   VISA ⬚   MASTERCARD ⬚   SWITCH ⬚

OTHER ⬚   TYPE ⬚⬚⬚⬚⬚⬚⬚⬚⬚⬚⬚

EXPIRY DATE ⬚⬚⬚⬚   SWITCH ISSUE NUMBER ⬚⬚

COMPLETE ALL DETAILS

A card transaction slip

Credit account transactions

Organisations that give credit on account may require the following details:

♦ details of the order or service
♦ the date the goods or service are required (where appropriate).

Such organisations usually only deliver to the name and address of the account holder, therefore there is no other requirement to ask or confirm any other details.

Check it out

♦ What transactions do you deal with? Make a list in your portfolio – you may like to add to this as you go on.

Case study 1 – Susan's experiences

The caller, Mrs Edwards, rang Castle Bank and said she would like to transfer some money to her current account and then to pay some of her bills. I asked for her name and account details. She gave them to me. I also asked her to confirm some of the personal details we have on file. She did so without hesitation.

I asked her which account she would like to transfer the funds from and she said the deposit account. I asked how much she would like to transfer; she said £800. When I accessed her deposit account I could see that there was only £600 remaining as £2000 had been transferred to a high interest account two months previously. I explained to the caller that there were insufficient funds in her deposit account to do as she asked. At first she seemed very puzzled and then she asked if her husband had actually transferred funds to a high interest account. I was able to confirm that he had. She asked what remained in the deposit account, I told her £600. She said in that case she would only transfer £500. I confirmed with her the amount and the details of the two bank accounts and completed the transfer. The caller then asked to pay two outstanding bills, an electricity bill and a telephone bill. I asked if she had both bills in front of her, she replied yes. I asked her for details of the bank to which the payments needed to be made, the amounts of each bill, and the customer account details from the top of each bill. I entered all the details into the system, which it accepted. I finally asked when she would like the bills paid, she said to pay them as soon as possible. I entered today's date and informed the caller that the bills would be processed overnight.

I asked if there was anything else I could help her with. She said no but thanked me for being patient as she had forgotten that her husband had actually transferred funds to their high interest account.

Think about it

Can you think of an occasion when you contacted an organisation by telephone only to find that things were not as you had expected? Maybe they were rude and unhelpful.

♦ How did it make you feel?

How to confirm the details of transactions with callers

One of the most important skills to develop if you are to be successful at handling financial transactions is your ability to listen and pick up information. It is a recognised fact that most people are too busy thinking about what they are going to say next to concentrate fully on what is being said to them. Active listening is a very important skill to develop if you are working with the telephone. Remember that any mistakes you make by not hearing correctly or by not getting the correct information could result in the transaction failing or being charged back to your organisation.

It is important to listen carefully as mistakes can be costly to the caller or to you and your organisation

When handling financial transactions you are normally dealing with numbers with many digits and it can be very easy to transpose two or more of the digits if you are not fully concentrating on what the caller is saying to you.

Case study I continued

Two weeks later Mrs Edwards rang in a very irate state. In the post this morning she had received a statement for her current account with Castle Bank and a red reminder for her electricity bill. She said the current account was in the red as a result of £500 being transferred out and although the telephone bill appeared to have been paid, there was no indication that the electricity bill had been paid. The red reminder from the electricity company had been dated last Friday. She wanted to know urgently what went wrong.

I Give three examples of what went wrong – and explain how this could have been avoided.

In the case study the person who handled the call had not listened properly and had obviously made a mistake when processing the transactions.

In order to avoid this type of situation happening you should confirm details of the transactions by:

♦ repeating details back to the caller to check that you have heard correctly
♦ ask questions to check mutual understanding
♦ clarify the situation where necessary.

Actions to take when problems are encountered obtaining information

Problems can arise for a multitude of reasons, some may be sinister and others can be genuine. If you are working in a bank or financial institution that uses personal details to confirm the identity of the caller, problems can arise because the caller has forgotten the original answer. Factual questions are always easy to remember, but where the question gives the person a choice they are easily forgotten. For questions such as *'What is your mother's maiden name?'* the person instinctively knows the answer or has never known. But if the question was *'Name your favourite place'*, the person has a choice, so the answer could vary and could well depend on the mood of the person at the time.

If a caller gave the wrong answer to the question *'What is your mother's maiden name?'* you are justified in treating the call with some suspicion, but if the wrong answer was given to the second question you may feel justified in asking further questions such as:

♦ what direct debits are there on the account?
♦ can you identify a recent transaction on the account?
♦ what other accounts do you hold with this branch?

If you think the caller is just confused you may need to be patient and encourage the caller to answer your questions, but if you suspect the caller has other intentions you may find it necessary to flag the situation to a supervisor or team leader. Whatever action you take it should always be

Did you know?

Plastic card fraud cost the UK a staggering £242.6 million in 2000, an increase of 55 per cent on the 1995 figure. Although large and increasing, this figure is only a fraction of total card spend. These losses represents just 0.45 of 1 per cent of all card total turnover in 2000. This includes credit, debit, charge and cheque guarantee cards.

The peak year for card frauds was 1991 when the majority of fraud was due to lost or stolen cards and the non-receipt of mailed cards, but these have now fallen and the majority of losses incurred today are due to counterfeit cards and cards not present.

in line with the guidelines laid down by your organisation. You need to be extra vigilant as card crimes are always on the increase.

From the above you can see that the majority of card frauds today are due to counterfeit cards or people attempting to complete a transaction without having the card present. If you encounter callers who are having difficulty in providing you with the information you require or are being vague, you will probably have to ask further questions to satisfy yourself that the card the caller is using is genuine and not stolen, lost, counterfeit or not available. Some of the further questions you could ask include:

◆ is there a number printed underneath the first few digits of the card number? If so what is it?
◆ is there a hologram on the card? What do you see if you tilt the card back and forth?
◆ are there any numbers printed on the signature strip on the rear of the card? What are they?

As a result of the answers to these questions you may like to ask the caller to confirm some of the details already given you such as:

◆ the start date on your card?
◆ the expiry date on the card?
◆ the address for the delivery?
◆ the postcode of the address?

Confirming these details may help any investigation should you suspect a fraud was being attempted.

Some organisations may have put in place procedures that allow you to flag cases where you think cards are being used fraudulently, while the call is still in progress. Whatever action you decide to take it should be in line with the guidelines set out by your organisation.

How to record details of transactions

All the information you have gathered concerning the transaction will need to be recorded so it can go ahead. You may record the details on paper transaction slips that will be processed later (either by yourself or another person). Alternatively you may record the information by inputting it straight into a computer system, where it is processed immediately or stored for processing later. Whichever system you use you should always check to confirm that the details you have recorded or entered into the computer system are correct.

You must never jot down details and information gathered from a caller or customer on scraps of paper that may be disposed of in a normal waste bin or basket. Information concerning an individual's bank account or credit card details that falls into the wrong hands could have major implications for the individual, you and the organisation you work for. If it is accepted practice to jot down information before the details are transferred to the recording system used by your organisation, all of the paper used for the jottings should be disposed of securely by shredding or burning and never disposed of with normal waste.

Any notes or jottings must be disposed of carefully

7.2 Compare transaction details with the authorisation criteria

- The authorisation criteria for transactions
- How to request additional information from callers when there are discrepancies in the information
- Some of the reasons why the authorisation criteria may not be met
- Actions to take when you encounter difficulties in meeting the authorisation criteria.

The authorisation criteria for transactions

The authorisation criteria are those criteria that need to be met before the transaction can be processed. Failure to meet any of the criteria will result in the transaction either being delayed until further checks are made, or failing altogether.

Banking transactions

The authorisation criteria used by individual banks and financial institutions may vary slightly but in general they all need to meet the following:

- confirm the caller's identity
- confirm the caller's account details
- confirm funds are available
- confirm details of the transaction.

◆ Confirm the caller's identity

The caller's identity is usually confirmed by running through and completing the security checks discussed earlier, e.g. confirming some of the personal details such as mother's maiden name, date of birth.

◆ Confirm the caller's account details

This is to confirm that the account numbers given by the caller belong to the caller, or the caller is authorised to carry out transactions with the account (i.e. authorised or able to sign).

◆ Confirm funds are available

This will involve checking the balance of the account and confirming that there are sufficient funds available to meet the demands of the transaction. This might also include an agreed overdraft limit.

◆ Confirm details of the transaction

The details of the transaction are the most important part of the transaction as far as the caller is concerned. All the other details are for your organisation's benefit, to ensure the caller has the authority to request the transaction and to identify attempts to commit fraud. It is therefore imperative that the details of the transaction are confirmed in order to satisfy the caller's demands.

The details usually include:

♦ the amount to be paid or transferred
♦ details of the receiving account
♦ the date when the payment or transfer is to take place.

Check it out

If you are working in the banking or financial sector what authorisation criteria does your organisation apply? Make a list of them for your porfolio.

Card transactions

The majority of organisations that accept debit and credit cards use the same authorisation criteria for authorising transactions. They are:

♦ confirming the caller's identity
♦ confirming the card is valid
♦ confirming the transaction details
♦ confirming the cards is not reported stolen or lost
♦ checking the transaction value against any organisation floor limits.

♦ Confirming the caller's identity

The type of information and details you will need to gather from the caller to confirm identity include:

♦ the caller's name and address
♦ the type of card and the card number
♦ the name and title displayed on the card
♦ whether the card belongs to the caller
♦ a contact telephone number
♦ the address to where the goods are to be sent.

If the name and address matches with the details held against the card number you have confirmed the caller identity as far as you can.

♦ Confirming the card is valid

This can easily be checked by confirming the expiry date and the start date on the card. Pre-dated or expired cards should be rejected and the transaction cancelled.

♦ Confirming the transaction details

This is a final check before authorising the transaction to confirm the details with the caller. Any misunderstanding or errors that could have resulted in incorrect information being entered can be corrected before authorisation.

♦ Confirming the card is not reported stolen or lost

If your organisation is licensed to accept credit and debit cards, the network's operators – through your provider – will provide your organisation with updated information about all known lost and stolen cards. The files that contain all this information are commonly known as the '**hot card files**'. They are updated at regular intervals.

Organisations are expected to check all cards that are offered as payment against these files. If a card is found to be on the list you are expected to refuse acceptance and notify the provider of any information gathered during the process, as this may help to catch the fraudsters. In such situations the more information you can gather the better.

◆ Floor limits

Most organisations that accept debit or credit cards set limits under which transactions can be processed without authorisation from the card issuing company. These are usually referred to as floor limits.

All transactions below the floor limit can be agreed by the organisation, but those above the floor limit will need authorisation from the card issuing company before they can be accepted by the organisation.

Organisations that deal with large numbers of card transactions can show considerable savings in both time and money by operating a floor limit. Many criminals and fraudsters who use stolen or forged cards know that organisations operate floor limits and they will operate below these limits to avoid their transaction requiring authorisation from the card issuing company. To try to prevent this happening nearly all organisations review their floor limit at regular intervals. Some organisations even go further and subject a small percentage of randomly selected transactions to the authorisation process, even though they are below the floor limit, in order to catch such people.

Check it out

Find out if your organisation operates a floor limit scheme.

◆ How does it operate?
◆ How often does your organisation change its floor limit?
◆ Does your organisation seek authorisation for any transactions below the floor limit? If yes, what percentage does it seek authorisation for?
◆ How are they selected?

Keep a note of your answers for your portfolio.

Credit account transactions

Most organisations that allow callers to operate credit accounts use authorisation criteria such as:

◆ confirming the account number is current and valid
◆ confirming that the name and address given by the caller agrees with that recorded against the account number
◆ confirming there is sufficient credit available to permit the transaction to proceed
◆ confirming details of the transaction.

If you work for an organisation that allows callers to buy products or services via the telephone and charge them to credit accounts, you usually have far more information available to you than an organisation that accepts credit or debit cards. You will be able to authorise most, if not all, transactions from the information available without reference to any other outside agency, such as bank or credit card provider.

♦ Confirming the account number

The account number is the linchpin of trading with credit accounts; only people that have applied and been accepted by the organisation can use such a system. Your first requirement is to confirm that the account number given by the caller is valid and current. From then on all the information asked for by you is to check that the person requesting the transaction is the account holder or a person who is authorised to use the account.

♦ Confirming the caller's name and address

This question is asked to confirm that the name and address given by the caller is the same as that recorded by the organisation, and not someone trying to use the account. Most accounts like this operate by only dispatching goods to the account holder's address, or if a bookmaker operates the account, any winnings from bets placed through the account are paid into the account. It is therefore difficult for anyone other than the account holder to benefit from any transactions made on the account.

♦ Confirming there is sufficient credit available

Such accounts work within very strict credit limits, and as all the account details are likely to be available to you when you access the account number, you will be able to see if sufficient credit is available to fund the transaction.

♦ Confirming details of the transaction

Again this is a final check before authorising the transaction to confirm the details with the caller. Any misunderstanding or errors that could have resulted in incorrect information being entered can be corrected before authorisation, as changes after authorisation may be impossible.

How to request additional information from callers when there are discrepancies in the information

In this context we can define discrepancies as either a shortage of available information, in which case additional information is required, or inconsistencies in the information given to you by the caller, or between the data you have available and that given to you by the caller.

How you request additional information from a caller will depend on the type of discrepancies you have identified. You could use direct questions such as: *'Could I have your full name and address?'* or, *'Could I have your telephone number?'*.

This type of question is straightforward and, as you are asking for direct information, the caller is unlikely to be evasive otherwise the transaction may fail. If you do meet with any reluctance to give such information you would be justified in treating the caller with some suspicion.

If the discrepancies you have identified are inconsistencies in the information already supplied you may need to ask for confirmation or clarification of the details. The type of question you ask will depend on the nature of the discrepancy. Major differences such as the address given by the caller not matching the details you have on file, could result in you asking the caller to repeat the address or to confirm the address. Either of these should prompt the caller to repeat the information and give you the chance to make amendments or confirm the details you had recorded. If necessary you can amend your records and check the details now agree with the information you already hold. But you may need to ask probing questions to discover why a discrepancy exists. This could involve explaining to the caller that the details given you do not match the details you hold on file.

You should remember that the information you are using to identify the discrepancies might also be wrong. For example, if the address given by the caller is not the same as the address on file for the card number you are checking it against, it may be that you have transposed several of the digits in the card number and are checking the wrong details. Do not always assume the worst.

Mistakes in recording the information given by the caller, or misunderstandings between the caller and yourself, are usually responsible for most discrepancies identified during the process of confirming a transaction.

Case study 2 – Ravi's experiences

The caller, Mrs Dodd, rang asking if she could book flight tickets for herself and her 12-year-old son to fly from Luton to Barcelona on the 23 December and return on the 5 January. I checked to see if there were any seats available as it was close to Christmas, and was surprised to find there were. I told her the times of departure and the price of the tickets and I also explained that I would have to book the tickets immediately as they were likely to go very quickly at this time of year. She agreed and I took all the details of her name and address and the name of her son, ready to book the tickets. I asked how she would like to pay for the tickets and she said by Visa card.

I asked for the card number and expiry date, and entered them into the computer system, I also repeated the number back to Mrs Dodd and she said yes. This computer system runs address verification when you enter the details, but this time it came up with details of a Mr T. Smith at an address in Brighton. I asked Mrs Dodd if I could just confirm her address, which she gave me without hesitation. I was beginning to wonder if I was dealing with a stolen or forged card, but I decided to ask Mrs Dodd to confirm the card number for me again. As she repeated it I realised two of the digits had been transposed. I corrected this and this time the correct details came up and I was able to complete the transaction.

If I learnt a lesson from this, it was not to jump to conclusions, but to check again if things go wrong.

1 Why did Ravi decide to ask to confirm the card details again?

2 How would you have reacted if the same situation had happened to you?

The case study illustrates how even when you think you have checked the details things can go wrong and you can get suspicious. The statistic quoted earlier was that the losses due to fraudulent use of cards represents less than one half of one per cent of the total card spend. This is about one in 200 transactions being fraudulent. Therefore the vast majority of cases showing information discrepancies are due to either misunderstanding of the information requested or transposed errors in recording the information.

In most cases, if you ask appropriate questions, you will resolve the problem. It is therefore extremely important that you work to maintain the goodwill of the caller, even when you are probing for information.

Remember that if you are still uncertain you have several options available. You can:

♦ seek advice from a senior colleague, team leader or line manager
♦ transfer the call to a senior colleague, team leader or line manager
♦ refuse the transaction.

Some of the reasons why the authorisation criteria may not be met

Some of the most common reasons are given here.

Bank transactions

If you are working in a bank or financial institution the reasons could include:

♦ you are unable to confirm the caller's identity
♦ there are insufficient funds in the account to complete the transaction
♦ there are insufficient cleared funds in the account to complete the transaction
♦ the transaction requested is outside your authority to complete.

♦ Caller identity

Establishing the caller's identity is the most crucial part of being able to complete transactions over the telephone, and if the caller's identity cannot be confirmed the transaction will always fail. This is why both banks and financial institutions build up databases of the personal details of their clients in order to make caller identification easier.

♦ Insufficient funds

All transactions depend on there being sufficient funds available for you to complete the transaction and when there aren't the caller is usually taken aback. This can be because:

♦ the caller has not monitored the account and has no idea of what funds are available
♦ direct debits have been paid that have been forgotten about

- expected regular payments into the account have not been made
- cheques paid into the account have not yet cleared
- the caller is trying to get money from the account, knowing there were insufficient funds to meet the demand.

It is possible that you may be able to advise the caller that funds are likely to be available at a later date, for example, callers who have funds awaiting clearance. You can then set the transaction completion date on or after that date.

This may also be possible for the caller who is expecting regular payments that have not yet arrived. You may be able to look back at the records and see that the payment is made regularly but the date of the deposit can vary over a short period. In such cases you may be able to advise the caller to call back in two or three days time when the payment may have been made.

In all the other cases you should advise the caller to contact their own branch in person and discuss the situation with their personal banker, as you are unable to authorise completion of the transaction requested.

Case study 3 – Michael's experiences

On the first day at work after the Christmas break we started to have a lot of calls from customers whose debit cards were being refused by shops in the town and they were referring them to the bank.

In the first two hours I personally dealt with five customers, all of them had been to the pre-new year sales and had attempted to pay for their purchases with their debit cards, only to find that the transactions had been refused due to lack of funds. It soon became apparent that all of the callers worked for the same company in the town and none of them had been paid before Christmas.

I remembered dealing with the salaries from the finance department at the works just before I left work the day before Christmas Eve. I started to check what had happened to their payment and discovered that all had been rejected in the overnight run because someone at the company had loaded the wrong database. No one was available at the factory on Christmas Eve and with all the rush to close business in the bank at midday Christmas Eve it was not followed through before Christmas.

When I discovered this I spoke to the manager and explained what had happened. It was agreed that we would extend credit to all our customers who were employed by the factory until the matter could be resolved. I was able to pass this information to the customers that I had dealt with and they were quite relieved.

◆ Outside your authority

Sometimes a caller requests a transaction that you consider may have implications either for the caller themselves or your bank or financial institution. In such cases you may need to inform the caller that it will be necessary for you to seek advice from a senior person or manager before you can authorise such a transaction. Authorising the transaction will depend on the advice you are given. If you have any doubt about your authority to authorise any transaction you should always consult your line manager as trying put things right after the event can be difficult and time consuming.

Card transactions

If you work for an organisation that accepts credit or debit card transactions, some reasons for not being able to process a caller's card transactions could include:

♦ being unable to confirm the caller's identity
♦ the card has expired or is pre-dated
♦ the card has been reported lost or stolen
♦ the transaction value exceeds your organisation's floor limit
♦ the caller requests the payment be split between two or more cards
♦ you are offered a type of card your organisation is not licensed to accept
♦ the card has been stopped by the credit card company or bank.

♦ Caller's identity

Establishing the card user's identity, whether it is in person or over the telephone, is a crucial part of the transaction. If it is in person, you have a signature on the card to compare with that of the person presenting the card. But over the telephone you have to reply on your knowledge of the card presented, your ability to get details from the caller, and the information supplied by the network provider in the form of address verification information and hot card files.

Some organisations may impose a ruling that they will not deliver goods to anywhere other than the card holder's address, in an attempt to prevent the fraudulent use of someone else's card.

♦ Expired or pre-dated cards

You cannot accept expired or pre-dated credit or debit cards. Callers may give very plausible reasons why the card they have offered you for payment has expired, such as, *'I have received a new one but I forgot to put it in my purse or wallet'*. Whatever the reason you should always refuse to accept it.

Many of the card issuing companies have now stopped including a start date on their card, but instead ask the customer to call a certain telephone number and have the card validated. The validation process involves the customer answering questions regarding personal information they gave at the time they applied for the card.

♦ Cards that are reported lost or stolen

Again you must never accept a card that has been reported lost or stolen, even though the caller may sound extremely plausible about the reason for using it. Such reasons may include temporarily losing the card, reporting it to the lost card telephone number, then subsequently finding it again. It sounds very plausible but once a card has been reported lost or stolen it is stopped and no further payments will be made on it. The only thing you can do is to explain to the caller that they will have to wait until the card issuing company replaces their card.

◆ The transaction exceeds floor limit

A transaction that exceeds your organisation's floor limit does not necessarily mean that it does not meet the authorisation criteria, it just means that you may need to seek authorisation from the card issuing company before you can complete the transaction. In some organisations it may be someone else's responsible to seek authorisation from the card issuing company before it can be processed. Your responsibility then ends when you pass all the necessary information over to them.

◆ The caller requests the payment be split between two or more cards

Occasionally you may get a request to split payment for services or goods over two or more cards. It could be that the caller is well aware of the state of the account and in an attempt to avoid the transaction being rejected they have decided to offer split payment. It could also be an attempt to avoid the transaction exceeding your organisation floor limit, therefore preventing the automatic seeking of authority for the transaction from the card issuing company. Many organisations would automatically refuse to accept such an offer, but others may accept – as long as all the parts of the transaction are subjected to the authorisation process from the card issuing companies.

◆ A card you are not licensed to accept

Occasionally you may be offered a card for payment you are not licensed to accept. In this case you will have no alternative but to refuse acceptance and ask if the caller can offer any other form of payment.

◆ A stopped card

Your service provider might also provide you with regular updates of cards that they have stopped or restricted for whatever reason, and if you are offered such a card you should refer the caller to the company or bank that issued the card. You should never become involved as to why the card has been stopped or restricted, that is a confidential matter between the caller and the issuer.

Credit account transactions

The authorisation criteria for credit accounts are basically the same as for bank and card transactions, therefore most of the reasons they are not met are the same. Several other reasons may arise such as:

◆ insufficient credit balance available to complete the transaction
◆ the caller's balance has not been cleared or monthly payment made.
Both of these reasons may be apparent when dealing with credit accounts, and could become reasons for rejecting a card transaction.

In order for a customer to be allowed to continue to have a credit account, the organisation expects the customer to operate the account within the credit limit and to make regular payments to pay off any sum outstanding.

◆ Insufficient credit balance available

This is where the caller is operating the account to the limit of his or her credit and at times there is insufficient available credit to allow the transaction to be processed. In such situations the transaction is either refused or the call is transferred to a manager or person with responsibility to extend the credit limit.

If this situation arose with a credit or debit card transaction your responsibility would be to refer the caller to their own bank or credit card company and not to become involved in discussing the reason why. In some circumstances you may have been given the reason why the transaction was refused but it is not up to you to tell the caller.

◆ The caller's balance has not been cleared or monthly payment made

The regular repayment of all or part of the outstanding balance is an essential part of being allowed to hold a credit account with any organisation. If the caller is in breach of this part of the agreement, you are entitled to refuse to allow any further transactions until the overdue payment is received. Your organisation may have issued strict guidelines regarding the procedures to adopt if this should happen.

Check it out

Find out the reasons why transactions fail to meet the authorisation criteria in your organisation. Make a list of them for your portfolio.

Actions to take when you encounter difficulties in meeting the authorisation criteria

It is assumed that at this stage of the transaction you have already tried to get the information you want from the caller, and you have either not been able to get it or the details given contradict the information available from other sources, such as address verification files or details held on the system. You have asked probing questions and asked the caller to reconfirm details, but you have been unable to confirm the information.

You have now reached the stage where you have to decide what further action you can take. The possible actions available to you could include:

◆ continue with your questioning and investigate further
◆ seek advice
◆ transfer the call
◆ refer to a relevant authority if appropriate
◆ inform the caller that you are unable to process their transaction further.

This may be decided by the attitude of the caller and the information and details you are trying to reconcile.

The option of continuing with the questioning and investigating further is only possible if you consider there is a chance to match the two sets of information. It may be appropriate if you consider the caller to be somewhat confused and, with additional encouragement and probing, you may gather the information you require. It is not an option if the caller is being evasive or obstructive with their answers, or where the caller is getting annoyed or abusive about the delay in processing the transaction.

Seeking advice from a colleague or team leader may be appropriate if you are unfamiliar with a situation explained by the caller or you are uncertain about how to handle information given by the caller. Seeking advice from a senior or more experienced colleague may be one of the best ways to learn as it may be the first time you have faced such a situation, but they may have faced it numerous times in the past.

Transferring the call to a colleague or team leader may be the next step after you have sought their advice. If you are totally inexperienced in handling such a situation, they may have suggested that it is better to transfer the call rather than spend time explaining to you how it can be handled. If this happens, it is suggested that you talk to the person to whom the call was transferred after the call has ended to learn what you should do if the situation arose again. This can be done at leisure with no pressure from a caller.

You may also want to transfer the call if the caller asks to be transferred to a particular person or department, or if you consider it appropriate. You may not have the authority to deal with the transaction as requested by the caller or feel the problem would be better handled by another department. This could include increasing the caller's credit limit or extending their overdraft facility.

If you are satisfied that you have done all you can for the caller, and you can still not satisfy the authorisation criteria of the transaction, you may have no other option than to tell the caller that you are unable to accept their transaction. Whatever the situation, you should always try and leave the caller on a positive note.

Case study 4 – Sonia's experiences

The other day I had a call from a man who said he had a copy of our UK holiday brochure and would like to book a short break for himself and his girlfriend at a quiet location in the Lake District. He told me the hotel and dates he required so I checked availability, but it was full. He said any hotel would do, but I soon discovered they were all fully booked. He then selected two or three hotels in and around York, but they were also fully booked. He kept telling me that cost was unimportant – he just wanted to get away. By this time I was getting suspicious but continued to try and find somewhere for him. We finally found and settled on a hotel in London. I took all his details for the hotel booking and asked how he would like to pay. He offered a Visa credit card, I took the details and found that the card was in the name of a Miss Jones; I asked if the card was his and he said that it belonged to his girlfriend who was at work. He gave me his address, which tied in with the information I had on screen. I asked where he wanted the tickets sent to and he said he would get a friend to pick them up. I was unhappy with this so I explained that I needed to consult a colleague about the procedures we adopted in such circumstances as I had only just started working here and was unsure.

I put him on hold and spoke to my manager who asked me to transfer the call to him and he would deal with it. When I returned to the caller and told him I was going to transfer him to a colleague who would agree where the tickets could be picked up he put down the telephone.

1 What would you have done in Sonia's position?

7.3 Confirm the transaction

WHAT YOU NEED TO KNOW OR LEARN

♦ Your organisation's procedures for confirming transactions

♦ How to inform the caller of the decision with regards to the transaction

♦ Action to take when you are unable to confirm the transaction

♦ Your organisation's procedures for recording details of transactions

♦ Who to pass details of the transactions to and the timescales that may apply

♦ Your organisation's procedures for maintaining the security and confidentiality of information

♦ Your obligations under the Data Protection Act.

Your organisation's procedures for confirming transactions

The procedures may depend on the volume of transactions and the nature of the business. Some organisations find it necessary to confirm all transactions while the caller is still online, while others are able to delay the confirmation of the transaction until later.

There are many factors that can influence an organisation's procedures. These could include:

♦ the volume of transactions it processes
♦ whether it operates a floor limit scheme
♦ the type of goods and services it sells
♦ its ability to seek authorisation for transactions while the caller is online.

Larger organisations that operate a floor limit scheme only need to seek authority for those sales where the value of the purchases exceeds the floor limit, whereas organisations that only deal with a relatively low volume of transactions may demand that all transactions are authorised by the card issuing company before they can be confirmed.

Having decided which transactions need to be authorised by the card issuing companies, your organisation must consider when it will seek the authority to complete these transactions. It can record the transaction details during the call for process later, or seek the authorisation for the transaction while the caller is online.

Whichever option your organisation chooses will depend on the nature of the business and the types of goods and services offered by your organisation. Some organisations rely on the rapid turnaround of goods, such as same day or next day delivery services; while others promise delivery within a period of anything from 10 to 28 days.

Organisations that rely on the rapid dispatch and delivery of goods will probably need to be able to seek authority from card issuing companies immediately while the caller is still on line, in order to achieve the timescales. Such organisations usually have big problems calling back an order once it has been put into the system. However, other organisations can delay confirming the transaction until later as their timescale allows them to delay or stop the order if there is any difficulty during the authorisation stage of the transaction. These organisations usually have systems and procedures in place that will allow you to record and store the information for access or retrieval later. There should be sufficient details about the transaction for someone to be able to retrieve and process the transaction without further reference to the caller. This is extremely important as it is possible that you may not be the person who will seek to authorise and confirm the transaction.

Two methods are used:

♦ paper transaction slips, that can be passed to any other person or stored safely until you have time to process them
♦ a computer system where you input the details and save them to retrieve later or email to another person for processing.

Check it out

Check out your organisation's method of authorising and confirming transactions.

♦ How does the process work?
♦ Make a note of this for your portfolio.

How to inform the caller of the decision with regards to the transaction

How you inform the caller of the decision about the transaction will depend on your organisation. Figure 7.2 shows the circumstances when it is appropriate to authorise a transaction.

Some organisations will have online facilities where you can seek authority while the call is in progress, which will allow you to inform the caller whether or not you can accept their order.

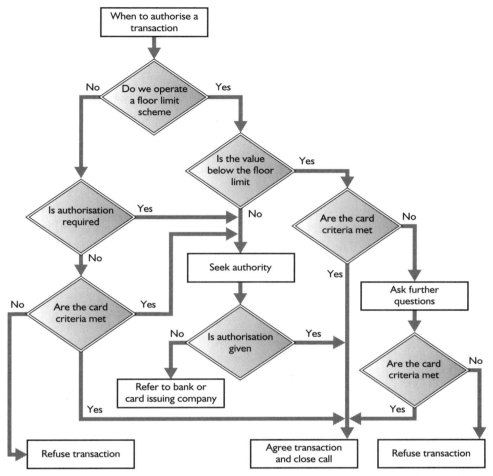

Figure 7.2 A flowchart to show how transactions are authorised

Other organisations prefer to delay seeking authority until later, so you will need to inform the caller that the transaction has been accepted subject to it being authorised by the card issuing company or bank later. Organisations that delay seeking authority for transactions usually ensure that the delay is kept to a minimum, as long delays can have implications for the customer.

Hopefully in the end you will be able to inform the caller that the order has been accepted and the goods will be dispatched or the service provided as agreed.

Case study 5 – Steve's experience

About a fortnight ago I took a call from a Mrs Jones who was booking a walking holiday for the club where she was secretary. After I had booked the holiday she asked for a quote for insurance. I gave it to her but she said she would shop around as the price I quoted appeared to be expensive. Yesterday she rang again and asked for me, she said she had shopped around and could get it cheaper elsewhere, but the cover was very limited, so they had decided to accept our offer.

I said I would need to check the details of the holiday's itinerary, the number of people going, and the period they were going to be away. I entered the details onto the screen and let it calculate the cost, which worked out at £350.00. I asked how she was going to pay and she said the only method of payment she had available at present was her own personal Visa card.

Within Fortress Travel we have a policy that all credit card transactions are subject to a handling fee of 1.5 % and that all transactions are authorised by the card issuing company before we request tickets or insurance documents. I informed Mrs Jones of the handling charge and told her that it would increase the price to £355.25. I took the card details and requested authorisation. The system refused to authorise the transaction, so I told Mrs Jones and she said she knew she had hit the plastic a lot in preparation for her holiday but thought there would have been sufficient to meet £355.25. She asked if I could try again; I said I would but warned her that the result was likely to be the same. It was, so I asked if she had any other way of paying and she said no. I told her that I could not accept the order and advised her to contact the company that issued the card. She thanked me for trying again and said she would talk to the card company. I said I would save the details so that when she sorted out the problem she could ask for me again and I would be able to retrieve the details

About two hours later, just before the end of my shift Mrs Jones rang again and asked to speak to me. I accepted the call and she told me that she had spoken to the bank and the situation was being sorted, but in the meantime could she pay with the club account. This time I was able to process the transaction and confirm the party would be covered by the insurance.

1   How did Steve handle Mrs Jones' card refusal?
2   Could he have handled it better? If so how?

Informing a caller that you can accept their order is relatively simple as the caller has achieved their objective. But what happens when you are unable to accept an order or request from a caller because the system will not authorise their transaction?

Action to take when you are unable to confirm the transaction

Here we will look at the reasons why transactions fail during the authorisation process. The basic purpose of seeking authorisation from a card issuing company or bank is to confirm that there are sufficient funds available in the account to meet the payment of the transaction the caller is requesting. Card transactions can fail at this stage because of:

♦ insufficient funds available
♦ a recent stop on the card
♦ transactions outside the norm for the account.

> **Personal note**
>
> It is likely that where you are unable to confirm a transaction the caller will be shocked and upset. You must remember that **this is not your problem – you must not become personally involved.**
>
> Some callers may well try to appeal to your better nature with stories of bad luck and misfortune in the hope that you will authorise this particular transaction to get them on the right road again. **Don't!**

Insufficient funds available

This is probably the most common reason why a card transaction is refused during the authorisation process. You must avoid being judgemental, as you do not know the circumstances that have led to this situation. You should remain calm and inform the caller that the transaction as been refused and they should contact the company that issued the card to discuss the matter. You should avoid become involved in any discussions or speculating as to the reason why it was refused.

A recent stop on the card

There may be times when cards have been stopped and the company or bank haven't had time to circulate the details, in which case transactions will be refused when they are submitted for authorisation. The reasons for such stops are numerous but can include:

♦ non receipt of the minimum repayment of the outstanding balance
♦ the caller has ignored attempts by the card issuer or bank to contact them
♦ the card has been suspected of being used by someone other than its rightful owner.

Again you must avoid being judgemental as to the reason why and should refuse to discuss or speculate about the reason. You must refer the caller to the card issuer or bank who will be in a position to discuss the reason for its refusal.

Transactions outside the norm for the account

Information is generated about each one of us every time we make a purchase, pay a bill and, in some cases, move around the country. Some credit card companies use this type of information in their fight against fraud. Using statistics of our past purchases they are able to predict our habits as far as purchases go, and if we vary from that prediction, warning bells will sound. Purchases they are asked to authorise which fall outside our usual pattern can and will be challenged, and the purchaser asked for more information before the authorisation is given. This can be very useful in detecting fraudulent use of your cards.

In such a case it is very unlikely that a person making a genuine transaction would be upset if challenged for more information. However that is not the case for everyone. Some are likely to be shocked and may hold you responsible for the refusal; they cannot accept that the card issuer has refused their transaction. In these circumstances you should assure them there is nothing personal and that the refusal is beyond your control. You should inform them that they should contact their card issuer to resolve the matter. Some callers may be upset and even embarrassed by the refusal.

However, in all circumstances you should always be polite and try and leave the caller on a positive note, such as, *'I will hold the details and when you have resolved the situation please ask for me again and I will complete the transaction'*. The majority of refusals are solved by the caller making contact with their card issuer, so if you are not polite and understanding you may never see them again as customers of your organisation.

Your organisation's procedures for recording details of transactions

There are many ways in which an organisation can record details of the transactions; some will be computer based and others will be paper based.

Computer-based recording

Computer based systems are fast and efficient; they can ensure that all the necessary information has been collected from the caller and input into the computer system before the system will allow you to proceed further. They are capable of carrying out basic validation checks on the information as it is being input, to confirm that the information being input into a particular field is in the correct format and within preset limits. They also have the ability to read information from other files to help speed up the process of completing the fields. Depending on which computer operating system is used they may also be capable of distributing relevant parts of the information to appropriate destinations via internal email.

Different computer systems work in different ways; some of you will be able to input data and information into the system and process the information online immediately. Others will only be able to input the information, where it is stored and processed when the system is quiet, which is usually overnight. If your system is like this then any delay in the processing will have to be taken into account when making commitments to the caller or customer as to the timescales of completing the transactions.

Paper-based recording

Paper-based systems are more labour intensive, with the transaction details being sent around the relevant departments, such as stores, dispatch and finance, as though they were in a chain. Each department extracts the details they require before the transaction slip is forwarded to the next department in the chain. This can be very time consuming as each department is reliant on the previous department to pass on the information.

Other organisations may rely on you completing multi-copy pre-carbonate packs, where completed packs are separated into the different colours and sent to the relevant department. This speeds up the process compared to the other paper based system, as all the departments can be working and processing the information in parallel.

Who to pass details of the transactions to and the timescales that may apply

Most organisations that sell their products and services via the telephone or through a retail outlet have a common structure that can be broken down into the same basic stages. These stages are:

♦ taking orders, preparing order details and payment information
♦ picking stores from order lists or making arrangements to provide service
♦ dispatching stores items to delivery address or provide service at required location
♦ process payment.

In order for the process to run smoothly the information prepared during the first stage of the process needs to be available to the later stages in time to fulfil the commitment to the customer or caller. If your organisation promises its customer that goods will be delivered later the same day or by the next day then the information needs to be available to the later stages of the process immediately. Even in organisations that promise delivery within 28 days, the overall process may include stages where your organisation has to manufacture the items or place orders with their suppliers before they can take possession and deliver them to the customer. Also, having delivered the goods or provided the service, your organisation needs to receive payment as soon as possible in order to maintain its cash flow.

If you work for a bank or financial institution you will have made commitments to the caller to process the transaction by a certain time. Callers that telephone requiring you to pay bills from their accounts have agreed with you dates when the transactions will be fulfilled. If they have arranged with you to transfer funds between accounts you will have a commitment to complete the transaction as soon as possible or by the time agreed with the caller. Therefore all the information you have gathered concerning the transactions has to be input into the system for the transaction to be completed and the system updated.

Check it out

Find out how your organisation processes its transactions.

♦ Do you use a computer system or paper records?
♦ If you use a computer system does it use *online processing* or *batch processing*?
♦ If batch processing, when is it run? Make a note for your portfolio.
♦ Who requires the information you produce?
♦ Do you have timescales to deliver the information? If so, what are they?

Your organisation's procedures for maintaining the security and confidentiality of information

In your job it is likely that you are handling personal information about the callers. Every time callers give you personal details concerning their financial situation, whether bank account details or credit or debit card details, they have a right to expect you to treat this information in confidence. You would not like your personal financial details being discussed around the office.

When you are processing transactions you will obtain information of a personal or private matter from other sources, which you must not give out even if pressed to do so; for example, if you are processing a credit card transaction and the transaction has not been authorised. In such cases you must not divulge the reason for the non-authorisation but advise the caller to contact their own bank or credit card company themselves to discuss the matter.

It is inevitable that most of the organisations that process financial transactions will gather and maintain information on all their clients and customers and this information will be confidential.

There are two aspects to confidentiality that you need to consider:

♦ some of the information may be of a sensitive nature about your organisation's clients and customers, which could cause your company considerable damage and embarrassment if it were to fall into the hands of a competitor. Therefore it needs to be protected
♦ your organisation is legally obliged to protect information that has been entrusted to it by other parties, such as personal details and credit ratings, and any other information that falls under the scope of the Data Protection Act and the Consumer Credit Acts.

If information is to remain confidential, it must be kept securely and it should only be accessible to those people who are authorised to see and handle the information.

Your obligations under the Data Protection Act

If you are authorising transactions for a bank, financial institution or an organisation that accepts payment by credit or debit card, you will be collecting, processing and storing data about the people you are dealing with. Because of the nature and sensitivity of these data it is very likely that your organisation will have laid down procedures that govern the way that you work. However, it is also important that you have a good overall understanding of the Data Protection Act and can appreciate the constraints it places on the way your organisation can operate.

The Data Protection Act 1998 came into force on 1 March 2000. It applies to the **processing** (collecting, using, disclosing, destroying or holding data) of computerised **personal data** (data that can be associated with identifiable living individuals – it can include facts and opinions about an individual). It also covers personal data held in structured manual files.

Organisations that process personal data are called **data controllers** and they are required by law to comply with the rules of good information handling, known as the **data protection principles** (Figure 7.3).

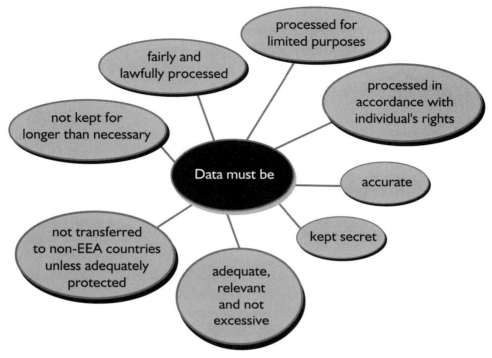

Figure 7.3 Data protection principles

Processing may only be carried out if one of the following conditions has been met:

♦ the individual has given his or her consent to the processing
♦ the processing is necessary for the performance of a contract with the individual
♦ the processing is required under a legal obligation
♦ the processing is necessary to protect the vital interests of the individual
♦ the processing is necessary to carry out public functions
♦ the processing is necessary in order to pursue the legitimate interests of the data controller or third parties (unless it could prejudice the interests of the individual).

The Data Protection Act also makes specific provision for sensitive personal data. This includes data relating to a person's racial or ethnic origins; religious or other beliefs; political opinions; trade union membership; health; sex life; and criminal proceedings or convictions.

Sensitive data can only be processed under strict conditions, which include:

♦ having the explicit consent of the individual
♦ being required by law to process the data for employment purposes
♦ needing to process the information in order to protect the vital interests of the data subject or another
♦ dealing with the administration of justice or legal proceedings.

Data controllers must take security measures to safeguard personal data. The 1998 Act requires data controllers to take appropriate technical or organisational measures to prevent unauthorised or unlawful processing or disclosure of data.

The Act strengthens individuals' rights to:

♦ gain access to their data
♦ seek compensation.

It also creates new rights for individuals to:

♦ prevent their data from being processed in certain circumstances
♦ opt out of having their data used for direct marketing
♦ opt out of fully automated decision making about them.

Case study 6 – Debbie's experiences

Debbie works as a telephone holiday booking clerk for Fortress Travel and lives at home with her mother and father. On Friday night she meets up with her friend at a local wine bar. Most of Debbie's friends live in the same area as Debbie and they have all been friends since they started school.

On friday night after a few drinks and a lot of jokes and tales, Debbie said, 'You know that snooty Mrs Jones that lives at the end of the road, the one who's always going on holiday? She tried to book a holiday to Spain with me yesterday, but when she came to pay for it the bank wouldn't accept her credit card as she was over her limit'.

One of her friends asked if she knew who she was dealing with. Debbie said, 'No, we only give our first name'. One of the friends asked, 'What did you do when the bank refused?' Debbie said, 'I told her to sort out her problems with the bank before she tried to book her holiday'.

1 What did Debbie do wrong?
2 Did she contravene the Data Protection Act?
3 If so, how?

Although in this case study it may be considered as just gossip on Debbie's part to disclose the information, it could still have serious consequences for Debbie and her employer. Disclosing such information in the first place is serious enough, but to make the disclosure in a public place while under the influence of alcohol makes the matter worse. Anyone in the wine bar could have heard what was said and reported the facts to Mrs Jones. This could result in Debbie losing her job and the company losing Mrs Jones's business as well as being taken to court under the Data Protection Act. It could also have wider implications for the travel company as anyone hearing such a disclosure would certainly avoid using the company in case details of their transactions became the topic of discussion in a public place.

The Data Protection Act was established to give people the right to have personal information about them protected and remain confidential.

In this section we have only looked at obligations you and your organisation have under the Data Protection Act but there are other Acts that you may have to comply with. These could include:

♦ the Consumer Credit Act
♦ the Distance Selling Act
♦ the Fair Trading Act
♦ the Financial Services and Marketing Act.

Check it out

♦ Do you or your organisation have to comply with any other regulations? What are they?
♦ Make a note of them for your portfolio.
♦ How do they apply to the work you undertake?

Keys to good practice

✓ Memorise the main features of the credit and debit cards you deal with most often.

✓ Treat callers as you would like to be treated yourself.

✓ Always ask the caller to confirm the details of the transaction before proceeding.

✓ Record details of the transactions accurately.

✓ Always be aware of any changes to the organisation's floor limit.

✓ Don't get personally involved when transactions cannot be authorised.

✓ Don't be drawn to speculate about the reason why a transaction cannot be authorised.

✓ Don't infringe the Data Protection Act – maintain the caller's confidentiality.

Check your knowledge

1 How many credit and debit cards are there in use in the UK?
2 Which credit card account number starts with a 4?
3 Which card contains a globe hologram?
4 Which card has a hologram depicting the head of Shakespeare?
5 Which card contains an issue number?
6 What information will you need to process a credit card transaction?
7 What information will you require to process a bank transaction?
8 What is the main cause of failure for credit card transactions?
9 Explain how a floor limit scheme works?
10 How would you deal with a caller who offers a stopped card as payment?

UNIT 9

Offer products and services over the telephone

This option unit is all about offering products and services to customers over the telephone. Calls will be planned in advance and you will be expected to have an in-depth knowledge of the products and services offered by your organisation.

This unit has four elements:

♦ prepare to offer products and services over the telephone
♦ identify customers' needs and their interest in your organisation's products and services
♦ promote the features and benefits of your organisation's products and services
♦ gain customer commitment and progress the transaction.

After you have completed this unit, you will be able to:

♦ understand the nature of the sales cycle
♦ determine how customers process information and know how to communicate more clearly and effectively
♦ develop and use questions effectively to diagnose customers' needs and overcome their objections
♦ explain the benefits and features of your organisation's products and services to promote a sale
♦ ensure that the products and services that you recommend fulfil the customer's requirements and support your objectives
♦ increase your success in cross-selling and up-selling your organisation's products and services.

The case studies in this chapter will be based around a fictitious member of the public – 'Mr John Clay'. We can look at the way 'John' is contacted by a number of different companies trying to sell him a variety of products and services. This allows us to look at a number of the techniques that are used.

Did you know?

Expenditure on telemarketing during 2000 was £2,419.1 million, an increase of 8 per cent from £2,232.3 million in 1998.

9.1 Prepare to offer products and services over the telephone

WHAT YOU NEED TO KNOW OR LEARN

♦ Familiarity with your organisation's products and services
♦ The nature of the sales cycle
♦ Who you can call and how you can contact them
♦ How to establish the objectives of your call and consider the questions that need to be asked
♦ How to structure your calls in line with your organisation's requirements
♦ How to anticipate any queries that the customer may raise and formulate apropriate responses.

Did you know?

Confucius said: 'In all things, success depends upon previous preparation, and without such preparation, there is failure.'

Familiarity with your organisation's products and services

Your customers need to know that you have the competence to help them. They want to feel confident that you can recommend or select the best option for them regarding your products and services. Product knowledge is vital if you are going to be successful. For example, you need to know about:

♦ what your products and services can do
♦ what your products and services cannot do
♦ your competitor's products and services
♦ your unique selling points – the benefits and features of your organisation's products and services
♦ the life expectancy of your products and services
♦ the type of maintenance or supplies needed for your products and services
♦ the target market for your products and services.

This list is just a start! You have to find out what you need to know in order to address your customers' needs, questions, challenges or problems.

Check it out

What do you need to know about your organisation's products and services so that your customers feel confident that you can help them? (Hint: you can always ask your more experienced colleagues for advice.)
Make a note of what you think you need to know.

Never try to fake product knowledge, especially when you are dealing with complex products or services. Do not assume that it is always just up to your company to educate you: you are responsible for taking an active part in your own learning. Product knowledge does not make up for poor people skills, weak selling skills or a bad attitude, but if you can be good at all four you are likely to be a successful salesperson.

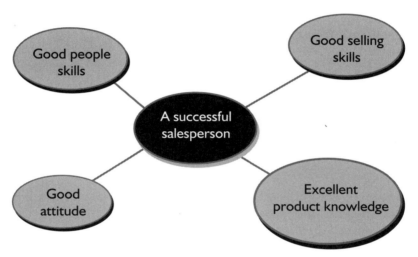

Figure 9.1 Successful selling involves a number of skills

Think about it

What do you think could happen if you pretended to know about something that you didn't?

If you pretended to know about a product in front of a customer who was knowledgeable about it, you would lose the customer's confidence and look very foolish. It is likely that the customer would never deal with your organisation again and could tell other people about their experience, which could ruin your company's reputation even further.

If the customer was not knowledgeable about the product, he or she will be relying on you to advise them correctly but you cannot do this if you do not genuinely understand your products. In these circumstances, faking product knowledge could lead you to offer the customer a product that is not suitable for them. This could be very inconvenient and disconcerting for the customer or it could even be harmful, depending upon the nature of the product.

Good product knowledge means:

♦ you are able to diagnose the customer's problems or needs
♦ you have pride and confidence in the product
♦ self assurance
♦ you can offer better customer service
♦ you have an air of competence
♦ you can sell to knowledgeable people as well as beginners.

As well as knowing about your organisation's products and services, your customers will also expect you to be knowledgeable about your company, for example:

♦ the history of your company
♦ how the products and services have evolved
♦ who are your customers – past and present.

Check it out

Find out what you need to know about your company in order to answer any questions your customers may have. (Hint: you can always ask your more experienced colleagues for advice about this too.)
Make a note of this for your portfolio.

If you are not knowledgeable about your company, you will not be able to gain the customer's confidence and trust.

The nature of the sales cycle

Never forget that preparation is the key to success. This will dramatically improve your ability to progress the call to a successful conclusion.

Three key steps to being prepared

1 Identify the features and benefits of your organisation's products and services.

2 Define and identify your target market.

3 Structure your calls – plan the call and set the call objectives.

Bear in mind that the first 30 to 40 seconds of your call are the most important. Once you have gathered information about the customer and their particular needs, you will need to move quickly on to the next stage, that is creating a sale, by presenting the customer with appropriate solutions and explaining the benefits of your proposed solutions.

Figure 9.2 The sales process involves six key stages

The diagram makes the sales process look very simple. However, you realise that it is not as simple as it looks when you also bear in mind that throughout the sales cycle you should be continually:

♦ asking questions
♦ listening
♦ building a rapport
♦ establishing trust
♦ developing credibility
♦ developing a valuable relationship
♦ addressing objections
♦ planning your next step
♦ confirming the customer's understanding
♦ seeking additional opportunities to cross-sell and up-sell.

Who you can call and how you can contact them

When you are trying to decide who to call, you will realise that it is not as simple as just deciding who you may *want* to call. You must remember that there are people that you are **not allowed** to call, so you will need to make sure that none of these people are included on your list.

The Telephone Preference Service (TPS) was set up in 1995 and is managed by the Direct Marketing Association. It exists to help those customers who do not want to receive cold calls from organisations that may wish to telephone them about special offers or other information. Customers can use the TPS to make sure that their telephone number is no longer available to such organisations.

The Telephone Preference Service Ltd which administers the Telephone Preference Service register is a subsidiary company of the Direct Marketing Association (UK) Ltd, which OFTEL has appointed to manage the opt-out registers.

Under government legislation introduced on 1 May 1999, it is unlawful to make unsolicited direct marketing calls to **individuals** who have indicated that they do not want to receive such calls. The term *individual* includes consumers at their residential address, sole traders and, except in Scotland, partnerships.

An overview of your organisation's legal obligations

The Telecommunications (Data Protection and Privacy) Regulations 1999 are intended to protect people – and in some cases businesses – against receiving unwanted direct marketing calls.

It is unlawful for someone in business (including charities or other voluntary organisations) to make such a call to any individual who either:

♦ told that business or organisation that he/she does not want to receive such calls
♦ registered with the TPS that they do not wish to receive such calls from *any* business or organisation.

All call centres must keep a 'do not call' list, which contains the numbers of any customers that have asked not to be contacted again. The company must abide by that list for any future unsolicited calls. If the company is a member of the Telephone Preference Service then they may also inform the client of its presence but the TPS is not a substitute for an in-house 'do not call' list.

Cold call lists and customer lists should be cleansed against the TPS register before calls are made to ensure compliance with the regulations. This is in addition to checking such lists against in-house 'do not call' lists. The only exception to this is where an individual has indicated to your organisation that they do not object to your organisation making direct marketing telephone calls.

Lists should be cleansed as often as is necessary to ensure that anybody who is protected by the regulations, who has registered with either of the registers 28 days or more ago, is **not** contacted.

Think about it

What might happen if you were to call someone who has registered with the Telephone Preference Service to indicate that they do not wish to receive cold calls?

If you were to call someone who does not wish to receive such calls, there could be several consequences. The person that you called would be within their rights to make a complaint to the Telephone Preference Service (TPS). The TPS investigates complaints made to it by anyone whose registration has not prevented a call, which it should have done, and the Office of the Data Protection Commissioner will determine any action required for breach of the regulations.

Even if the person does not make a formal complaint, he or she will not be happy. The person may be abusive to you for having called or may just hang up. The person might also tell other people about the 'nuisance' call that they have received which could be detrimental to your company's reputation.

How does your organisation carry out its legal obligations?

Use the 'check it out' activity (below) to investigate how your organisation makes sure that it does not make direct marketing calls to individuals who have indicated that they do not wish to be called.

Check it out

- Does your organisation make direct marketing calls? If it does, how does your organisation cleanse its call lists against the TPS register? Make a note for your portfolio of how it is done.
- How often is it done and who is responsible for doing it?
- Does your organisation have an in-house 'do not call list? If it does, make a note of where you would find it.
- How is it kept up to date and by whom?

Self-regulation covering the restriction of contacts

The UK Direct Marketing Association has issued a Code of Practice that sets standards of ethical conduct and best practice that its members must adhere to as a condition of membership.

Check it out

- Is your organisation a member of the UK Direct Marketing Association? If it is, make a note of how it makes sure it complies with the DMA Code of Practice.
- Does it abide by the DMA Code of Practice anyway?

The following sections of the code specifically relate to the restriction of contacts. They describe those people that you may not contact.

Direct Marketing Association Code of Practice	
Section no.	Section content
9.19	Members must take all reasonable steps not to make outbound marketing calls to minors.
9.20	Sales, marketing and service calls must not be generated by random number or sequential number dialling, manually or by computer.
9.21	Members must not knowingly make calls to unlisted or ex-directory numbers unless the number has been provided by the customer concerned.
9.22	Members must not make consumer calls to individuals at their place of work unless the individual has given this number for that purpose.
9.23	Members using the telephone for marketing, sales or service purposes to consumers with whom they have no established commercial or charitable relationship, must use the Telephone Preference Service and abide by the rules.
9.24	Members must block from their telephone contact lists those people who have specifically requested not to be contacted by telephone. They must keep a record of these names and telephone numbers and have documented procedures to ensure that all such names have been blocked from the telephone contact lists used on the members' behalf.
9.25	Members intending to initiate outbound sales and marketing calls involving the use of wholly automated messages must: (a) have obtained the prior written permission of the person being called (b) have available for inspection by OFTEL a record of those who have given such permission using an individual's telephone number as identification.

Manual dialling

Did you know?

When operators manually dial telephone numbers they could be wasting 70 per cent of each hour just trying to reach someone to talk to.

Manual dialling means that first the operator has to pick up the telephone, check the number and then dial it. After dialling the operator then may encounter busy signals, operator intercept tones (disconnected lines, etc.) and answering machines or the telephone may just not be answered. When all of this is taken into account it can have a dramatic effect on an operator's productivity, which is why automated dialling was developed.

Automated dialling

Predictive dialling is the most automated and sophisticated of all outbound calling methods.

How predictive dialling works

1 A number of agents are logged into the same campaign, which may consist of hundreds or possibly even thousands of records, all containing the telephone numbers of the people or businesses that are going to be called. This information is held on a network server with links to all agents. The network server has a link to a predictive dialling engine, which may be a physical device (hard dialler) connected directly into the Public Switched Telephone Network (PSTN) or it may be a piece of software (soft dialler).

2 As agents become available, the server and the dialler decide in which order to dial the campaign numbers and then initiate the calls.

3 If there is no answer after a defined number of seconds, the dialler hangs up. For those calls that connect, the dialler strives to filter out such things as answering machines and puts the remaining calls through to agents.

4 At the same time as the connected call is being put through to the agent's headset, details of the called party are brought up on the agent's screen.

5 The dialler monitors the results of all the calls, such as the percentage of no answers, busy signals, etc., and it also measures agent performance in terms of average talk time. It then uses this information to calculate how many lines it should be dialling out on. At times of high 'no answer' levels the dialler initiates several calls for each agent who is either waiting or about to finish a call.

Dialling in this way obviously keeps down the waiting time between calls for agents. However, if it is not controlled, it can lead to lots of abandoned calls as the dialler will hang up if it reaches a live voice before an agent is available. The dialler is therefore programmed to achieve low waiting times whilst keeping the level of abandoned calls down to an acceptable level.

Most of the better predictive diallers also offer the function of call blending, which means that if agents who typically handle inbound calls are idle for a period of time, the dialler will work with the Automatic Call Distributor and start to feed outbound calls to these agents. However, as soon as the incoming call volume is back up to where more inbound agents are required, it will put them back on inbound calls.

This process works the same way for agents that typically handle outbound calls. If the inbound call volume increases beyond pre-determined levels, the dialler will send incoming calls to agents that primarily handle outbound calls.

The benefits of predictive diallers are:

◆ they can make many more calls in a much shorter period of time than if an agent had to manually dial each phone number
◆ if the dialler encounters a busy signal or no answer it will dial the number again later without any human intervention
◆ the system can also keep track of an entire campaign's progress in real time, which would be virtually impossible to do manually
◆ they can also be fed 'do not call' lists.

Legislation governing the use of automated dialling equipment

Different regulations apply to the use of automatic calling equipment, depending on the use to which the equipment is being put – it all depends on whether the equipment is being used for direct marketing purposes or not.

If use does relate to direct marketing then the Telecommunications (Data Protection and Privacy) Regulations 1999 apply, which implement part of the European Telecoms Data Protection Directive (Directive 97/66/EC). These regulations state that automatic calling equipment may only be used for direct marketing when the called party has previously consented to receive such calls.

Enforcement of the regulations is the responsibility of the Data Protection Commissioner (DPC), formerly the Data Protection Registrar. Where the DPC finds that there has been a breach of the regulations, the DPC has the power to issue an Enforcement Notice against the company concerned. Should that company breach the terms of the Enforcement Notice then the DPC has the power to impose a fine.

If automatic calling equipment is being used for calls other than direct marketing then use of that equipment may be in breach of the Self Provision Licence (SPL) and the Telecommunications Service Licence (TSL), which are the main class licences under which the majority of telecommunications systems are run. These class licence requirements are enforced by OFTEL.

Self-regulation covering the use of automated dialling equipment

If your organisation is a member of the Direct Marketing Association (DMA), then the DMA Code of Practice also contains guidance that you will be expected to comply with if you use automated dialling equipment.

The following sections of the code relate specifically to the use of automated dialling equipment and will be incorporated into the third edition of the code which is being revised and updated.

Direct Marketing Association Code of Practice	
Section no.	Section content
9.31	Members must ensure their dialling equipment is adjusted to ensure a minimum ring time of 15 seconds before the call is abandoned as unanswered.
9.32	If a 'live' operator is unavailable to take the call generated by the dialling equipment, the equipment should abandon the call and release the line as quickly as possible and within a maximum of 1 second from when the line is picked up (going offhook).
9.33	The dialling equipment must at all times be adjusted to ensure that the rate of calls abandoned is no more than 5 per cent of live calls on each individual campaign over any 24 hour period.
9.34	Where a number has received an abandoned call, any further calls to that number within the next 72 hour period must be handled by a dedicated operator.
9.35	For each individual campaign, members must maintain an up to date archive of dialler statistics which clearly demonstrate compliance with 9.31 – 9.33 of this code. This must include a daily summary of: (a) The number of calls attempted (b) The number of calls answered (c) The number of calls connected (d) The number of calls passed to a live operator (e) The number of live calls abandoned by the dialling equipment.
9.36	Records of dialler statistics must be retained for a minimum of 24 months and must be available for inspection on reasonable notice from the DMA and other appropriate authorities.
9.37	When undertaking outbound calls members must provide relevant caller line identification.
9.38	Consumers calling back on the number provided should, either by live operator or a recorded message, be informed: (a) where possible, the name of the company on whose behalf the call was made or the name of the call centre from which the call originated (b) relevant information to allay any fears as to the purpose of the call (c) where the call is unsolicited, relevant information to allow the recipient to indicate that they do not wish to receive further direct marketing calls relating to the campaign.
9.39	Calls to the telephone number provided in accordance with 9.38 above should not be charged at a rate exceeding national call rate.

How to establish the objectives of your call

The objectives of your call may often be set by your organisation. If this is the case, it is quite likely that your objective will be to sell products and services to the customer. You may be required to follow a pre-set script and your organisation may have set performance targets that you are expected to meet.

Check it out

- ◆ Are you expected to follow a pre-set script when offering products and services over the telephone?
- ◆ If your organisation uses more than one standard script, are you also provided with guidance on which script to use on any particular occasion? If you are, then make a note of it or if the guidance is detailed, write down where it can be found.
- ◆ Are you also set sales targets that you are expected to meet?
- ◆ Do you think that you will meet your targets?

If your organisation does not expect you to just follow a pre-set script and you are also responsible for establishing the objectives of your call, the three most important questions that you need to ask yourself before you start are:

- ◆ *what do I want to achieve?*
- ◆ *who am I going to call?*
- ◆ *what am I going to say?*

Once you know what you hope to achieve, you will then be able to focus on the **purpose** of your call; for example, stimulate customer interest and generate orders for the new product that your organisation is launching.

You should then be able to go on and determine the **objectives** of your call, which in this instance could be to:

- ◆ let existing customers know about the new product and attempt to generate orders
- ◆ contact prospective customers to stimulate further interest
- ◆ make the general public aware of the new product and what it has to offer.

You should always be as specific as possible when setting sales call objectives as there is a very high correlation between specific objectives and desired results. When you plan exactly what you want to achieve during a sales call, you become incredibly focused and so does the customer.

Outbound Calls

Good Morning / Afternoon / Evening. My name is (*First Name*)
I am calling on behalf of (*State name of Organisation*) am I speaking to (*State the name of the person you expect to be speaking to*)

We are conducting research into (*State the nature of the campaign*) can I take a few minutes of your time to ask you a few questions?

If yes proceed:
This research will be used to inform _____

If no – can I call you back at a time convenient for you to spend 5 minutes answering these questions?

After gathering the information thank the caller for their participation, ask if they have any questions for you?

Reinforce purpose for the research, thank the caller again and close the call.

Inbound Calls

Good Morning / Afternoon / Evening. Thank you for calling (*State name of Organisation*) my name is (*First Name*) how can I help you?

Good Morning / Afternoon / Evening. Thank you for calling (*State name of Organisation*) you are speaking to (*First Name*) May I/Can I take your customer reference number?

Thank you, Can you confirm your name and postcode please? (If no postcode first line of address).

Thank you Mrs/Miss/Ms/Mr (*State their name*) how can I help you?

At this point the script would become organisational specific.

Examples for a catalogue could include:

♦ Do you have an order number?

or

May I take your first catalogue number, colour number and size please . . . .

And the next item please . . . . etc until order complete.

That's fine Mrs/Miss/Ms/Mr (*State their name*) I've put the order through for you,

Press F7

Thank you for shopping with _____

Examples of a pre-set scripts

> **Five reasons to set very specific sales call objectives:**
>
> **1** You will achieve definition of purpose.
>
> **2** The objective will direct and guide the call.
>
> **3** The customer will know why you have called.
>
> **4** You will not waste any time as your efforts will be focused.
>
> **5** You will be able to measure results on every call.

You will find that the better you plan, the better your results will be. If you set very specific call objectives you will focus your effort which will, in turn, improve your performance.

Once you have determined the objectives of your call, you have to decide who to call and the best approach to use. For example, if your objective is to increase sales to existing customers, you may want to offer a special bonus to those who purchase the product within a specified time period.

However, if your objective is to contact prospective customers who have never heard of your organisation before, you may want to use a softer approach and ask them if you could send them some information to introduce your organisation's products and services. This could include a coupon or special introductory offer and you could plan a follow-up call to review the information.

How to structure your calls in line with your organisation's requirements

You must always structure calls in line with your organisation's requirements. The 'Check it out' activity (below) will help you to find out what these are so that you can make sure you meet them.

Check it out

♦ Does your organisation expect you to structure calls in a certain way?

If it does, make a note of how calls should be structured or, if the guidelines are detailed, write down where they can be found.

How to anticipate any queries that the customer may raise and formulate appropriate responses

When you offer products and services over the phone, you will have to deal with any queries or comments that the customer may raise. These are likely to fall into two distinct categories (Figure 9.3).

The majority of questions raised by the customer fall into the category of 'buying signals' and are considered on page 265. The remaining queries or comments are likely to be **objections**, i.e. anything that the customer raises that you need to address in order to progress the sale.

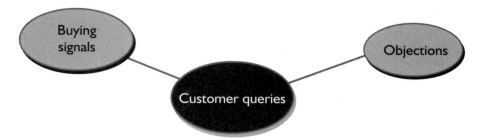

Figure 9.3 There are two main categories of customer queries

The key to handling objections successfully is being able to anticipate them in advance. Therefore, the best way that you can prepare yourself for dealing with any possible objections or queries that your customer may raise is by:

♦ identifying the strengths and weaknesses of your products and services
♦ asking your colleagues about any objections or queries that they have encountered in the past and finding out how they responded to them
♦ keeping a list of any objections or questions that you encounter and using it to give answers to future objections.

Check it out

Find out about the sort of objections or queries that your colleagues have been faced with, ask them how they responded and if the customer appeared satisfied with their response.
Make a table of the results like the one below.

Nature of objection/query	Nature of response given	Was customer satisfied?

This exercise will allow you to pinpoint any major objections that there are likely to be to your organisation's products and services so that you will be prepared and can respond in a manner that will satisfy the customer.

You should always expect the customer to raise objections – welcome them as a sign of the customer's interest that can be turned to your advantage. If you expect objections to be raised they will not come as a surprise and you will be prepared to deal with them.

There are many kinds of objection that may be raised – the list is endless. Some examples are:

♦ *'I can get it quicker than that elsewhere'*
♦ *'That's more than I am currently paying'*

- *'I am happy with the level of service provided by my existing supplier'*
- *'I don't have to pay for delivery at the moment'*

Most of the objections that you are likely to come across will arise from:

- the customer having insufficient information
- the customer's particular circumstances
- procrastination on the part of the customer
- the price or running costs of the product or service.

The best way of dealing with an objection is to ask the customer a further question. For example, if the customer says *'I would like to think about it'*, you could respond by saying *'I can fully appreciate that you would like to think it over. However, can I just make sure that you have all the information that you need by asking you which particular aspects you would like to think about?'*.

We will be looking at ways of dealing with objections in more detail on page 252.

Keys to good practice

✓ Product knowledge is vital to your success – you must therefore learn what you need to know as quickly as you can.

✓ Make sure that you fully understand the strengths and weaknesses of your products or services.

✓ Never assume that it is solely the responsibility of your company to educate you.

✓ You should be knowledgeable about your company.

✓ Never forget that preparation is the key to success.

✓ Make sure that you are familiar with the sales process and that you have identified your call objectives.

✓ Remember that there are people who you are not allowed to call and make sure that you know how to identify them and eliminate them from your call lists.

✓ If you are expected to follow any pre-set scripts, make sure that you are familiar enough with them for them to sound natural.

✓ Always expect the customer to raise objections and be prepared to deal with them.

✓ Keep a record of any objections that you come across so that you are better prepared for any future objections.

9.2 Identify customers' needs and their interest in your organisation's products and services

WHAT YOU NEED TO KNOW OR LEARN

♦ When to contact customers

♦ How to introduce yourself and the organisation that you represent

♦ How to identify if it is convenient for the customer to continue with the call

♦ How to use questions to identify the customer's needs and evaluate their interest in your organisation's products and services

♦ How to confirm with the customer your understanding of their needs

♦ How to answer questions raised by the customer in a way that promotes a sale

♦ Your organisation's requirements for recording and using the information that you gather

♦ Your organisation's sales procedures and any relevant legal requirements.

When to contact customers

The hours associated with outbound calling are left to self-regulation by individual call centres. If your organisation is a member of the Direct Marketing Association (DMA), then the DMA Code of Practice contains guidance that you will be expected to comply with regarding what constitutes reasonable hours.

The following section of the code relates specifically to the timing of outbound calls.

Direct Marketing Association Code of Practice	
Section no.	Section content
9.12	Members must not make sales, marketing or service calls during hours which are unreasonable to the person called, recognising that what is regarded as reasonable can vary in different locations and in different types of households or businesses. In general, members should not make calls between the hours of 9.00 p.m. and 8.00 a.m., unless an express invitation to do so is received. Members should also be aware that many consumers might consider it unreasonable to be called on a Sunday or on national/religious holidays.

In general, customers are likely to fall into two groups, i.e. those who:

♦ are usually at home all day, such as retired people or people who work from home

♦ are normally out all day and who you need to contact after they have finished work.

There is probably no ideal time to call a customer unless you have knowledge of their particular circumstances. However, if you were to phone after about 8.00 p.m. and start trying to sell things you will probably not get a very good reception.

You will need to consider the type of product or services that you are offering in order to decide what time of day to contact the potential customer. These will fall into two distinct categories: business and domestic.

If you are offering products or services to businesses, such as selling a company a franking machine, then you will need to contact the customer on Monday to Friday, during business hours. However, if you are offering domestic products or services, it is more likely that you would choose to contact the customer during the early evening or on Saturdays.

Your organisation's shift patterns may also dictate the times at which you are able to contact customers.

How to introduce yourself and the organisation that you represent

Your introduction is without a doubt the most critical part of your call. Your opening statement must:

♦ identify you
♦ put your listener into a positive frame of mind
♦ allow you to move on effectively to the next part of the call.

Identifying yourself and your company

Your organisation may well have a standard introduction that it expects you to use when you are introducing both yourself and your company to the customer.

Check it out

♦ Does your organisation have a standard introduction that it expects you to use when you introduce yourself and the organisation that you represent? If it does, make a note of it, or if it is detailed write down where it can be found.

If your organisation does not have a standard introduction, you will need to make up your own. You must say something in the first 20 seconds of the call that will let the customer know who you are and what you want and will also gain their trust and put them in a positive frame of mind. Your opening statement should be clear and non-intrusive.

You could start with a simple greeting 'Good afternoon Mrs Smith' followed by an identifier 'my name is Jenny Page, I am calling from Direct Office Supplies'. Then follow it up with your call purpose statement 'we have just opened a new branch in your area and we have a number of special offers that may interest you' and finish by establishing if it is convenient for you to continue 'do you have a moment to talk?'.

You should avoid using opening statements that are manipulative, for example, *'Good afternoon Mr Jones, I have a proposal for you that will save you money on local telephone calls – you would like to save money wouldn't you?'*. This is designed to make the customer say 'Yes'. However, most people are wise to this sort of sales pitch and do not appreciate being manipulated.

It would be much better to say *'Good afternoon Mr Jones, my name is Sue Reed, calling from Telephones Direct. I would like to let you know about our new and very economical local telephone service. Can you spare a moment to talk?'*. This opening statement is non-manipulative, it grabs the customer's interest by alluding to a money saving opportunity and it asks for permission to continue.

Customers are more likely to stay on the line if they feel that you are pleasant and safe to talk to.

If your organisation is a member of the Direct Marketing Association (DMA), then the DMA Code of Practice contains guidance that you will be expected to comply with – this should have been taken into account when your organisation devised its standard introduction. The following sections of the code relate specifically to the conduct of calls.

Direct Marketing Association Code of Practice	
Section no.	*Section content*
9.3	Members making sales, marketing or service calls must volunteer the name of the advertiser at the beginning of the call and must repeat this information on request at any time during the conversation.
9.5	Members must clearly state at the beginning of the conversation the purpose of the call and must restrict the content of the call to matters directly relevant to this purpose.
9.6	When acting as a telephone marketer and making calls on behalf of another organisation, members must disclose their own name, address and telephone number at any time during the conversation.
9.7	If a person is telephoned as a result of a referral by a third party, they must be informed of this at the beginning of the call, told the identity of the third party and given an opportunity to ask for the call to be discontinued.
9.9	Sales, marketing or service calls must not be made under the guise of research or a survey. When collecting information for legitimate research or a survey, members must not use this information to form the basis of a sales approach either during or after the call.

Putting your listener into a positive frame of mind

As a telephone salesperson, your voice is crucial because customers cannot see you; all they can hear is your voice. So make sure that your voice is clear and pleasant and always have a ready smile. A smile on your face reflects in your voice, so smile and give the customer a good impression.

Did you know?

When people communicate, only 7 per cent of the message is verbally communicated whilst 93 per cent is transmitted non-verbally.
Of the 93 per cent of non-verbal communication that takes place, 38 per cent of it is through vocal tones and 55 per cent of it is via facial expressions.

The image the customer has of you as a salesperson is vital and in telesales the image is created through the voice alone. There is no smartly dressed representative for the customer to see and no glittering product for the customer to touch – there is just a voice on the other end of the telephone.

A lot of successful people who rely on the quality of their voice such as politicians, singers and actors record their voices so that they can monitor their voice tone and find out if there are areas where it can be improved.

Try it out

♦ Record your voice and play it back to find out what it sounds like to a customer.
♦ Practise your sales pitch and see if there are areas where you think that your vocal presentation could be improved.

Make sure that you do not speak in a monotone manner as this not only makes you sound boring and unenthusiastic, it could give the customer the impression that your product or service is lacking in substance too.

Did you know?

The quality of the sound of the human voice is partially lost through transmission via a telephone system.

Your voice therefore needs to sound enthusiastic, caring and confident. Try to radiate sunshine by making your conversation bright and cheerful. Try to be positive and optimistic and always be enthusiastic. The customer will be irritated by a tone that is indifferent, hostile or too reserved.

Be careful with your choice of words so as to allow speech to be heard clearly. Use simple words. Avoid using jargon or local expressions that may not be understood by the customer. Bear in mind that people will judge you based on the words that you use so you should develop good verbal skills.

Never forget that the tone of your voice, the speed at which you speak and the way that you articulate your words communicates many things about you to your customers. They will be able to tell:

♦ if you are comfortable using the telephone
♦ what your state of mind is
♦ whether you have any emotion behind your voice
♦ whether you are confident and knowledgeable about your business.

The first 15 seconds are crucial to building a relationship of trust with the customer. The customer should see you not as a salesperson but as a friend who is helping them to invest their money wisely. Try to relax when you are talking by imagining that you are talking to a friend.

Six tips for a successful approach

1 Act in a natural way and be yourself.

2 Smile and you will sound pleasant and friendly.

3 Have ready all the information that you need.

4 Be precise and clear.

5 Be professional.

6 Give customers what they need.

Moving effectively on to the next part of the call

You can influence the customer to do business with your company by being professional in your approach. You need to create a climate in which new customers want to do business with you and existing customers wish to continue the relationship.

The easiest way to set the right atmosphere is to consider the customer – their needs, their preferences and their emotions. Try to know your customers as well as your products. Treat each customer as the most important person and always think to yourself that they are doing you a favour by giving you the opportunity to do business with them.

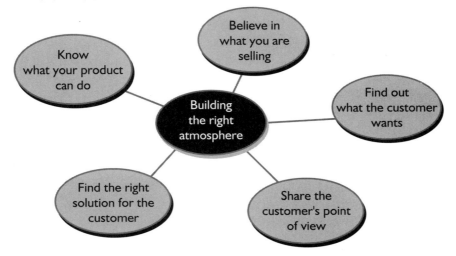

Figure 9.4 Five key steps that help to build the right atmosphere

---

Building a rapport is also very important in building trust and creating a relationship with the customer. This subject has been dealt with in detail in Unit 2 on page 137. If you build a good rapport with the customer, it will help them to feel comfortable with you and it will create a feeling of warmth and understanding. It will help your customer to feel that what you are saying is aimed directly towards their particular needs and desires. If you cannot establish a rapport with your customer, it is very unlikely that you will make a sale.

It is important to build a rapport with your customer

Case study 1 – John Clay's experiences

I recently received a call from a travel company, 'Leisure Breaks' I think they were called. This very nice friendly young lady introduced herself and said that their computer had selected my telephone number and that I was the lucky recipient of a week's free holiday to Spain.

Well, that immediately got my attention, as I thought that there must have been some sort of competition if my telephone number had been selected at random and she seemed such a pleasant person.

1 Do you think that John had really won a free holiday?
2 Do you think that there was anything other than the chance of a free holiday that gained John's attention?
3 How would you feel if you received such a call?
4 Do you think that this sort of approach is ethical?

How to identify if it is convenient for the customer to continue with the call

As your call is likely to be an intrusion into the customer's busy day, you should always remember to be considerate and *seek permission* to continue with the call.

So many people call us at home or at work and just launch straight into what they have to say – without even thinking about what we may be in the middle of doing. If someone is busy and you just begin speaking, they will not pay attention to you. You should therefore ask for permission before you open up with what you have to say.

Plenty of people will speak to you if you are polite. Just be prepared to introduce yourself quickly and then find out if it is convenient for you to continue with the call. An example of an opener that you could use is:

> *Hello, my name is* [insert your first and last name] *and I am calling on behalf of* [insert your company name]. *Do you have a minute to speak with me?'*

If the person that you have called is busy, offer to call back at a different time, and explain that you would prefer to call back when it is convenient for them to talk. Your organisation may well have a set of procedures for this circumstance.

Check it out

◆ Does your organisation have a set of procedures that you are expected to follow when you are trying to find out if the recipient finds it convenient to continue with a call?

Self-regulation regarding the convenience of calls

If your organisation is a member of the Direct Marketing Association (DMA), then the DMA Code of Practice also contains guidance that you will be expected to comply with when establishing the convenience of your calls. The following sections of the code relate specifically to the recipient's view of the convenience of your call and their right to end the call.

Direct Marketing Association Code of Practice	
Section no.	*Section content*
9.13	Members initiating a sales or marketing call must ask the recipient if the call is convenient. If it is not, members should offer to telephone again at a more convenient time, or not at all if so required.
9.16	Members must always recognise the right of the other party to end the telephone conversation at any stage, and must accept any request to end a call promptly and courteously.

How to use questions to identify the caller's needs and evaluate their interest in your organisation's products and services

Selling is not trying to convince someone of something – it is helping them to get what they want or need. The key to effective selling and communication is the ability and willingness to ask questions. Being able to ask the right questions will enable you to learn valuable information that is critical to the achievement of your objectives. However, more importantly, asking thoughtful, genuine questions also shows that you are interested and that you care.

To be successful in sales, you need to become a master questioner so that you can 'open up' your customer and unlock their needs, concerns or desires. You want to be able to move them into a state of mind where they begin to want a product or service like yours even before you start to tell them about it.

Think about it

If you offer someone a drink of water when that person is not thirsty, he or she will decline. However, when the person is parched, they will actively seek out the water. You should think of it as your job to help customers to recognise that they are thirsty!

- ◆ How do you draw people to you and what you have to offer?
- ◆ How do you show potential customers that you know something about them, what they want and how best to get it?
- ◆ What is the best way to get people to notice you and develop enough interest to talk seriously with you about themselves?

You ask the right questions.

Properly posed questions will make your customer take notice and think about their situation and what they might want to do about it. Good questions are often deceptively simple.

Did you know?

Studies have shown that dialogues that start when customers begin to answer questions that are important to them create the most meaningful relationships and the most sales.

Once you have introduced yourself to the customer and you have explained the reason for your call, you should continue the call with an **inviting question**. Inviting questions are used to invite the customer into the conversation, they:

- initiate the conversation
- begin the rapport-building process
- start the customer speaking.

If you are calling a prospective customer, some examples of inviting questions are:

- *'Do you have the time to speak with me?'*
- *'Are you the right person for me to be speaking to?'*

If you are calling an existing customer, some examples of inviting questions are:

- *'Is this a good time for us to talk?'*
- *'Have things been going well since we last spoke?'*
- *'Have you thought of any more information that I can help you with?'*

One of the key things to being successful in selling is to ask lots of questions and to listen intently to the answers you receive. You could ask questions about your customer's work, their organisation or anything else that interests them and you should listen to their answers with genuine interest.

If you do this, the customer is more likely to be friendly and start talking to you. You will then find that when you start talking about the benefits of the product or service that you are selling, the customer is more likely to listen to you.

Asking questions also allows you to remain in control of the conversation. If you find yourself doing most of the talking, it is an indication that you are losing control of the situation. So if you find that the customer is dominating the conversation by asking you lots of questions, try answering their questions with a question.

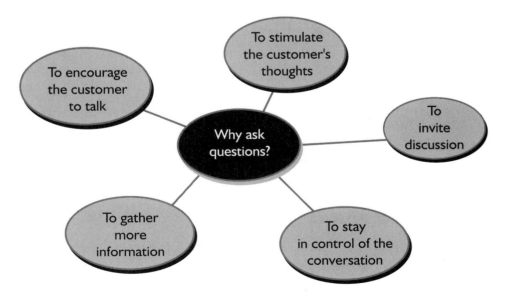

Figure 9.5 Five good reasons to ask questions

Questioning techniques in general have been covered in detail in Unit 1 on page 30. However, probing questions are particularly useful in sales. We will look at those in more depth now.

How to use probing questions to get the information that you need

Think about it

What do you think is the difference between a gentle probing question and an irritatingly asked question that the customer resents, gets angry with or hangs up on?

The answer to the activity above lies in the purpose of the question and the technique used to obtain the information that you need. Questions that probe into the business affairs or personal life of a customer must be phrased carefully and administered gently.

If you want to be able to get the information that you need, think about how the question is going to sound to the person you are talking to and how they are going to feel about it.

Think about it

Has a sales person ever asked you questions like: '*Who are you buying from now?*' or '*Are you ready to make a decision now?*'

◆ How did it make you feel?
◆ Did it give you the urge to say: '*That's none of your business?*'

The act of probing for information can be perceived as a very intrusive experience unless a great deal of thought goes into planning both what to say and how to say it. If you are making cold calls, people are likely to be wary and may even be suspicious of both you and your motives. If you are overtly nice or patronising that will only make it worse as it arouses people's suspicions.

Your only option is to sound pleasant and polite; state who you are and why you are calling and to ask if you can speak with them for a moment. If the caller grants you permission, that is when you can begin to probe for information. The information that you gather can then become the framework around which you can build your sales presentation.

Think about it

What sort of information would you like to gain from a customer so that you are able to make them an offer that they do not feel able to turn down?

The information that you would like to have is probably the answers to these sorts of questions:

- Does the prospective customer use the products or services that you are selling?
- How often do they buy and in what quantities?
- How much are they currently paying?
- Are they happy with their current supplier and product or service?
- Who is their current supplier and why did they choose them?

Life would be very simple if you could just ask the above questions straight out and get honest answers to all of them. Unfortunately, this does not happen because it is not polite and it is not acceptable practice. You must therefore learn to ask for information in a way that will be perceived by the prospective customer as non-intrusive and non-manipulative.

All questions should be phrased in a way that will make the customer willing to respond. Make sure the questions have no hint of sarcasm and that they are not patronising. Questions that insult like, *'You would like to save money, wouldn't you?'* can seriously damage a relationship with the prospective customer.

Soften every question by prefacing it with a statement of interest or information. Give the customer adequate time to think and prepare a response to the next question. You need to create a safe environment for customers through the use of questioning. The objective is to control the path of the call, not to control or manipulate the customer. The use of a statement prior to a question gives the prospective customer time to prepare an answer and the statement can also be used to show interest in the subject the customer wants to talk about.

If you ask questions that make the prospective customer curious or feel that you may have a solution to a troublesome situation then you will have a better chance of continuing the conversation. This is because you assume the role of a valuable and informed consultant.

You should also work to make the prospective customer feel that you have their best interests at heart rather than your own. The tone of your voice and the attitude that you project can help here. You should adopt a tone of voice that displays your confidence and willingness to help as well as showing your concern for the customer's situation.

Whenever you probe for information, remember to listen actively to the customer so that you can fully understand what they are saying. Always try to detect any message that might lie between the lines and make sure that you acknowledge what the customer is saying. You can use probing questions to determine if there is a gap between what your prospective customer has or is using now and what they would really like to have. If this probing is done in a subtle manner, the prospective customer will also become aware of the gap, which will provide you with an opening to make a suggestion or recommendation.

Make sure that your questions are not too direct or too personal. They must not insult or irritate the customer or make them feel stupid. Always ask yourself: *'If I were the customer, would I be happy to respond to this question?'*.

If possible, ask questions that can be answered in several different ways by the customer, who is then less likely to feel that they are being backed into a corner or manipulated. However, if you ask the customer a question that offers different choices, phrase the question so that the choice that you would most like them to choose is the last one.

Case study 2 – more of John Clay's experiences

When I phoned up to renew my contents insurance last week, they were ever-so-good. The girl, Sue, did a search on the computer for me and found me a company that was offering the same amount of cover for less money. To start with I was a bit worried that the cover wouldn't be as good, as you usually get what you pay for and I was sceptical about this other company being so cheap.

I think the girl must have picked up on the fact that I was worried as she then asked me a series of questions like *'Do I own any single items that are valued over £1000?'* and *'Does the total value of my contents come to more than £50,000?'* I said *'No'* to both of those. She said that was fine but pointed out that I would have to have the item valued for it to be covered on the new contents insurance if I ever own anything worth more than £1000 or if the total value of my goods is worth more than £50,000.

She then asked me if there were any factors that they needed to be aware of like did my house suffer from damp or was it built on a flood plain or anything like that. She seemed very thorough. By the time she had finished asking me questions I was confident that she knew what she was talking about so I decided to go with the cheaper quote and changed my insurance company in the end. I saved quite a bit of money by doing that.

1 How did Sue make sure that the alternative cover she was offering John would be suitable for him?
2 What made John confident enough to change insurance company in the end?
3 Do you think that John was happy will the level of service that he received?

How to confirm with the customer your understanding of their needs

After you have discussed the customer's needs with them and asked questions to clarify things or make sure that you have gathered sufficient information, you should summarise your understanding of what the customer has said. This can help you to avoid any confusion that could arise due to a lack of understanding. It is a good way of checking that the customer has the same understanding as you of any agreements that may have been reached during the course of the conversation.

It will also help you to build a good relationship with the customer, who will feel more secure if they know that you fully understand and appreciate their needs. The customer will also have more confidence in your ability to help and may be more willing to consider any solutions that you propose.

In order to summarise your understanding of the customer's needs, you will first need to listen very carefully to what the customer tells you. You should then paraphrase what you believe you heard.

It is important to realise that being able to listen effectively is crucial to your success as a salesperson. Very few people are good listeners as most of us find it very hard to listen properly.

Think about it

Do you fully listen to your customers?

Stop and think for a minute – do you **really** listen? On your next few sales calls, listen to yourself and see how quickly you respond to a customer's statement or question. Do you answer immediately? A second or two later? Can you be truly listening if you are able to:

◆ hear the customer
◆ process everything that they say in your brain
◆ formulate a response
◆ deliver that response

all in an instant?

Even worse, have you ever been so excited about your response that you have actually cut the customer off?

Unfortunately, many people believe that it is powerful to be good at speaking and that listening is a less useful skill. They tend to think that salespeople need to be good talkers rather than good listeners, for example, someone might say '*He's a born salesman – he's got the gift of the gab*'. However, in reality, being a good listener in a conversation has much more power as the listener is able to get more information than the talker. The job of a salesperson is to **listen** to customers.

Listening is an essential skill for making and keeping relationships. Once you are a good listener people will confide in you and trust you.

Five tips for being a good listener

1 Give your full attention to the person who is speaking.

2 Make sure that your mind is focused – if you feel your mind wandering, change the position of your body and try to concentrate on the speaker's words.

3 Let the speaker finish before you begin to talk – speakers appreciate having the chance to say everything they would like to say without being interrupted. If you interrupt, it looks like you are not listening – even if you really are.

4 Listen for the main ideas as these are the most important points the speaker wants to get across – pay special attention to statements that begin with phrases such as *'my point is . . .'* or *'the thing to remember is . . .'*.

5 Ask questions if you are not sure that you understand what the speaker has said – it is a good idea to repeat in your own words what the speaker has just said so that you can be sure that your understanding is correct.

How to answer questions raised by the customer in a way that promotes a sale

If your organisation is a member of the Direct Marketing Association (DMA), then the DMA Code of Practice contains guidance that you will be expected to comply with when it comes to answering questions raised by the customer. The following section of the code specifically relates to how you should answer questions raised by the customer.

Direct Marketing Association Code of Practice	
Section no.	*Section content*
9.18	Members must not evade the truth and must take care not to mislead. Any questions must be answered honestly and to the best of available knowledge.

You should always encourage the customer to ask questions and pay attention to them when they do. When customers talk to you they want you to know how they feel, what they believe and what they want.

This information is exactly what you need to know so that you can correctly position your sales pitch to satisfy this person. Therefore, the more the customer talks to you, the better chance you have of making a sale.

However, even in the best sales conversations, you may find yourself running into objections raised by the customer. Remember that an objection is anything that the customer raises that you need to address in order to progress the sale. Objections tend to happen when customers lack information and feel unsure about the suitability of what you are offering. Therefore, if you are going to be able to overcome any objections you need to make sure that you understand what is worrying the customer and that you deal with their concerns.

Customers' objections offer a window of opportunity for closing a sale. Until a customer reveals what they are thinking during the sales process, no salesperson (no matter how good) can start to close a sale.

Never avoid an objection or argue with it. The customer believes that they have raised a valid point and they will expect you to deal with it in a courteous and helpful manner. If you get into an argument you will only antagonise the customer and risk ruining your relationship with them.

Objections can usually be easily overcome if you possess a deep passion for your product and in depth knowledge of it.

Four steps for overcoming objections

1 Empathise with the customer – make them feel listened to and understood by using a statement like '*I understand how you feel*'.

2 Clarify your understanding of the customer's concerns – ask a question that helps you to understand like '*Is it the cost that you are concerned about?*'.

3 Present the customer with a solution – use the customer's words to tailor the solution so that the customer can see that it addresses their concerns. For example, '*I see, based on what you've told me, this is right for you because . . .*'.

4 Gain the customer's agreement – attempt to move the customer onto the next stage of the buying process by trying to close the sale, '*Can you see why this makes sense for you?*'.

As you deal with objections, you must remain confident throughout all the ups and downs of the customer's thought processes. You will find that customers that are getting ready to make a buying decision usually go through six different stages of behaviour (see page 254).

You should aim to become a logical and clear communicator with a comprehensive knowledge of your organisation's products and services. You can then give your customer a clear understanding of your proposition, so that they can weigh up the pros and cons in their own minds and overcome any negatives themselves.

Always remember that if you are not able to overcome an objection, you can still learn something valuable from it. You should get into the habit of analysing any lost sales and writing down anything that you should have said that may work next time you encounter the same objection or query.

Your organisation's requirements for recording and using the information that you gather

Your organisation may well have procedures for you to follow when you record or use the information that you gather.

Check it out

Does your organisation have a set of procedures that you are expected to follow when you record or use the information that you gather?

♦ If it does, then make a note of them or, if they are detailed, write down where they can be found.

The six stages of customer behaviour

1 Exploration

When customers begin researching a product or service, they do not always recognise their exact needs or the available options. In the early stages of the sales process, you are the informer, enabling the customer to explore the possibilities. At this stage customers are still investigating and you must gain their confidence by letting them feel free to make comments and objections. This is your opportunity to start making positive points about your products or services. If you answer the customer's objections with honest answers they will eventually realise that you know what you are talking about.

2 Slight withdrawal

Some customers react enthusiastically from the outset, but most refrain from showing early excitement. You should remain positive, upbeat and confident and you need to accept that the customer may not be ready to be influenced at this point.

3 Asking more questions and showing interest

If you keep moving forward with your sales pitch and successfully counter the customer's objections you will normally find that their interest becomes heightened and they will start to ask you more questions. You should respond to the customer's questions with calm, confident answers.

4 Deliberate pondering and brainstorming

At this stage, you may find that the customer seems nervous or edgy as they are close to making a buying decision. The customer may also make meaningless comments and objections one minute and positive acknowledgements the next – they will often contradict themselves.

5 More doubt, questions and anxiety

If you do not have a logical answer to the customer's questions at this stage, the customer could assume that you have a faulty product or poor product knowledge. The customer may also ask you to run through things again at this stage.

6 Resolving and finalising doubt

When the customer is close to making a buying decision, you will often find that they need one last bit of reassurance from you that they have reached the right decision. However, you must then have the confidence to back off and allow the customer to make the final decision alone – based on your expert guidance.

An overview of the legislative requirements

When recording and using information related to customers, you are required to comply with the obligations contained within the Data Protection Act 1998. This applies to the processing (which includes collecting, using, disclosing, destroying or holding data) of computerised personal data (data that can be associated with identifiable living individuals – it can include facts and opinions about an individual) and personal data held in structured manual files. Any organisation (data user) that wants to store personal information is required to register with the Data Protection Commissioner and must follow the Data Protection Principles. The Data Protection Commissioner has the right to inspect an organisation's computer systems to ensure that they are complying with the Act.

The principles of data protection basically state that the data user must ensure that the information is:

♦ obtained fairly and lawfully
♦ kept accurate and up to date
♦ surrounded by proper security
♦ only used for the registered purpose.

The data subject has the right to: see the information stored about themselves; have the data corrected if it is wrong; and claim compensation in some cases.

There is more information on the Data Protection Act in Unit 2, page 148.

Self-regulation regarding the recording of customer information

If your organisation is a member of the Direct Marketing Association (DMA), then the DMA Code of Practice contains guidance that you will be expected to comply with when it comes to recording and using customer information.

The following sections of the code specifically relate to how you deal with information about the customer.

Direct Marketing Association Code of Practice	
Section no.	*Section content*
4.5	Members collecting personal information from individuals must inform them at the time of collection: (a) who is collecting it (b) why it is being collected except where this is obvious from the context or where the individuals already know. If it is intended to disclose that information to others (including to associated companies), the member must also inform the individuals of that intention, unless they already know, and give them an opportunity to object before first disclosure.
4.7	If, after collecting personal information from individuals, members decide to use it for a purpose that is significantly different from the one originally intended, they must first advise those individuals and allow 30 days for objections to be received. A significantly different use is: (a) the disclosure of personal information to third parties for their direct marketing purposes (b) the use or disclosure of personal information for any purpose(s) substantially different from the purpose(s) for which it was collected and which individuals could not reasonably have foreseen and to which it is probable that they would have objected if they had known.
4.10	The extent and detail of personal information held for any purpose must be adequate, relevant and not excessive for that purpose.
4.11	Personal information held by members must be accurate and, where necessary, kept up to date.
4.12	Personal information must always be held securely and must be safeguarded against unauthorised use, disclosure, alteration or destruction.

Your organisation's sales procedures and any relevant legal requirements

Case study 3 – more of John Clay's experiences

I received another call from a company who said, '*Mr Clay, can I confirm your name and address please? Your property has been selected to feature in our summer magazine and as part of that, if we could feature pictures of your home, we will give you £1000 towards a new kitchen.*'

I told them that I wasn't interested, as I guessed that it was just a scam to try and sell me a kitchen. It's quite clever really, because if you buy the kitchen they then come and take pictures of their wonderful work so that they can try and sell it to other people.

1 Have you ever received a call like this?
2 If you have, did you suspect that the company was really just trying to sell you something?
3 What would your response have been?
4 Do you think that this is good practice?

Check it out

Does your organisation have a set of procedures that you are expected to follow when offering products and services over the telephone?

♦ If it does, make a note of them or, if they are detailed, write down where they can be found.

Relevant legal requirements

There is a wide range of legislation that may have an effect when you are offering products and services over the telephone, such as:

♦ The Charities Act 1992
♦ The Consumer Credit Act 1974
♦ The Consumer Protection Act 1987
♦ The Consumer Transactions Order 1976
♦ Fair Trading Act 1973
♦ Financial Services Act 1986
♦ Mail Order Transactions Order 1976
♦ Sale of Goods Act 1994
♦ Supply of Goods and Services Act 1982
♦ Trade Descriptions Act 1968
♦ Unsolicited Goods and Services Act 1971 and 1975.

In general, the type of products and services you are offering and how they are made available will determine which particular pieces of legislation are applicable.

Check it out

Find out which particular pieces of legislation apply to your circumstances when you are offering products and services over the telephone and the effect that they have.

Keys to good practice

✓ It is best not to call people after about 8.00 p.m. It is also a good idea to avoid Sundays and public or religious holidays.

✓ Your introduction should identify you, put your listener into a positive frame of mind and allow you to move effectively on to the next part of the call.

✓ Your voice should be enthusiastic, caring and confident and you should make your conversation bright and cheerful.

✓ Always act natural and be yourself.

✓ Remember to be considerate and seek the listener's permission to continue with the call.

✓ If the person that you have called is busy, offer to call back at a different time.

✓ Being able to ask the right questions will enable you to learn valuable information that is critical for the achievement of your objectives.

✓ Always check with the customer that you have accurately understood their needs.

✓ Being able to listen effectively is crucial to your success as a salesperson.

9.3 Promote the features and benefits of your organisation's products and services

WHAT YOU NEED TO KNOW OR LEARN

♦ How to explain the features and benefits of the products and services that you have identified as meeting the needs of the customer

♦ How to make sure the customer understands what you are saying

♦ How to recognise and act on any buying signals expressed by the customer

♦ Your organisation's procedures for recording the outcome and closing the call effectively when you are unable to meet the customer's needs.

How to explain the features and benefits of the products and services that you have identified as meeting the needs of the customer

Every product or service has lots of features. A **feature** is a fact that is true about a product or service, tangible or intangible.

Think about it

Consider an everyday object like a ball-point pen, what do you think some of its features are?

Some of the features of a ball-point pen are: the lid that covers its point; its rotating ball point; the colour of the ink; the outer plastic casing; the stopper at the end; its weight and the length of it; there are plenty more!

A feature becomes a **benefit** when it fulfils the customer's needs. Let's consider the ball-point pen again. If, for example, the customer particularly needs a *black* ball-point pen then the fact that the ink in the pen that you are offering them is also *black* becomes a benefit because it fulfils the customer's need.

You will need to be very familiar with the features of your organisation's products and services, as it is this knowledge that will make it possible for you to describe the benefits of those products and services.

Get to know your product very well

You will also need to be able to determine what is motivating the customer to buy and which stage of the buying process the customer is at. Research has shown that every consumer goes through five steps when they decide to buy something (see page 260).

The five stages of buying

1 **Problem recognition** – the consumer feels that their current situation is lacking something. It could be anything from a tin of beans to a new house. Most marketing techniques attempt to stimulate problem recognition by suggesting to consumers that they need a particular product.

2 **Information search** – during this stage, the consumer looks into their options and tries to decide which product fulfils their needs best.

3 **Alternative evaluation** – the consumer draws up criteria against which they can evaluate their options, such as:
   ◆ what will the product do for them?
   ◆ how long will it last?
   ◆ how much does it cost?

   Retailers can influence consumers at this stage by suggesting criteria for consumers to use and also by taking the consumer's criteria into account when promoting the benefits of their products.

4 **Purchase decision** – the consumer judges the choices and finalises their purchase. This is the point at which the salesperson has the most influence. It is at this stage that purchase incentives can affect the customer's decision to buy.

5 **Post-purchase evaluation** – this stage can be disconcerting for the consumer, especially if there was more than one attractive option and the product was expensive. Contact with the retailer is still important during this stage as it can help the customer to decide if they are satisfied with their purchase and it may affect their decision to return to the same retailer.

The first stage – problem recognition – may occur when the consumer receives information via advertising, or through a conversation with friends, that causes them to become aware of a need. It may also occur when the consumer re-evaluates their current situation and perceives an area of dissatisfaction or a void in their life.

You will also find that no matter what kind of need exists, some consumers will never consciously recognise it. Sometimes you have to use your abilities as a salesperson to help the consumer uncover a need that they did not initially realise they had.

Imagine that you have decided that you need a new car, what would your next step be?

Before you could go out and buy a new car, you would need to at least decide what type of car you may want as there are so many to choose from. You may also need to find out what an average car costs so that you can decide what sort of car you are likely to be able to afford. In other words, you would need to carry out your own information search before you could even narrow down the choice enough to visit a car showroom.

Think about it

If you were going to buy a new car, what sort of things would you need to know before you could evaluate all the alternatives and know what sort of car you want to buy?

It is your job to help the customer with their information search, as your product knowledge can be invaluable to them. The customer's own search for suitable products is usually limited by several factors, such as:

♦ the time they have available
♦ their level of experience
♦ the urgency of their need
♦ the value of the purchase.

You can provide customers with a wealth of information about the features of your organisation's products and services and can also help them to evaluate the alternatives by considering the benefits of those products and services. In this way you can help them to reach a purchasing decision.

You can also play an important role in the post-purchase evaluation as you can help to alleviate any possible purchase worries the customer may have. You can:

♦ sell the customer the products and services that meet their needs
♦ reinforce the buyer's belief that the right decision has been made
♦ re-iterate the capabilities and quality of the product or service
♦ offer a post-purchase follow up to check that the customer has received the correct goods and that the product or service is functioning as expected.

Selling is all about helping people to buy. You should never push a sale, you should just help people to make the right decision, as the more you try to sell, the less likely people will be to buy.

People buy for a variety of reasons, so it is your responsibility to meet their expectations. Generally, people do not buy a product or service, they buy what that product or service can do *for them*. In other words, people do not buy features they buy benefits.

To summarise:

1 Give your customer useful information.

2 Discuss features and benefits with your customer and help them to find a solution.

3 Offer them the product or service that best suits their needs.

How to make sure the customer understands what you are saying

In order to communicate well with the customer you must be able to speak their language – you basically need to know how the customer thinks. If you begin to understand how your customer's mind works, then you will know how to communicate effectively and when the customer understands the meaning of your words they will start to trust you.

It is therefore crucial to establish a connection with the customer if you are going to be able to understand what the customer wants and what is important to them so that you can match their needs.

Did you know?

Research has shown that your customers fit into one of three basic groups:

1 Visuals
2 Auditories
3 Kinesthetics.

Visuals are those people who **see** the world – they prefer maps to verbal or written directions when they are trying to find somewhere. Auditories are people who **hear** the world – they prefer to follow verbal instructions rather than written ones or diagrams. Kinesthetics are people who **feel** the world around them – they like to write things down because it clarifies their thoughts.

Did you know?

Approximately 35 per cent of your customers will be visuals, 25 per cent will be auditories and 40 per cent will be kinesthetics.

Visuals

These are customers who understand more from what they can see than from what they hear or feel. These people like colourful brochures or pictures.

Visual people take your words and translate them into pictures, so if you use words that prevent them from making pictures you will not be able to build a rapport with them and they will probably not buy from you.

People who think in pictures use words like '**see**'; '**look**'; '**vision**' and '**scene**' and phrases like '**I can see what you are saying**' or '**I see your point of view**'. They may think that auditory and kinesthetic people do not have vision.

When dealing with someone who is a visual, you need to use words that can help them to make pictures. Use phrases like:

◆ *'It looks good to me.'*
◆ *'How do you see the situation?'*
◆ *'Do you see what I mean?'*
◆ *'I can see that working for you.'*
◆ *'I'll see if we can do that for you.'*

A visual buyer will enjoy looking at colourful catalogues

Auditories

These people are influenced by what they hear rather than what they see or feel, so how you talk about your products or ideas is important as auditories listen more closely to how you say things than to what you actually say.

People who are auditories are interested in your voice inflection and the pace, pitch and tone of your voice. These people are more likely to buy over the telephone than face to face.

People who think in sounds or hear an internal voice use words like '**say**'; '**tell**'; '**speak**' and '**questions**' and phrases like '**It sounds good to me**' or '**I like the sound of that**'. They may think that visual and kinesthetic people do not listen.

When dealing with someone who is an auditory, you need to use words and phrases like:

♦ *'I have heard good things about it.'*
♦ *'It sounds like it should work.'*
♦ *'It doesn't ring a bell.'*
♦ *'I hear what you are saying.'*
♦ *'I'll speak to you soon.'*

Kinesthetics

These people are influenced by their emotions and gut feeling rather than what they see or hear. They will want to touch and feel your suggestions and ideas.

People who think using feelings use words like '**touch**', '**grasp**', '**feel**' and '**solid**' and use phrases like, '**It feels good to me**' or '**I have a good feeling about it**'. They may think that visuals and auditories are insensitive.

When dealing with someone who is a kinesthetic, you need to use words and phrases like:

◆ *'How do you feel about it?'*
◆ *'We touched on that before.'*
◆ *'Hold onto that idea.'*
◆ *'Have you grasped what I mean?'*
◆ *'Keep in touch.'*

If you are unable to decide which category a customer fits into, you should try to use all the different representational systems when you talk to them. The customer will then understand what you are saying whichever type they are.

Try it out

The words and phrases used by people can reveal information about the way that they perceive the world and can give you clues about which representational system they use. Consider the three snippets of conversation below and decide if the speaker is a visual, an auditory or a kinesthetic.

1 *'I'm sorry, I can't quite grasp the idea, as it is not something that I have come into contact with before. Could you please explain it to me again so that I can try to get a better feel for it.'*
2 *'The way I see it, I need to look into the various possibilities and clarify which ones appear to be the most relevant.'*
3 *'I hear what you're saying and it sounds interesting. Perhaps we could discuss it more tomorrow.'*

Try it out

Which sort of representational system do you use?

1 Are you a visual?
   ◆ Do you like people to draw you a picture if they are trying to explain something to you?
   ◆ Do you gesticulate when you are trying to explain something to someone else?
2 Are you an auditory?
   ◆ Do you have to read a passage out loud if you are trying to understand it?
   ◆ Do you like to discuss your ideas with other people?
3 Are you a kinesthetic?
   ◆ Do you need to experience something for yourself in order to believe it?
   ◆ Do you learn best by trial and error and trying things for yourself?

Make a note of which sensory type you think you are and why.

How to recognise and act on any buying signals expressed by the customer

If you listen effectively to your customers, they will give you signals when they are ready to buy. It is your job to recognise these signals as they are your cues to close the sale. This is critical to your success as a salesperson as you could end up going past the point of sale if you are not able to spot them.

Did you know?

As a rule of thumb, any question asked by the prospective customer could be considered a buying signal.

The most blatant buying signal of all and also the easiest to recognise is when the customer asks you *'What's the next step?'*. If you hear this, then you **know** that it is time to close the sale!

However, there are a number of other, less obvious buying signals that the customer may give (see page 266). Any of the signals on page 266 indicate that the customer is interested in the products or services that you are offering.

As a salesperson, your highest skills will be called upon when the prospective customer asks you a question or shows an interest in buying. This is because you must know how to act on buying signals as well as being able to recognise them.

Did you know?

If the customer asks you a question which could be answered 'Yes' or 'No', **never** just answer 'Yes' or 'No'. Otherwise, you could end up going past the sale without making it.

When the customer asks you a question, you should try to answer them with a question or ask a question at the end of your answer, as this establishes the two central objectives of selling:

1 Stay in control of the conversation.
2 Try to put yourself in a position where you are able to close the sale.

When the prospective customer asks you a question, it is often a buying signal and your first instinct will be to say yes if you know it to be true. For example:

◆ *'Does that model come in red?'*   **'Yes'**
◆ *'Do you have it in stock?'*   **'Yes'**
◆ *'Can you deliver on Thursday?'*   **'Yes'**

However, answering **'Yes'** is the wrong response, as it will only prolong the sale.

20 other buying signals to look out for

1 Specific questions about rates or prices or statements about affordability such as, *'How much does it cost?'* or *'I am not sure that I can afford it'*.

2 Any questions or statements about money such as, *'How much money would I have to put down as a deposit?'*

3 Questions about availability or time such as, *'Are these in stock?'* or *'How often do you receive new shipments?'*

4 Questions about delivery such as, *'How soon could it be delivered?'*

5 Questions that indicate that the customer wants you to repeat something you have said such as, *'Tell me about the . . . again'* or *'What was that you said before about financing?'*.

6 Statements about problems with previous suppliers such as, *'Our current supplier does not offer us very good service, how quickly does your organisation respond to an emergency call out?'*

7 Positive questions about you or your organisation such as, *'How long have you been with the company?'* or *'How long has your company been in business?'*

8 Questions about qualifications – either yours or your company's such as, *'Are all your staff qualified to . . . '.*

9 Specific positive questions about your company such as, *'What other services do you offer?'*

10 Questions about quality, guarantees or warranties such as, *'How long is the warranty?'* or *'Is that covered by the guarantee?'*

11 Questions about features and options such as, *'What does the . . . do?'* or *'Does that come as standard?'*

12 Questions about productivity such as, *'How many copies per minute can it do?'*

13 Specific product or service questions such as, *'How does the . . . work?'*

14 Specific statements about ownership of the product such as, *'So it would be mine at the end of the second year?'*

15 Questions about other satisfied customers such as, *'Who is already using your products?'*

16 Questions about references such as, *'Do you have a list of satisfied customers?'*

17 Buying noises such as, *'Oh, I didn't realise that!'* or *'That's worth knowing'*.

18 Concerned questions such as, *'What if I get it home and it is not the right size?'*

19 Questions that seek support such as, *'What would you do?*

20 Indications of interest such as asking for a free trial or wanting to see samples.

You will also find that you will be inclined to answer the prospective customer in the most straightforward way. For example:

◆ *'When will the new model be available?'* **'At the end of the month'**
◆ *'How soon after that would you be able to deliver?'* **'Two weeks later'**

These answers are also the wrong response!

Did you know?

The rule of thumb is: use the prospective customer's question to confirm the sale.

When you receive a buying signal from the customer, you should respond in the form of a question that implies the answer and also confirms that the customer wants to buy whatever you are selling. This is not as complicated as it sounds and it should become clearer as we consider some examples of confirming questions.

If the customer asks:	An appropriate response would be:
'Does that model come in red?'	*'Is red the colour that you want?'*
'Do you have it in stock?'	*'Would you like it delivered immediately?'*
'Can you deliver on Thursday?'	*'Do you want it delivered on Thursday?'*

You could also answer directly but you should pose a closing question immediately afterwards. For example:

If the customer asks:	An appropriate response would be:
'When will the new model be out?'	*'At the end of the month but we are doing a special deal if you order it now.'*
'Do you have it in stock?'	*'Yes. When would you like it delivered?'*

Constructing an appropriate response is more difficult. It requires creativity and practice, as does delivering the response softly and smoothly. However, being able to do this is the mark of a professional salesperson and it can be achieved with practice.

Try it out

Ask a colleague to role play with you so that you can try spotting buying signals and practise responding to them in a way that closes the sale.

Your organisation's procedures for recording the outcome and closing the call effectively when you are unable to meet the customer's needs

You must make sure that you are prepared if you are ever faced with the situation of being unable to meet the customer's needs. The following exercise will enable you to find out how your organisation expects you to deal with such a situation.

Check it out

Find out what your organisation expects you to do if you are ever faced with the situation of being unable to meet the customer's needs.

◆ Is there a procedure to follow?
◆ Does your organisation expect you to record any such instances? If it does, note down how and where the information should be recorded.
◆ How does your organisation expect you to close the call in such instances?

Keys to good practice

✓ Make sure that you know all about your organisation's products and services so that you can describe their benefits.

✓ Ensure that you are familiar with the five stages that people go through when they decide to buy something.

✓ Try to understand how the customer's mind works as it will help you to speak their language, enable you to communicate more effectively with them and allow you to gain their trust.

✓ Always look out for any buying signals that the customer may give and make sure that you respond to them in the appropriate manner.

✓ Make sure that you know what to do if you are unable to meet the customer's needs.

9.4 Gain customer commitment and progress the transaction

WHAT YOU NEED TO KNOW OR LEARN

◆ How to establish which products and services your customer prefers and agree a way forward
◆ How to identify and take advantage of any opportunities for cross-selling and up-selling
◆ How to maintain a professional manner throughout the call and close calls on a positive note
◆ Your organisation's procedures for recording the details of the sale, progressing documentation and forwarding information

♦ How to evaluate objectively the effectiveness of your techniques to improve your future performance.

How to establish which products and services your customer prefers and agree a way forward

Any buying signals that your customer gives you should point you towards their preferred product or service. However, if this does not become clear, you will need to discuss further the options available.

Bear in mind that the customer may need you to summarise the features and benefits of each of the options for them so that the information they need to make their decision is fresh in their mind. Always be ready to do this for them.

It is also possible that the customer may need time to go away and think about all the information that you have presented them with and may wish to discuss the possible options with other people. You may therefore not be able to establish which product or service they prefer straight away and might arrange to call back at a later date so that you give the customer enough time to feel comfortable about their decision.

It is always best to try to close the sale straight away if that is possible. However, you should never put the customer under pressure to make a decision there and then if they feel they need more time to consider the information. It is also possible that the way forward for the customer may be further sales contact in the form of a demonstration of the product or service. You will need to play it by ear and use your experience to judge the best way forward for your customer.

How to identify and take advantage of any opportunities for cross-selling and up-selling

Cross-selling is the conscious strategy of switching your customers across your product range to see if there is a match. It is usually a natural process, for example, if you were selling a skirt, you could offer the customer a belt that matches it. Often all it takes to gain the extra sale is to tell the customer about the product or service. It is very likely that you have already experienced cross-selling first hand for yourself.

Think about it

Have you ever been to a fast food restaurant?
If you have, think about what the sales assistant said to you when you ordered a burger. The chances are that you were asked, '*Do you want fries with that?*'.

The example above is one of the most well known forms of cross-selling that you are likely to come across, although you probably did not realise it at the time!

Some people worry that they will irritate customers by cross-selling. However, in reality, the reverse is usually true – you are demonstrating that you are interested in the customer.

There is one major rule that you should always follow when you are attempting to cross-sell – *make sure that you have the original order in hand*. In other words, always make sure that you have achieved your **primary** objective first. Close the sale, take down the customer's particulars, process the order and then, and only then, attempt the cross sell. If you try to sell additional items too early in a call, you might turn the customer off and you could lose the original sale.

Once the order has been taken, you can then bridge across to the cross-sell item. For example, *'Thank you Mr Ali for ordering an ink jet printer from us. Incidentally, did you know that we have our ink jet cartridges on special offer this month at 20 per cent off? If you were to buy a set of spare cartridges now, you could save money and also avoid the hassle of having to get hold of new cartridges when they eventually need replacing. Would you like me to add a set of replacement cartridges to your order?'*

The cross-sell item should relate directly to the purchase and the item offered should be relatively low cost in comparison with the original order. Also, by including the word *'incidentally'*, the remark becomes something casual and you avoid the possibility of the customer feeling that they have been exposed to hard sell tactics.

Up-selling is the practice of selling more of the same product when a customer asks for it – this typically takes the form of an additional enticement, such as a bulk-buying discount. Good examples of this are the 'multi-saver' or 'three for two' offers that you see in many of the shops these days where if you buy two of a particular item you then get one free. This is a form of enticement to stop you buying only one – it works on the principle that most people find it hard to resist a bargain.

Most businesses will tell you that cross-selling and up-selling are the keys to their success. It is good to get a sale, however it is far better to increase the size of that sale, as real profits come when you get the customer to buy more or they buy larger, more expensive or more comprehensive products or services.

Successful cross-selling and up-selling should be at the core of every business as they are techniques that can instantly multiply profits.

You will find cross-selling easy if you think of your main business as helping customers. Consider the problems that your customers come to you with. What does it *really* take to solve their problems? The chances are that your customer needs a lot more than the simple inexpensive solution that they first consider. By grouping together several different products and services, you can give the customer a more advanced package that goes much further towards providing a satisfying solution.

Your customers are intelligent people who make decisions every day. If they do not need or want the item that you have offered, they will tell you. If you offer the cross-sell politely and they are not interested, they will usually politely decline.

Up-selling has more to do with good planning than special selling skills. If you find that you are good at fulfilling a need then you just need to create packages and strategies that sell even more of your solution to every customer.

Three ways to increase the opportunity for up-selling and cross-selling

1 Bundle several related products or services together and drop the price below what the total would be if the customer bought all the products separately. If a customer then enquires about a single item, point out that they can get that item *plus* a great deal more by purchasing your bundle.

2 If your product or service works much better when it is combined with another item, make sure that you tell your customers about it. You will be surprised how many products and services go together in a way that makes it hard to have one without needing the other.

3 If you find that a customer likes your product or service, offer them a good deal if they buy even more of it.

It is even possible, with the right approach, to up-sell and cross-sell successfully when the customer has called in with a complaint – as it is not what has happened to the customer that counts but how you deal with the situation. The key is to address the problem first. By doing so, you can build a rapport with the customer that lays the groundwork for a sale. Once you have resolved the customer's problem you can then move from offering them a service to pursuing a sale.

The techniques listed in the box on page 272 show that using the right words can make all the difference when it comes to convincing the customer to buy more. You should practise using the techniques until you feel comfortable with them.

Try it out

Ask a colleague if they will role play with you so that you can try out the suggested techniques and practise them until you are able to use them comfortably.

Always remember that if you approach up-selling and cross-selling with an 'extra service' rather than a 'sales' attitude you will not find it difficult to master.

Cross-selling and up-selling techniques

1 Take charge of the call.

It is essential that you control the customer's reaction by assuming a positive ending to the conversation. For example, instead of asking *'Would you like to hear about our special offers?'* you should say *'By the way, did you know that we have . . . on special offer this week at just £10?'*.

2 Use command words.

Using words like *'must'*, *'need'* and *'have to'* can help to close a sale. For example, if you have just suggested the perfect add-on item, you can tell the customer *'You have to have this! It would . . .'* and add the benefit that the customer would like to hear – based on the customer's own words if possible.

3 Sell a product's benefits not its features.

Remember that from the customer's point of view, 90 per cent of a sale is emotional. Active verbs such as *'gain'*, *'improve'*, and *'save'* along with words that express benefits such as *'new'*, *'free'* and *'proven'* are likely to appeal to the customer's emotions. The impact of these words is greatest if you combine them with any needs that the customer may have expressed earlier. For example, *'You will save 25 per cent on your order if you buy two today and you did say that you like to have a spare just in case you run out'*.

4 Appeal to the customer's emotions not their intellect.

You should ask your customer *how they feel*, not *what they think*, about adding the suggested item to their order. If you ask them to think it may cause them to question the appropriateness of the item whereas testing their feelings about it tends to help them to see how it could be suitable.

How to maintain a professional manner throughout the call and close calls on a positive note

Maintaining a professional manner

If your organisation is a member of the Direct Marketing Association (DMA), then the DMA Code of Practice contains guidance that you will be expected to comply with regarding what constitutes professional behaviour.

The following sections of the code relate specifically to courtesy and procedures.

Direct Marketing Association Code of Practice	
Section no.	Section content
9.14	Members must at all times be courteous and efficient during sales, marketing and service calls.
9.15	Members must avoid the use of high pressure tactics which could be construed as harassment.
9.17	If a member arranges to visit the recipient of a sales, marketing or service call, a telephone number or address must be provided in advance of the visit to enable the recipient to cancel or change the appointment.

Closing calls on a positive note

Your organisation may have a standard closing statement that it expects you to use when you close a call.

Check it out

♦ Does your organisation have a standard closing statement that it expects you to use when you close calls? If it does, make a note of it for your portfolio.

You should always close on an upbeat note, as the last comment that the customer hears is what he or she will remember. Rather than just ending with a pleasantry, you should invite the customer to call back again (especially if they were upset when they called) and then say *'goodbye'* with a pleasant upward inflection at the end of the word.

Your organisation's procedures for recording the details of the sale, progressing documentation and forwarding information

Most recording is normally done electronically. The whole system is usually screen driven with very little paperwork being involved. Data are normally input straight into a database, along with the customer's billing details or credit card number and the delivery address.

Check it out

Find out how your organisation expects you to record the details of the sale and how this information should be forwarded to the people involved in the way forward.

♦ Does your organisation have a procedure that you are expected to follow when you are recording the details of the sale?
♦ Do you generate any paperwork when you record the details of the sale?
♦ Does your organisation have a procedure that you are expected to follow when forwarding information to the people involved in the way forward?

How to evaluate objectively the effectiveness of your techniques to improve your future performance

We all learn from our experiences and evolve our own techniques in the light of those experiences. It is a natural process – the more calls that you make, the more competent you become and the more knowledgeable you will be.

We have already looked in detail at how you can evaluate your own performance and draw up a self-development plan in Unit 25. You may wish to review this now.

Keys to good practice

✓ Be ready to summarise the features and benefits of each of the options available to the customer if required.

✓ Never pressurise the customer to make a decision.

✓ Use your experience to judge the best way forward for the customer.

✓ If you approach up-selling and cross-selling with an 'extra service' attitude rather than a 'sales' attitude you are more likely to succeed.

✓ Remember that the last thing that the customer hears is what they will remember so always close calls on an upbeat note and invite the customer to call again.

✓ Make sure that you know how to record the details of the sale, progress any documentation that may be necessary and pass on information to any people involved in the way forward.

✓ Periodically review your performance and look at ways in which you can improve your techniques.

✓ Always remember that the more calls that you make, the more competent you will become and the more knowledgeable you will be.

Check your knowledge

1. List the features and benefits of the products and services you offer.
2. What are the six steps of the sales process?
3. What is the Telephone Preference Service?
4. Why must all call centres keep an in-house 'do not call' list?
5. What is the DMA Code of Practice?
6. How does predictive dialling work? What are the benefits of it?
7. What are the three most important questions to ask yourself before you start a telemarketing/telesales campaign?
8. List five reasons why you should set very specific call objectives.
9. What makes customers raise objections?
10. What should a good introduction achieve?
11. Why should you seek the customer's permission to continue with a call?
12. List five things that good listeners do.
13. List four steps for overcoming objections.
14. What are the five stages of buying?
15. What are the two main objectives of selling?

UNIT 11 Enter and retrieve information using a computer system

This option unit is all about using a computer system, as part of your call handling activity, to enter, store and retrieve data. It includes ensuring that you enter information accurately and that you follow the correct procedures for identifying and correcting errors. You will need to be familiar with your organisation's procedures for maintaining the security and confidentiality of the data you enter and retrieve, and will also need to know how to safeguard your computer equipment and data from damage.

This unit has two elements:

◆ enter information into a computer system
◆ retrieve information from a computer system.

There are also initial sections on computer basics, health and safety issues and data and equipment protection issues.

After you have completed this unit, you will be able to:

◆ gain access to an appropriate computer system and accurately input new data
◆ process, amend, store and delete data within an appropriate computer system
◆ demonstrate your understanding of the provisions contained within the Data Protection Act 1998
◆ recognise and minimise any risks there may be to your personal safety when using computer equipment long term.

The case studies in this chapter have been based on a fictitious company – 'Direct Communications', a supplier of telephone, internet and cable television services. Examples from other sectors such as banking, insurance, telemarketing and office supplies will be covered in other chapters.

Computer basics

This section is aimed at new, or relatively new, computer users. If you are a confident computer user, you may wish to go straight to the next section. However, if you know how to use a computer but you do not know how it works, you could find this section useful as it may help you to understand why computers do not always do what you expect them to do.

WHAT YOU NEED TO KNOW OR LEARN

◆ The basic components of a computer system
◆ How computers work

- How computers store data
- How to start up your computer
- How to shut down your computer
- How to use a mouse.

The basic components of a computer system

Every computer consists of both **hardware** and **software**. The hardware is everything 'physical' about your computer, that is, all the parts that you can see and feel, whilst the software is made up of the programs (sometimes also called **applications**) that are installed on the computer to make it function and perform certain types of activities. A computer cannot do anything without software.

The software installed on your computer consists of two types of programs:

- the **operating system**, such as Microsoft's Windows software
- the applications, such as word processing software, spreadsheets or databases.

Without an operating system, your computer would not be able to run any other programs. The operating system only exists for one reason – to make it as easy as possible for you to operate your computer.

Did you know?

Microsoft's Windows software is the operating system that is currently in use on 90 per cent of the world's personal computers.

The operating system allows you to:

- run other programs
- change the way your computer screen looks
- customise the way your computer works according to your own personal preferences
- organise, move, copy and delete data
- rapidly find lost or missing documents
- perform periodic maintenance on your hard disk drive to keep your computer working at optimal efficiency.

The basic components that make up the hardware of your computer are the:

- monitor (sometimes also called the visual display unit)
- system unit
- keyboard
- mouse
- printer.

The basic components of a computer

We will now take a brief look at each of the components that make up your computer system and their function.

The monitor

This is sometimes also called a Visual Display Unit (VDU) and is the part of your computer that looks a bit like a television screen. It may be powered independently of the main computer and so may have its own on/off switch. Like televisions, monitors usually have a set of controls for adjusting contrast and brightness.

The text and images that you see on the screen are made up of tiny dots called 'pixels'. The greater the number of pixels that make up the picture, the more detailed the image is. The screen resolution is measured in pixels. For example, a screen resolution of 1024 × 768 describes a screen which is made up of 1024 pixels along the horizontal axis and 768 pixels along the vertical axis. You can increase the screen's resolution (the number of pixels it contains) without making the screen bigger – the pixels become smaller which is what makes the image shown on the screen clearer.

The system unit

This is the main 'body' of the computer. It houses the computer's processing circuitry, hard disk storage, power supply and other hardware elements such as floppy disk drives, modems and CD-ROM drives.

The keyboard

The keyboard is a standard typewriter-style keyboard that allows you to interact with the computer.

The mouse

The mouse is used to move a pointer or cursor around the screen. If you are going to be able to use your computer efficiently, you will need to be able to use both the mouse and keyboard in tandem.

The printer

As you might imagine, a printer allows you to produce a paper version of the information on your screen. Nowadays, the most common types of printer are inkjet and laser printers.

Both types of printer produce excellent results, but for high-quality black and white output, laser printers are best. If you want to print in colour, it is most likely that you would use an inkjet printer as although colour laser printers exist they are expensive to buy.

The photo below shows how these different items of hardware can be connected together to make up a stand-alone personal computer.

A typical personal computer set up

It is also possible to connect several computers together into a computer network. This is commonly done in business, as computer networks have a number of advantages over stand-alone personal computers:

♦ all the computers in the system are able to communicate with each other via the network
♦ data and information that are likely to be used by more than one person are kept on a **file server** (a sort of 'super' computer that runs the network) which means that they can be shared by many users
♦ several users can also share a printer.

The diagram opposite shows how the different items of hardware can be connected together into a computer network.

Other items of computer hardware	
Floppy disk drives	A floppy drive is a commonly used type of storage device. You can use this type of drive to write information onto a floppy disk as well as reading information that has already been written onto a floppy disk. However, the drawback of floppy disks is that they cannot hold very much data.
Zip drives	These are similar to floppy drives but they use zip disks, which can hold more information than floppy disks.
CD-ROM drives	This is another type of storage device that uses compact disks, which can store far more information than 'floppies'. However, the disadvantage to this type of drive is that it can only read CDs – you cannot use it to write on a CD.
DVD drives	Another type of storage device which is becoming more common. DVDs (Digital Versatile Discs) are the same size as compact disks and look very similar but they can hold even more data. The same disadvantage applies to this drive as the CD-ROM drive in that you can only use it to read DVDs – you cannot use it to write to a DVD.
CD writers	This is a special type of drive that allows you to write information onto a CD. With a CD writer, you can transfer files to a recordable CD. There are two types of recordable CD: ♦ one that can only be used once (CD-R) ♦ the more costly alternative that can be used many times (CD-RW).
DVD writers	This is a special type of drive that allows you to write information onto a DVD. They are still expensive at the moment, so they are not yet commonly used.
Modems	A 'modulator/demodulator' (modem for short) allows your computer to connect to a telephone line so that you can send faxes and emails or browse the World Wide Web. A modem can either be an external box that connects between your system unit and the telephone line or, more commonly these days, it can be a piece of electronic circuitry that sits inside the case of your system unit.
Scanners	A scanner operates rather like a photocopier in that you place a picture on a flat glass 'bed' and scan the image into your computer. You can then change the image using a photo-manipulation program.

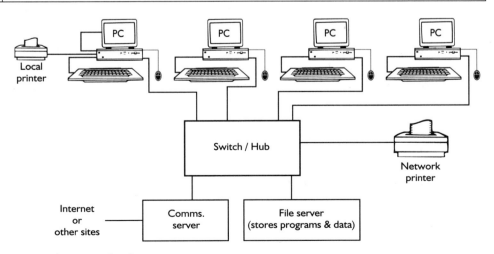

A typical networked computer system

How computers work

In simple terms:

♦ you tell the computer what to do whenever you provide input by typing in a command or clicking on an icon

♦ the software installed on the computer allows it to perform certain types of activities

♦ the hardware processes the commands that it receives from the software, and performs tasks or calculations.

Initially, you provide the computer with input when you turn it on, this results in the system software telling the processing circuitry to start up certain programs and to turn on some hardware devices so that they are ready for more input from you. This whole process is called **booting up**.

The next step happens when you choose the program that you want to use. You click on the icon or enter a command to start the program. Let's use the example of an Internet browser. Once the program has started, it is ready for your instructions. You either enter an address or click on an address that you saved earlier. In either case, the computer now knows what you want it to do. The browser software then goes out to find that address, starting up other hardware devices, such as a modem, when it needs them. If it is able to find the correct address, the browser will then tell your computer to send the information from the web page over the telephone line to your computer. Eventually, you will see the website that you were looking for.

If you decide that you want to print the page, you click on the printer icon. Again, you have provided input to tell the computer what to do. The browser software then determines whether you have a printer attached to your computer or not and whether it is turned on. If the printer is not switched on, it will remind you to turn the printer on. It will then send the information about the web page from your computer over the cable to the printer, where it is printed out.

How computers store data

There are three distinct forms of data storage used in all computers:

♦ Random Access Memory (RAM)
♦ the computer's hard drive
♦ external storage media, such as floppy disks, CD-ROMs, etc.

Random Access Memory

RAM is a form of temporary storage, it only stores data whilst you are actually working on it. When you switch off your computer everything that is held in the RAM memory is lost.

The computer's hard drive

The computer's hard drive is a magnetic storage medium that is made up of a series of spinning disks. A small drive head moves across the surface of the disks to locate the data. When you switch off your computer, the hard disk retains any information that has been stored so that when you switch your computer back on again the data that you stored will be unaltered.

External storage media

Some of the different external storage media devices which are currently in use, like floppy disks and CD-ROMs, were considered on page 281.

All these type of storage media have several common characteristics:

♦ like the computer's own hard drive, these are permanent storage devices – the data stored on these devices is retained when your computer is switched off
♦ unlike the computer's own hard drive, these devices are portable – they can be removed from the media drive and taken away. You can therefore use these type of devices to transport data from one computer system to another
♦ you need to have the correct media drive fitted to your computer for it to be able to read the data stored on that type of storage medium.

The main difference between these types of storage media, other than appearance, is in the amount of data they can hold.

The size of a data storage device is described in terms of how many **bytes** of data it can hold. A byte is the memory needed to store a single character or number. As most storage devices are capable of storing lots of bytes, you will often hear a number of terms used to describe multiples of bytes – the commonest ones are shown in the table below, along with just how many bytes they equate to.

Term used	Its common abbreviation	The number of bytes
Kilobyte	K, KB or Kb	1,000 – one thousand
Megabyte	M, MB, Mb or meg	1,000,000 – one million
Gigabyte	G, GB, Gb or gig	1,000,000,000 – one billion
Terabyte	T, TB, Tb or tera	1,000,000,000,000 – one trillion

The amount of data each of the most common types of data storage device can hold is given in the table below.

Type of storage medium	Its volume	The number of bytes it can hold
Floppy disk	1.4MB	1,400,000
Zip 100	100MB	100,000,000
Zip 250	250MB	250,000,000
CD-ROM	650–700MB	650,000,000 – 700,000,000
DVD	5.2GB	5,200,000,000

Although floppy disks are cheap, and have been commonly used in the past, they are being used less and less now because they hold such a small amount of data compared to other storage devices.

Check it out

Find out about how data are stored within the computer system(s) used in your company.

♦ What types of data storage devices are used by your company and how much data do they hold?

How to start up your computer

Before you operate the power switch, make sure that your monitor is switched on and that there is no disk in the floppy disk drive. Now turn on your computer's power switch. After a few seconds, your operating system will start to boot up – the technical term for starting up the operating system.

If you try to start up your computer when a disk has accidentally been left in the floppy disk drive, you will get a rather confusing error message that reads '*Invalid system disk*'. The message then reads '*Replace the disk, and then press any key*'. If you eject the disk from the drive and then press any key on the keyboard your computer will now boot up as normal.

Logging on to the computer

Logging on is the process of identifying yourself to the computer by giving your user name and password. This process identifies you as an authorised user and helps maintain security.

The first thing that you will see when you boot up is the main screen of your operating system, followed shortly by a box that asks you for a user name and password. As the majority of computer systems within call centres are currently running Microsoft's Windows NT4 software, we shall use this operating system to illustrate our examples.

You will now need to type in your user name and password in the Logon Information dialogue box. If you have not yet been given a user name or password, you will need to contact your system administrator and ask them to set you up as a user. They will set up your user name and password when they establish your user account.

Your password is a security measure that stops unauthorised users accessing your computer. A password can contain up to 14 characters and can include uppercase and lowercase letters. Although your password will initially be set by your system administrator, you will probably be asked to change it periodically as an additional security precaution.

Now that you are logged on to the computer, you will be able to open any of the programs that you are allowed to access.

How do I open the program that I want to use?

Use your mouse to click on the 田 **Start** button in the bottom left hand corner of your screen. When you have done this, a menu will pop up.

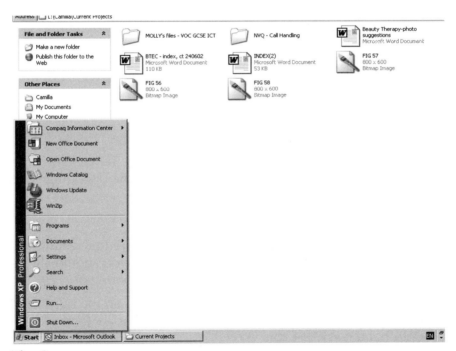

The Start menu

If you now select the **Programs** option by clicking on it with your mouse, a further menu opens (as shown overleaf) which shows a list of the programs which are available to you.

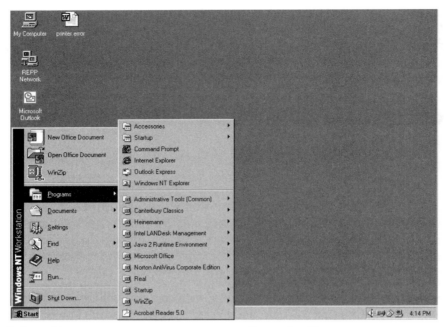

Select the program you want to open from the Programs menu

You can now select the program that you wish to open by clicking on it with your mouse. The program that you have selected will now be started and will open on your screen ready for your next command.

It is possible to have more than one program running at a time, so you do not need to close a program down before you can open another one. However, unless you need to have several programs open at once, it is always best to shut your current program down when you have finished using it, as your computer will run faster if you do not keep open programs that you are not using.

How to shut down your computer

You should always close down any programs that you may have running and shut down your computer (this closes down the operating system) before you switch it off.

How do I close a program?

When you have finished working within your selected program, you should close it down. However, before you do so, you should always make sure that you save anything that you have been working on.

To close a program down, use your mouse to click on the right hand button (the cross) of the bank of three buttons that are located at the very top right hand corner of your screen.

If you have forgotten to save your work before you do this, the computer will remind you to save your work by opening a dialogue box which asks you if you want to save your work before it closes down the program. If you select the **Yes** button by clicking on it with your mouse, your work will be saved before the program is closed down.

Shutting down your computer

To shut down your computer, after you have closed any programs that you have had open, click on the ⊞**Start** button in the bottom left hand corner of your screen. When you have done this, a menu will pop up. You now need to select the **Shut Down** option by clicking on it with your mouse. The Shut Down Windows dialogue box will now open, as shown below.

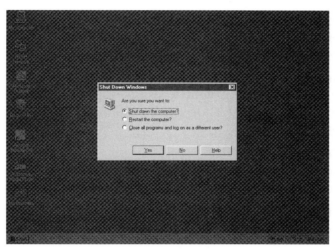

The Shut Down Windows dialogue box

The **Shut Down** option will normally be selected – if it is not, just click on it with your mouse and then click on OK. It is very unlikely that you will ever want to choose one of the other options.

A message appears on your screen to tell you that your computer is shutting down and warns you not to switch your computer off. A second message then lets you know when you can safely switch off your computer.

You can now operate the power switch on your computer and turn it off. Remember to make sure that your monitor is also switched off.

How to use a mouse

Practise holding and moving your mouse until it becomes second nature

Don't worry if you have never used a mouse before – in no time at all it will become second nature. Most right-handed people use both hands for typing on the keyboard and use their right hand to shift between using the keyboard and navigating using the mouse. It is standard practice to hold the mouse loosely between your thumb and third finger as this leaves your first and second fingers free to click on the mouse buttons.

You should always use your mouse on a flat, clean surface – specially made mouse mats with a hard plastic surface and soft foam underside are ideal.

The buttons on your mouse

Although mice come in a variety of styles, they generally have at least two buttons, which are located on the top at the front of the mouse. The 'primary' button is normally on the left and the 'secondary' button is on the right.

If you are left-handed, it is possible to use the operating system to swap these buttons round. You may wish to approach your system administrator and ask them to do this for you if you intend to use your mouse with your left hand.

Operating your mouse

By combining the movements of the mouse with clicking or holding down either of the buttons, just a few of the things that you can do are:

◆ activate objects
◆ move objects around
◆ select options from menus
◆ draw graphics.

With just six basic manoeuvres, you can make your mouse do just about anything short of typing in text. You will need to be familiar with each of these movements if you are going to be able to use your mouse effectively.

The box below describes each of the six basic movements – practise these until they become second nature and you can make each of the moves without having to think about it.

The six basic mouse movements

1 **Point:** this is rather like 'taking aim' with your mouse. You move it around so that the pointer is 'touching' an object on the screen.

2 **Click:** press and release the primary mouse button while pointing at an object on the screen.

3 **Double-click:** press and release the primary mouse button twice in quick succession while pointing at an object on the screen.

4 **Right-click:** press and release the secondary mouse button while pointing at an object on the screen.

5 **Drag-and-drop:** Press and hold down the primary mouse button while pointing at an object on the screen. You can then drag the object to a new location and drop it in place by releasing the mouse button.

6 **Right-drag:** as drag-and-drop but holding down the secondary mouse button.

A possibly confusing aspect about using a mouse for the first time is understanding that the position where the mouse is pointing on a screen has (in most cases) nothing to do with the place where text will appear if you were to start typing on the keyboard. This is because the mouse pointer is *not* the same thing as the cursor. If you point and *click* in the middle of a text document, then the cursor will move to that point – text will then appear at that position when you start to type.

How to use your mouse safely

If you are going to be spending a lot of time using a mouse, you need to be aware of the risk of repetitive strain injury, which can result from long term use. Long periods of clutching and dragging with mice can slowly accumulate damage to the body. This subject has been covered in detail in Unit 25, page 77. So we will just summarise the main points that you need to bear in mind here.

Tips for using your mouse safely

1 Make sure that your mouse is within easy reach so that your elbow can remain next to your side when you are using it.

2 Adjust the height of your chair so that your keyboard and mouse are at or below elbow height – if you use a mouse mat, remember to take its thickness into account when you make any height adjustments.

3 Hold your wrist in a neutral position (relaxed and straight), as this reduces the risk of a problem occurring due to overuse as your muscles are using the minimum amount of effort.

4 Avoid placing or supporting your wrists on sharp edges or on your desktop.

5 Try to avoid becoming stressed, as this can cause increased muscle tension and also generally sensitises the nervous system, which can increase your ability to perceive pain. Dealing with stress is covered in detail in Unit 25, page 83.

Remember, damage is more likely to occur if poor body posture is adopted as this can place unnecessary stress on the tendons and nerves in the hand, wrist, arms and even the shoulders and neck. Also, lack of adequate rest and breaks can further increase the risk of injury.

Cleaning your mouse

You will find that, from time to time, your mouse will not run as smoothly as it has done in the past. This is usually due to a build up of fluff or crumbs on the rubber ball in the base of your mouse as it has a tendency to gather bits of debris as it is used, which build up over time. If you find that your mouse is not rolling as well as it should, it is probably an indication that it is time to clean the rubber ball in the base of your mouse.

To clean the ball in your mouse:

1 First shut down your computer system.

2 Turn your mouse upside down – you will normally see something that looks rather like a rubber ball protruding from the bottom of your mouse. You need to remove this rubber ball – it is usually held in by a plastic panel, which should drop out if rotated. Look for any symbols on the plastic casing near to the ball which show that the panel can be rotated and which direction to rotate it.

3 Rotate the plastic panel which keeps the ball in place – both the ball and the panel should then come away.

4 Rub the ball around between your palms. This will remove any debris and fluff that has stuck to the ball, which is what stops it from rolling smoothly in your mouse.

5 Now give the ball a good blow to remove any debris that has become loose.

6 You also need to clean the little rollers that you should be able to see inside the hole in the base of your mouse where the ball normally sits as they can often pick up debris too – you should be able to do this by blowing hard into the hole.

7 Put the ball back into the base of the mouse, place the plastic panel back over the top and rotate it in the opposite direction until it locks.

8 You can now switch your computer back on and try your mouse out. Hopefully, it should now run smoothly again. If it is still not running smoothly, it is possible that it was very dirty and you may need to repeat the procedure again.

If your mouse still does not roll smoothly, it is possible that it could be damaged. If you suspect that it is, then you will need to report it as faulty.

Try it out

Take your mouse apart and clean it.

Keys to good practice

✓ Before you switch on your computer, make sure that the floppy disk drive is empty.

✓ Make sure that you commit your user name and password to memory.

✓ Keep your mouse clean and free of debris.

✓ Close down any programs that you are finished with as it improves the efficiency of your computer.

✓ Remember to save your work before you close a program down.

✓ Always close down all open programs before you shut down your computer.

✓ Make sure you shut your computer down before you switch it off.

Health and safety issues

WHAT YOU NEED TO KNOW OR LEARN

◆ The effect of the Health and Safety (Display Screen Equipment) Regulations 1992

◆ How to minimise the possibility of personal injury when using computer equipment long term.

The effect of the Health and Safety (Display Screen Equipment) Regulations 1992

If you spend most of your working day using a computer, then this piece of legislation is particularly relevant to you. The provisions contained within the Health and Safety (Display Screen Equipment) Regulations 1992 exist to help make display screen work safer and more comfortable.

The Health and Safety (Display Screen Equipment) Regulations 1992 set out six obligations that all employers have towards users of display screen equipment.

Your employer must:

1 Assess the risks arising from the use of display screen workstations and take steps to reduce them to the **lowest extent reasonably practicable**.

2 Ensure that any new workstations installed meet the minimum ergonomic standards that are set out in the regulations.

3 Inform users about the results of the assessments, any actions that the employer is taking and the users' entitlements under the regulations.

4 Plan display screen work so that users are provided with regular breaks or changes of activity.

5 Offer eye tests before display screen use, at regular intervals and if the user is experiencing visual problems. If the eye test shows that they are necessary, and normal reading glasses are unsuitable, the employer must pay for basic prescription glasses for display screen work.

6 Provide appropriate health and safety training for users before display screen use or whenever a workstation is **suitably modified**.

It is important that you understand the possible health implications that may be associated with working with a computer all day long. You should actively take precautions to minimise any risks there may be to your well being.

We will be covering the basic precautions that you should take to minimise the possibility of personal injury when using computer equipment long term in the next section. If you require more detail, the health and safety issues in general, and the Display Screen Equipment Regulations in particular, are covered in detail in Unit 25, in the section on 'Monitor and maintain health and safety in the workplace', which starts on page 69.

How to minimise the possibility of personal injury when using computer equipment long term

Think about it

♦ What risks to your health and well being do you think that there may be when you spend many hours of the day (or night) using a computer?
♦ Are you currently doing anything to minimise these risks?

The main health and safety risks associated with working on a computer for long periods at a time are work-related upper limb disorders (also sometimes referred to as repetitive strain injury or RSI) and eye strain. RSI and visual fatigue are covered in detail in Unit 25. You may wish to review these sections (see page 77).

It is the duty of your employer to make sure that any potential health risks are minimised by controlling and optimising your working environment, remember that you are also personally responsible for minimising those risks.

You need to make sure that your working environment is suitably tailored to your personal needs by adjusting your workstation. You need to pay particular attention to the adjustment and positioning of your:

◆ chair and footrest
◆ display screen equipment
◆ microphone.

These things are particularly important if your organisation uses '**hot-desking**' – where workstations are not assigned to individuals so you may end up sitting at a different workstation each day.

If you are required to work in this way, then you must ensure that you adjust each new workstation to meet your physical needs. This will help to minimise any risks there may be to your physical well being. You can use the checklist below to remind you about the adjustments that you may need to make.

Workstation checklist

1 Adjust the height of your chair so that your keyboard and mouse are at or below elbow height.

2 Your keyboard and your monitor should be directly in front of you with your mouse next to it. Make sure that your mouse is within easy reach so that your elbow can remain next to your side when you are using it.

3 The top of your monitor should be at eye level, as when your eyes are relaxed, your natural viewing angle is a downward gaze of about 15° below the horizontal. Therefore if you position the monitor so that your eyes are level with the top of it, providing it is the correct distance away, you will naturally focus on the middle of the screen.

4 It is recommended that you should be about 400mm away from your monitor and you should take breaks away from the screen every 45–60 minutes to prevent the onset of visual fatigue, during which time you should refocus your eyes on a distant object for a few minutes.

5 Make sure that your feet are well supported and that your shoulders are relaxed.

6 Use a document holder to hold any documents that you need whilst typing close to the monitor to reduce frequent head turning and changing of eye focus.

7 Place the materials on your desk in accordance with how frequently you use them. Make sure that the things you use most frequently are closest to you and put materials that you use occasionally no farther than an arm's length away. Things that you use infrequently can be placed further away, but still consider convenience.

A picture of a properly set up workstation is shown on page 77.

Keys to good practice

✓ Make sure that you take advantage of your employer's obligation to pay for eye tests by having your eyes tested at regular intervals.

✓ Always adjust your workstation to suit your needs.

✓ Ensure that you are fully aware of the symptoms and causes of RSI and that you take adequate precautions to avoid it.

Data and equipment protection issues

♦ How to store and back up data
♦ Why the Data Protection Act exists and the effect it has
♦ Your organisation's procedures for maintaining the security and confidentiality of data
♦ How to safeguard your computer equipment and data against damage
♦ How to report faults in your computer system
♦ The Computer Misuse Act 1990

How to store and back up data

In the earlier section on how computers store data, (page 282), we briefly looked at the different types of computer storage. You will remember that Random Access Memory (RAM) is where the computer stores what you are working on and also that when you switch off your computer, everything that is held in RAM is lost.

You must therefore make sure that you always save your work to the computer's hard drive before you shut your computer down as anything stored on the hard drive is retained when your computer is switched off.

The reason for the different types of memory is to do with speed. Unlike hard disk memory, RAM is not accessed by mechanical means – it is a microchip on a circuit board. This means that it can read and write information many, many times faster. When you run a program, although the program is stored on the hard disk, its functions are performed in RAM – this is the only way that your computer can work so quickly.

If you understand the difference between these two forms of memory, then you will understand the golden rule of computing.

Did you know?

The golden rule of computing is **do not forget to save your work!**

When you save a file, the program takes the work that you have done since the last time that you saved the file and stores it safely on the computer's hard drive. You therefore need to get into the habit of saving your work regularly. Then, if you were to have a power failure or the system were to crash, your work would not be lost because you could call it back up from the hard drive. You should make a habit of saving files about every 10 minutes or so, or when you have completed a tedious task that you could not bear to have to do all over again.

There are several ways of saving a file. You can:

♦ click on the **save** icon (the floppy disk symbol)
♦ choose **File** and then **Save** or
♦ hold down **CTRL** and press **S**.

When you save a file for the first time, a dialogue box appears (as shown below) which invites you to give the file a name. So the first time that you save, you do two things at once – you save your work and you name your file. Filenames can be 255 characters long and can include numbers, characters and blank spaces. However, the following characters cannot be part of a file name / ? : * " < > or |.

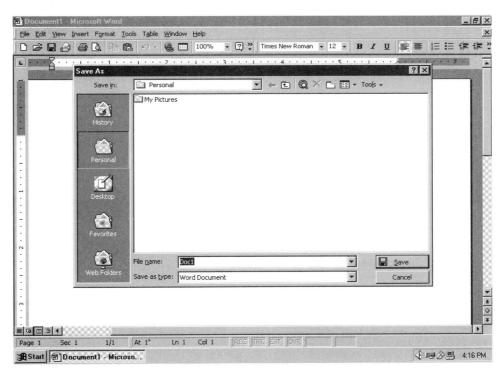

The computer will always remind you to save your work

How safe is my hard drive?
Like anything mechanical, it is possible that your hard drive could stop working at some point or that your computer could break down. The data stored on the hard disk could then be trapped inside and might never be seen again.

This leads us on to the second rule of computing.

Did you know?

The second rule of computing is always to make a **copy** of your work away from your hard disk!

This process is called **backing up**. As well as storing your work on your hard drive, you should always make at least one copy of it on another medium, such as a floppy disk or CD-ROM, which you should keep in a safe place where nothing can harm it.

Case study 1 – Gheeta's experiences

At Direct Communications, our database systems are backed up by our Database Administrator on a daily basis. Several generations of back-up are kept, which means that we do not just keep writing over the same back-up copy each time. We do this so that if anything goes wrong while we are making a new back-up we do not risk losing our only back-up copy. The back-ups are then kept in a fireproof safe as an extra precaution.

Although our IT Department is responsible for backing up our database systems, each of us is also individually responsible for backing up our own work. For example, if we send out a letter to a customer, we are expected to save the letter to our hard drive and also save a back-up copy on the file server.

1 Why is it good practice to make more than one generation of back-up copy?
2 What other precautions do Direct Communications take to safeguard their back-up copies?

Many organisations have set procedures for backing up computer files and sometimes whole computer systems.

Check it out

Find out if your organisation has a set of procedures that you are expected to follow with regard to backing up files or computer systems.

♦ What are your responsibilities are far as backing up data is concerned?
♦ How often are back-ups made?
♦ How many generations of back-up are kept and for how long?

Why the Data Protection Act exists and the effect it has

More and more organisations now use computers to store and process **personal data** gathered about people (**data subjects**), such as their:

♦ name and address
♦ financial history
♦ credit rating
♦ criminal record.

The Data Protection Act was brought in as a response to concerns about who has access to this information and whether it is accurate and kept up to date. The Act gives rights to data subjects and exists to protect their privacy.

It is very likely that your organisation collects and uses personal data and that you may well be involved in the processing of those data. Your organisation will also have laid down procedures that govern the way that you work. However, it is important that you have a good overall understanding of the Data Protection Act and can appreciate the constraints it places on the way your organisation can operate.

The Data Protection Act 1998 came into force on 1 March 2000. It applies to the **processing** (which includes collecting, using, disclosing, destroying or holding data) of computerised **personal data** (data that can be associated with identifiable living individuals – it can include facts and opinions about an individual) and personal data held in structured manual files.

Any organisation (data user) that wants to store personal information is required to register with the **Data Protection Commissioner** and must follow the **Data Protection Principles**. The Data Protection Commissioner has the right to inspect an organisation's computer systems to ensure that they are complying with the Act.

The principles of data protection state that the data user must ensure that the information is:

♦ obtained fairly and lawfully
♦ kept accurate and up to date
♦ surrounded by proper security
♦ only used for the registered purpose.

Data subjects have the right to:

♦ see the information stored about themselves
♦ have the data corrected if it is wrong
♦ claim compensation in some cases.

The Data Protection Act is covered in more detail in Unit 2, page 148.

We will now look at an example of how the Data Protection Act can affect the way someone carries out their job role.

Case study 2 – Melanie's experiences

I work for Direct Communications as a sales advisor. I regularly handle enquiries from customers who wish to receive cable television services over their telephone line. It is my job to answer any questions that the customer may have about our services, including how they work, how much they cost and how quickly they can be installed.

I usually run through all the options with the client whilst they are on the line, in case they have any questions that they want to ask. I then take down all their personal details so that I can arrange to have an information pack sent out to them that they can look through at their leisure. Because of the Data Protection Act, when I ask the customer for their details, I also have to ask the client if they would like to receive information from other areas of the company, such as special offers, or if I can pass their information on to another company. I then normally repeat the customer's personal details back to them to check that I have taken them down correctly.

It is company policy not to pressurise the caller for a sale when they initially contact us with an enquiry, as the caller often wants to discuss the options available with their partner before they make a decision. We find that high pressure sales tactics just turn the customer off and lose us sales.

I then make a follow up call to the client about a week later to check that they have received the information pack and to ask them if they require any further assistance.

1 Does Melanie take steps to ensure that she records the customer's personal details correctly?
2 How does Melanie make the customer aware of how their personal data will be used by Direct Communications?
3 Do you think that the customer will feel satisfied that they have control over the way that Direct Communications uses their personal data?

Your organisation's procedures for maintaining the security and confidentiality of data

Information is an asset just like any other important business asset and it needs to be protected. Keeping information secure helps to:

◆ minimise business damage
◆ maximise return on investment and business opportunity
◆ ensure business continuity.

However, many companies still fail to protect information properly and the risk of data being lost, corrupted, disclosed or stolen is growing.

Did you know?

Last year, one business in every five was a victim of computer crime.

Check it out

♦ What information does your organisation hold?
♦ How is it held?
♦ What is it used for?
♦ Who has access to it?
♦ What steps does your organisation take to keep information confidential and secure?
♦ How is information kept confidential?
♦ What is your contribution to the security and confidentiality of information?

How to safeguard your computer equipment and data against damage

Keep your workstation clean

In the earlier section on Cleaning your mouse (see page 291) we saw how your mouse can become clogged up with fluff and crumbs as it is used. You therefore need to keep your working area clean and free of crumbs and debris.

Some companies do not allow computer users to eat or drink at their desk because of the possibility that this could cause damage to the company's computer systems.

Check it out

Does your organisation let you eat and drink at your desk?

If you should ever accidentally spill tea or coffee on the computer keyboard you should:

♦ shut down your computer and turn it off
♦ mop up as much of the fluid as possible
♦ turn your keyboard over so that any liquid trapped in it gets a chance to drain out
♦ report the problem to the appropriate authority.

Shut your computer down correctly

Always make sure that you follow the standard shutdown procedure (as discussed on page 288) when you have finished using your computer. Never just be tempted to turn it off without closing it down properly as this could cause data loss or corruption and may even damage the hard drive.

If you are faced with the worst case scenario and your computer crashes so that turning off your computer proves to be the only way to shut down, wait half a minute before turning your computer back on to allow the hard disk to stop spinning.

Avoid the possibility of introducing a computer virus

A computer virus is a program that is designed to cause harm to someone else's computer. Viruses are written by malicious programmers who wish to cause problems for other computer users.

It is possible to 'catch' a virus by:

♦ putting an infected disk into your computer – a virus can automatically copy itself from the infected disk into your computer
♦ downloading infected files from the Internet
♦ using software that has been obtained from an unreliable source.

There is usually no evidence of the presence of the virus and you will often not be aware of it until something goes wrong. The extent of the damage that can be caused by viruses varies and there are thousands of viruses in existence. Some virus damage is insignificant but inconvenient, whilst the damage caused by others can be disastrous and can put computer systems out of action.

Fortunately, it is possible to avoid the introduction of viruses by taking a few precautions, such as:

♦ write-protecting disks
♦ using virus checking software – anti-virus software can inspect disks to check for viruses and remove them before they can cause any harm
♦ not allowing other users to use their own disks on your system
♦ not allowing users to take company disks home to use on their own home computers
♦ avoiding software from unreliable sources
♦ only downloading files from reputable Internet sites.

Check it out

Find out what precautions your organisation takes to avoid the introduction of viruses. For example, does your organisation use anti-virus software?

♦ Does your organisation have a set of procedures that staff are expected to follow so that the introduction of viruses is avoided?

How to report faults in your computer system

If you suspect that your computer system may be faulty because it displays an error message, make sure that you write down what the message says as this could help to solve the problem.

Most organisations have set procedures that their staff are expected to follow when reporting suspected faults. You need to find out how your organisation wants you to react and to whom you are supposed to report faults.

Check it out

♦ Does your organisation have a procedure that you are expected to follow when reporting faults in your computer system? If it does, make a note of it or, if it is detailed, write down where it can be found.

You should also note down who you are expected to report faults to and their contact details.

Keys to good practice

✓ Do not forget to save your work.

✓ Always make a back-up copy of your work and keep it in a safe place.

✓ Make sure that you understand why the Data Protection Act exists and the effects of this Act.

✓ Always keep your workstation clean.

✓ Make sure that you always shut your computer down properly.

✓ Avoid introducing computer viruses.

✓ If you suspect that your computer may be faulty, make sure that you report this promptly to the appropriate authority.

11.1 Enter information into a computer system

WHAT YOU NEED TO KNOW OR LEARN

♦ How to access the appropriate computer system and enter data accurately

♦ How to report your inability to meet any deadlines for inputting data.

How to access the appropriate computer system and enter data accurately

The type of computer system used varies from one organisation to another, as does the level of security involved, so it is not possible for this section to give you specific instructions on how to use your company's systems – we can only point you in the right direction.

Check it out

♦ Does your organisation have a procedure that you are expected to follow when accessing your company's computer system in order to enter data? If it does, make a note of it or, if it is detailed, write down where it can be found.

♦ Do you need a user name and password to be able to gain access to your company's computer system?

♦ Do you know what they are?

♦ Does your organisation have a procedure that you are expected to follow when entering data into your company's computer system?

♦ Does your organisation have a set procedure to identify and correct any errors there may be in the data that you have entered in your company's computer system?

♦ Is there a procedure that you are expected to follow when storing data in your company's computer system?

♦ Is there a procedure for exiting your company's computer system?

Again, make a note of all these procedures or, if they are detailed, write down where they can be found.

How to report your inability to meet any deadlines for inputting data

You need to make sure that you know what you are expected to do if you are unable to meet any deadlines that you have been set for inputting data.

Check it out

♦ Does your organisation have a procedure that you are expected to follow if you are unable to meet specified deadlines when inputting data into your company's computer system? If it does, make a note of it or, if it is detailed, write down where it can be found.

Keys to good practice

✓ Make sure that you know your user name and password and that you know how to access the correct computer system.

✓ Ensure that you are familiar with your organisation's procedures for entering data accurately and that you know how and where to store it.

✓ Also make sure that you report any inability to meet set data entry deadlines.

11.2 Retrieve information from a computer system

WHAT YOU NEED TO KNOW OR LEARN

♦ How to use the appropriate computer system to locate and retrieve existing data
♦ How to amend or delete existing data
♦ How to report your inability to retrieve data within specified timescales.

The type of computer system used varies from one organisation to another, as does the level of security involved, so again it is not possible to give you specific instructions on how to use your company's systems.

How to use the appropriate computer system to locate and retrieve existing data

Check it out

♦ Does your organisation have a procedure that you are expected to follow when you need to find and retrieve existing data? If it does, make a note of it or, if it is detailed, write down where it can be found.

How to amend or delete existing data

Check it out

♦ Does your organisation have a procedure that you are expected to follow when you need to amend or delete existing data? If it does, make a note of it or, if it is detailed, write down where it can be found.

How to report your inability to retrieve data within specified timescales

Check it out

♦ Does your organisation have a procedure that you are expected to follow if you are unable to locate and retrieve data within specified timescales? If it does, make a note of it or, if it is detailed, write down where it can be found.

The Computer Misuse Act 1990

The Computer Misuse Act 1990 came into force on the 1st of September 1990 as a result of the concern that the computer hacking (accessing a computer without the owner's permission) was becoming a widespread problem.

The Computer Misuse Act introduced three new criminal offences:

1 *unauthorised access to computer material*
  This offence means that it is illegal to access a computer system unless you are authorised to do so – it therefore makes the activity of hacking a crime. It also means that it is an offence for any legitimate computer user (such as an employee), who may have limited authorisation to use a computer system, to knowingly exceed that authority. This includes the use of another person's ID and password to gain access to a computer, data or programs.

2 *unauthorised access to a computer system with intent to commit or facilitate the commission of a further offence*
  This offence covers a range of situations. For example, gaining access to someone's bank account and re-directing the funds into your own account.

3 *unauthorised modification of computer material*
  This offence covers the deliberate deletion of data or corruption of programs, including the intentional introduction of viruses.

Keys to good practice

✓ If your organisation has more than one computer system, make sure that you know which system you should use to find any particular data and that you know how to access it.

✓ Make sure that you are familiar with your organisation's procedures for locating and retrieving data.

✓ Ensure that you report any inability to retrieve data within specified timescales.

✓ Also make sure that you are familiar with your organisation's procedures for amending or deleting existing data.

Check your knowledge

1 Name five items of computer hardware.
2 List two advantages of a computer network.
3 What are the three forms of data storage used in all computers?
4 Which kind of external data storage device holds the most amount of data?
5 What is 'logging on'?
6 How many obligations do employers have towards users of display screen equipment?
7 Why do you need to make sure that your workstation is suitably tailored to your personal needs?
8 Why should you save your work?
9 Why must we create back ups?
10 Why was the Data Protection Act brought into existence?
11 Why does data need to be kept secure?
12 List three ways that you can safeguard your computer equipment and data against damage.
13 If you think that your computer equipment is faulty, who should you report it to?
14 Do you know your user name and password?

UNIT 17 Process telephone calls

This option units is primarily for people working in front office reception areas, but it may also have applications in some call handling facilities. It is all about processing incoming and outgoing telephone calls with respect to their priority and sensitivity. It is also about reporting faults that occur in the telephone equipment.

This unit has three elements:

♦ receive telephone calls
♦ make telephone calls
♦ report faults in telephone equipment.

After you have completed this unit, you will be able to:

♦ handle calls efficiently, by identifying the callers, establishing their needs and meeting their needs
♦ identify and respond to calls with different priorities
♦ identify problems and find ways to overcome them
♦ make telephone calls, having prepared well beforehand
♦ identify types of sensitive information and take appropriate actions to safeguard such information
♦ recognise common faults in telephone equipment
♦ assess the priority to be given to a fault in the telephone equipment and report the faults to the appropriate authority in line with the service level agreement
♦ implement appropriate contingency plans to maintain communications if a fault occurs to the telephone equipment.

The case studies in this chapter have been based on a fictitious organisation called 'Rayner Engineering'. Examples from other sectors such as an office supplies company, insurance and telemarketing will be covered in other chapters.

A receptionist is the interface between the callers and the people who work in the organisation

17.1 Receive telephone calls

Working in the front office reception area you are the interface between the callers and the people who work in the area you front. The reception area could be in a small dental practice or doctor's surgery, or be part of a large organisation. The people involved could include everyone from general workers, through to the chief executive or chairman of the organisation and the professionals of the practices. You will be required to handle calls for all of these people, therefore the way in which you answer the calls and introduce yourself not only reflects on you but also on the people who work in the area you front.

The type of calls that you could handle may include:

♦ calls to the people you front directly
♦ calls from people asking to make an appointment to see the people you front.

The types of callers you are likely to deal with will depend on the type of organisation you work for. If you work for a dental practice or doctor's surgery the callers could be the patients or the general public. But if you work for a large organisation the callers could well be a mirror image of the people employed by the organisation. For example, callers who ask to speak to the chairman are usually in the same position within another organisation. It is possible that some of the callers will be employees of the organisation who are working away from the office, which could include the chairman.

WHAT YOU NEED TO KNOW OR LEARN

♦ How to answer incoming telephone calls
♦ How to identify callers and establish their needs
♦ The importance of maintaining confidentiality
♦ How to respond to calls with different priorities
♦ How to transfer calls
♦ The types of problems that may be encountered
♦ Ways of overcoming some of the problems that may be encountered.

How to answer incoming telephone calls

Unit 1 explained that how you answered a call was in fact an introduction to the organisation and to yourself. Remember that your introduction might be the first contact that the caller has with your organisation.

You are the interface between the people you represent within your organisation and the caller. Unlike most call centre agents who own a call from its receipt to its end, you have the responsibility of answering the call, identifying the caller and their requirements, and then either transferring the call to the appropriate person or making arrangements for them. In such situations, how do you answer incoming calls?

The basic requirements for answering incoming calls are:

♦ the call is answered promptly
♦ your voice is clear
♦ your introduction is positive, clear and concise
♦ you project an air of confidence.

Where possible all calls should be answered promptly, as delays can build up resentment and frustrations within the caller. It is very annoying to wait and listen to the ringing tone, particularly if the caller has other important things to do. From your point of view, you have no idea how important or urgent the call may be until it is answered. It could be the company chairman or chief executive wanting to speak to the department head urgently before going into a meeting or it could be the office cleaner ringing to report that he is ill and unable to report for work. A caller ringing a call centre may well hang up and take their business elsewhere if the call is not answered immediately. But the caller who has no option but to speak to a person within the organisation, is very likely to make adverse comments to that person if the call is not answered in a reasonable time. Your lack of promptness in answering a call might have dire consequences for you.

Whenever you answer a call your voice should be clear and the words unmuffled so that the caller can clearly hear what you have to say. You should ensure that you are not consuming food or drink when you are required to answer a call as this is unacceptable practice. You should also ensure that any background noise is kept to a minimum as it can adversely affect the caller's hearing ability. Where noise is present and is unavoidable, and is likely to be heard by the caller, then you should explain the circumstances and apologise.

When answering a call your introduction should be clear, concise and positive. The caller wants to know that they have called the right number without listening to a long drawn out speech about the organisation and its business. The caller wants to know that the person who has answered the call is there to help them.

The caller will also need to be assured that you know what you are doing and are in a position to take whatever action is required. This can best be achieved by projecting an air of confidence; that is not to say that you are supremely confident at all times, but you give the impression you are.

There are many ways you can answer a call and here are a few examples:

♦ *'Good morning, Zebra Communications, how may I help you?'*
♦ *'Zebra Communications, good morning, how may I help you?'*
♦ *'Thank you for calling Zebra Communications, Linda speaking, how may I help you?'*
♦ *'Zebra Communications, Linda speaking, how may I help you?'*

As you can see, all of these introductions are basically the same; they all introduce the organisation, some introduce the person answering the call, they all greet the caller, and they all end on a positive note by asking how they can help.

Some organisations will expect you to give your name to create a friendly atmosphere, while others prefer you to remain anonymous. Some will expect you to use a salutation and others won't; but they will all expect you to ask how you can help. It is probable that your organisation will have guidelines or instructions on how you answer and greet callers.

Check it out

Find out how your organisation expects you to answer calls and greet the caller.

♦ Do you have written guidelines or instructions?
♦ Does your organisation have a preferred greeting you are expected to use when answering calls?

Whether your organisation gives you guidelines to follow on how you answer calls or whether you have designed your own, your organisation will always expect you to be professional with your introduction.

How to identify callers and establish their needs

How you identify the caller will depend very much on the callers themselves; most people will automatically give their name when you ask how you can help, but a few will always wait to be asked. If the caller's name is not forthcoming then it is better to ask for it at an early stage as this will help draw them directly into the conversation. It will also allow you to personalise the call by directing any comments and questions to them by name.

Whenever the caller gives you their name, always be in a position to note it down, so that you do not need to ask for it to be repeated because you have forgotten. It is also good practice to ask if the caller would spell it for you in order to avoid any embarrassment or confusion later.

There will be situations where you may need to obtain more information than just the name of the caller. If, for example, you work in an organisation where callers telephone to make appointments to see employees it may be prudent to enquire where the caller is from and who he or she represents. This may help the person decide whether they want to see the caller.

Having identified the caller you are now in a position to enquire about the purpose of the call and establish their needs.

Callers you know or recognise

If you work in a reception area it is very possible that you will know many of the callers either because they work for the organisation or they are regular callers. Callers that fall into these categories are usually very familiar with the organisation and know who is responsible for what, and will just ask to speak to that person. Their requests and needs are usually straightforward and can easily be identified.

Depending on the position of the person the caller asks to speak to, you may need to enquire about the purpose of the call. This ensures that the person they require is not going to be involved in a call that is more appropriate for another person. An example of this is someone asking to speak to a senior manager on the assumption that it is better to go to the top if you want action, rather than speak to someone in a lower position. By asking to know the purpose of the call you may well be able to identify someone in a less senior position that could easily solve the problem without involving the senior manager.

Unknown callers

Identifying the needs and requirements of unknown callers may not be so straightforward. Many of them will have little or no knowledge of your organisation and it will be your responsibility to identify an appropriate person to deal with their request. You can do this by asking suitable questions to discover the purpose of the call. You can then advise or recommend a suitable person within the organisation to take the call.

Whether you recognise the caller or not, it is important that you discover the reason and purpose of the call. The more information you gather from the caller, the more information you will be able to pass on to the person taking the call before you complete the transfer.

Case study – Robert's experience

I am the relief receptionist and telephone operator at Rayner Engineering. I usually cover the lunch break. The other day I had just taken over when I answered a call from a person asking to speak to the works manager.

I asked the person's name and enquired about the reason for the call. He gave his name as Mr Evans but was evasive about the reason for making the call. I probed but the only information I could gather was that he wanted to speak to the works manager.

I explained that the works manager was very busy and had probably gone to lunch. He said he needed to talk to him quite urgently, so I asked if he would give me more information and I would see what I could do. In the end he explained he needed to talk to someone in authority about some work he needed carrying out.

Having gained this information I told him I would have to place him on hold while I checked to see if there was anyone who could help. I rang and spoke to the works manager and explained that I had a Mr Evans on hold asking to speak with him. I gave him the details and he said to pass the call to Bill Edwards, who runs the drawing office.

I went back on the line and informed Mr Evans that the works manager was out to lunch but I was going to transfer him to Mr Edwards who should be able to help him. I rang Mr Edwards and explained the situation and he agreed to take the call.

As it turned out, Mr Evans wanted to identify an engineering company who would be able to produce a prototype of a structure which he was trying to persuade his bank to finance. I hear on the grapevine that if he manages to get the money he would like our company to manufacture it.

1 How did Robert perform?
2 Should he have lied to the caller?
3 Could you have done better?

The importance of maintaining confidentiality

Working in a reception area there will be times when callers give you sensitive information that must not become public knowledge because it could have consequences for the caller, yourself and even the organisation. Such information will need to be treated as confidential.

There are two aspects to confidentiality that you need to consider. First, the impact such information could have on the business:

♦ it may contain details about your organisation's clients and customers
♦ it may concern the way the organisation is run and carries out its business
♦ it may contain future plans for the organisation.

If any of the above information became public knowledge its release could have serious consequences for the organisation. Its relationships with its clients and customers could be irreparably damaged and its reputation tarnished. It would also be a major coup for a competitor if the information fell into their hands. In fact, the release of any of this type of information could be of considerable embarrassment to the organisation and may well affect its future prospects.

Second, the information may be of a personal nature such as:

♦ the promotional prospects of a particular individual or group of people
♦ a person's medical records
♦ personal details about an individual or a group
♦ financial details about an individual or group.

The release of such information could cause considerable embarrassment to the individuals concerned and the company. The release of personal or financial details about an individual could have very serious consequences for the organisation itself. Organisations have a legal obligation under the Data Protection Act to protect any information they have generated or have been entrusted to hold of a personal nature regarding an individual. The Act covers such information as personal details, medical records, financial details, political tendencies and many more. For more details concerning the Data Protection Act and its consequences you should turn to Unit 11, page 297, where it is explained more fully.

Where information is protected under the Data Protection Act it is essential that it be kept securely and it should only be accessible to those people who are authorised to see and handle the information.

How to respond to calls with different priorities

In general there are two classes of call that you may need to respond to: routine calls and priority calls.

Routine calls

The vast majority of calls that you handle will be routine calls; that you will handle in the normal way every day. Each call is answered and dealt with before the next call is answered. The calls are answered in the order they are received. The type of calls that are considered routine could include:

♦ enquiries
♦ passing on information
♦ ordering or selling goods and services
♦ making or confirming arrangements
♦ personal calls.

Priority calls

Priority calls are the few calls that you receive that you need to react to immediately – even though you may be involved in other work. Examples of such calls could include:

♦ calls for emergency assistance; such as fire, ambulance or police
♦ bomb threats
♦ requests for assistance other than emergency calls.

It is very likely that because you work in the reception area of an organisation you will be the focal point for all calls to the emergency services. In this case it could well be your responsibility to summon the appropriate service when an emergency call is received from within the organisation. In such cases you would be expected to stop whatever you are doing and summon assistance immediately.

Bomb threats are another type of priority call where you will need to stop whatever you are doing and implement the procedures your organisation has for dealing with such situations.

There may also be other times when you receive calls asking for assistance which do not require the involvement of emergency services but where you may need to stop what you are doing and arrange for assistance to be given. Such situations could include someone trapped in a lift or locked in a room. In both cases immediate action is required in order to avoid the people panicking or getting distressed.

Case study – Adam's experience

It was only two weeks after I had started the job when I received an emergency call from the workshop saying they had a fire. I was in a panic immediately – I didn't know what to do. Jim who made the call said call the emergency services, so I did.

I dialled 999 and a woman asked which service, I remember saying all of them. Someone then asked me where I was and what was the matter. I said we had a fire, gave her the telephone number, the name of the company and the location. Then I put the telephone down. Halfway through my conversation the fire alarm sounded and everyone started trooping out of the building. I followed.

In five minutes a police car pulled up followed by two fire engines. The person who took charge outside directed them to the workshop. In about ten minutes the police and a person from the fire people came around the front and said it was safe to go back into the office block.

I had to go and speak to my manger when everything had died down and everyone had returned to work. I was thanked for my quick action, but I was questioned as to why I had summoned all three services. Apparently the ambulance people were on their way when the police arrived and reported that their presence was not required.

1 How do you feel Adam reacted?
2 How do you think you would react under the same pressure?
3 Would you know what to do if faced with such an emergency?

Check it out

♦ Do you have to deal with priority calls? If so, what type do you deal with?
♦ Does your organisation have procedures for handling such situations?

How to transfer calls

Working in the reception area of an organisation, the majority of your work will involve you answering calls, identifying callers, establishing their requirements and then transferring them to the appropriate person or department. Every call that you handle therefore involves a transfer of some kind, so it is essential that you are able to do this successfully.

Here are a few pointers that may assist you in your task:

♦ always keep the caller informed as to what you are going to do, how you are going to do it, and why you are going to do it
♦ always tell the caller that you are going to put them on hold before you do it

- when you return to the call always thank the caller for holding, using their name where possible
- always confirm that the other person is available and willing to accept the call before transferring the call
- where possible always offer the caller an alternative if the person the caller asks to speak to is not available or is unwilling to accept the call.

A typical procedure for transferring a call

1   Identify the caller, establish the person or department they require, and identify the purpose of the call.

2   Explain to the caller that you will need to place them on hold while you check if the person is available.

3   Place the caller on hold while you find out if the person is available.

4   If available, give them the following information:

    a the caller's name
    b the name of the company they represent, if applicable
    c the purpose of the call
    d any other relevant facts.

5   Confirm whether the person is available and willing to accept the call.

6   If the person is willing to accept the call, return to the caller, thank them for holding and explain that the person is available and will accept the call.

7   Transfer the call.

8   Where the person is busy on another call, not available or is unwilling to accept the call you will need to return to the caller and explain that the person is not available.

9   Offer the caller the option of either waiting, speaking to another person or any other feasible alternative.

Check it out

- Does your organisation have documented procedures for transferring calls? If so, how does it differ from the example given above?

The types of problems that may be encountered

It is inevitable that you will experience some problems when you are handling incoming calls. The following are a few of the most common problems that you may come across:

- the caller has dialled the wrong number
- the person asked for is unknown in the organisation
- the person asked for is no longer employed by the organisation

- the person is already busy on a call
- the person asked for is unavailable or to busy to accept the call
- the person asked for is unwilling to accept the call
- difficult callers.

Solving some of these problems will be relatively straightforward, but there are others that will test your professionalism to the full before the problems are solved.

Ways of overcoming some of the problems that may be encountered

There are many ways that each of the above problems can be overcome; here we look at some of the more common solutions.

Callers who have dialled the wrong number

This type of problem is quite common and it can easily be solved by repeating the name of your organisation. This is usually enough to trigger the caller into realising their mistake.

The person asked for is unknown in the organisation

Your first course of action in such a situation would be to confirm the spelling of the person's name. You may then have to ask the purpose of the call. If the purpose is business, you will need to ask for more details about the purpose of the call. If you can narrow down the search to a department you may be able to contact someone there who can identify the person required. If this is still not possible, you could suggest that the caller speaks to someone else in that department.

The person asked for is no longer employed by the organisation

This is very similar to the situation above, only this time you are able to identify the person required. The first requirement is to establish whether the call is business or personal. If it is personal you should inform the caller that the person is no longer employed by the organisation and if you know his or her whereabouts you may decide to give that information. If the purpose is business, you may need to ask for further details so that you can identify another person to accept the call.

It may be unwise to give details of the person's whereabouts if the purpose of the call is business, as a high proportion of people that leave organisations do so to take up positions at rival companies and organisations.

The person is already busy on a call

If the person the caller has asked to speak to is already occupied on a call, you could ask if they would like:

- to hold until the person is available
- to leave a message
- you to arrange for the person to call them back
- to leave a message on the person's voicemail.

Whenever you place a caller on hold, waiting for a person to finish a call, you should always check at regular intervals to keep the caller informed of the situation and to confirm that they wish to remain on hold. With the increasing use of voicemail and voice boxes, the requirement for you to take a message or arrange for a person to return a call is becoming a thing of the past.

The person asked for is unavailable or is to busy to accept the call

This is probably the most common cause of callers being unable to complete their call. In such situations you may be able to offer the caller one of the options discussed above.

The person asked for is unwilling to accept the call

This type of situation happens occasionally, where the person who has been asked to accept the call is either too busy with other commitments or is unwilling to accept the call for whatever reason. It is then up to you to explain to the caller that the person is busy at present in which case you can give them the same options as above, or suggest they might like to talk to someone else.

There may well be occasions when the person refuses point blank to speak to the caller, in which case the suggestion that they might like to speak to someone else may be the most appropriate option. If so you will need to be very diplomatic and not admit the real reason why the person was unwilling to accept the call.

Difficult callers

This is probably the most difficult part of handling any call, and unless you get it right you may well inflame the situation further. In Unit 1 we looked at five categories of difficult callers: aggressive, abusive, confused, distressed and insistent.

It was also suggested that:

◆ you should try not to panic; remain calm
◆ if callers are abusive or aggressive do not be tempted to react in a similar way or take the remarks personally
◆ you should be patient
◆ you try to calm the situation by addressing the caller by name
◆ you let the caller have their say
◆ you should listen, giving verbal nods to reaffirm you are listening
◆ you explain calmly the options available to them
◆ where possible, ask closed questions, giving the caller options to choose from
◆ you should give reassurance, where necessary.

This list is general and not every point is appropriate in all situations. Look back at Unit 1 for further information.

Think about it

Above we have listed some of the more common problems that you may encounter, but there may well be others.

♦ Can you identify any other problems? If so, make a note of them.
♦ What can you do or which actions can you take to overcome such problems?

17.2 Make telephone calls

Making a telephone call is something most of us have been doing for as long as we can remember, and is considered an essential part of life. Many of us would feel isolated if we didn't have access to the telephone; we use it to gain information, to make arrangements or just to have a chat. We pick up the telephone, dial the number and away we go – usually with an objective but without giving much thought to how we will achieve our objective.

This section looks at the processes you automatically go through when you make these calls on behalf of yourself or someone else. It is assumed that although you are primarily employed in a reception area you will be given other work to complete during quiet periods. This work could well involve making telephone calls to gather information or to arrange appointments.

WHAT YOU NEED TO KNOW OR LEARN

♦ Preparing for making telephone calls
♦ Making telephone calls
♦ Types of sensitive information
♦ Handling sensitive information
♦ Your organisation's standards with regards to service and quality of calls.

Preparing for making telephone calls

First, you have to identify the type of information you will require and where you can get it. The list should look something like this:

♦ why do you want to make the call?
♦ who do you want to call?
♦ what do you want to say?
♦ what information do you require to make the call?
♦ is the information sensitive?
♦ when is the best time to make the call?
♦ how urgent is the call?

This list is not definitive but it does contain most of the important information you are likely to need to make most telephone calls.

Why do you want to make the call?

The telephone is an essential part of our lives for the collecting and spreading of the vast array of information needed for our survival and well being. Therefore there are many reasons why you may want to make a telephone call. These reasons could include:

◆ to make arrangements
◆ to confirm arrangements
◆ to order goods and services
◆ to sell goods and services
◆ to pass on information to others
◆ to gather information from others.

The arrangements could be appointments, hotel or theatre bookings or just to arrange a meeting; similarly the telephone can be used to confirm these arrangements.

The goods and services you buy could include the bulk supplies your organisation converts into the products it later sells via the telephone. It could also include the consumables you use in the process of running the business, such as stationery, or the ancillary services such as transport and even telephones.

The gathering and passing of information can be formal where information is required to fulfil a purpose, such as in a police enquiry or to give warning of possible power cuts. There are also informal ways of gathering and passing information, such as a chat between friends.

Who do you want to call?

There will be times when it will be more appropriate to call a company than a person. Whether you call a person or a company will depend on the reason you want to make the call in the first place. Calls where you need to order goods or services are usually made to the company; you are not particularly interested in the person's name, only whether they are capable of taking the order and arranging for its delivery.

When you are making calls to sell your organisation's goods and services you may target a particular person by name, in the knowledge that they are the person responsible for placing orders. But there will be other times when you will make a call to a particular telephone number, hoping that you will be able to interest the person into making a purchase. It is only when the person has agreed to listen to your sales pitch that you ask for their name.

When making or confirming appointments or bookings, the name of the other person is unimportant as long as they are in a position to agree or reject the details. Where calls are to be made to arrange or confirm attendance at meetings it is better to speak to the person who is to attend, or to someone who has the authority to commit them to attend.

Calls where you need to gather or pass on information can be made to a particular person or to a location. The decision will be made when the contents of the message or the nature of the request is known. Where this is sensitive, the call is usually made to a named person. But if the contents of the message or nature of the request is general then the call can be directed to a location rather than a person.

What do you want to say?

No matter why you need to make a call or who you need to speak to, it is better to be prepared and know what you need to say. It is annoying to answer a call where the person on the other end is uncertain why they have rung. Some people know what they want to say but get flustered when the telephone is answered. There is no cure for this other than experience; don't give up just prepare yourself.

How you prepare will depend on the nature of the call. If you need to get over as much information as quickly as possible in order to maintain the person's interest, then it is best to prepare thoroughly. This occurs when you are trying to sell to people over the telephone – maintaining their interest stops them putting the telephone down. In order to prepare for such occasions it will be necessary for you to make notes and practise what you have to say; but even then success cannot be guaranteed.

There can even be advantages in making notes for calls to your family and friends. If you have prepared notes you are less likely to forget things you should tell them about and questions you need to ask.

What information do you require to make the call?

The amount and type of information you require will depend on the reason why you need to make the call. We looked at the different reasons above so we will take each of those and examine the different information you are likely to require.

◆ Make arrangements

In order to make arrangements for yourself or another person you will need to gather all or most of the following information:

- what arrangements are to be made
- when are the arrangements to be made for
- the location where the arrangements are to be made (if applicable)
- if anyone else is involved, if so who
- what authority you have to negotiate the date and location.

This may appear to be a lot of information but if it is not available when you start to make the call, you may need to keep rethinking your ideas or referring back to the person who asked you to make the arrangements. Arrangements that involve more than one person may well involve you in making a series of calls.

◆ Confirm arrangements

The preparation required to confirm details of arrangements made by someone else is minimal compared to that required for making the arrangement in the first place. The preparation will involve you gathering all of the following information:

- the name and telephone number of the person requiring the confirmation
- the details of the arrangement
- the decision as to whether the arrangements are agreeable or not.

When confirming the details of arrangements, it is best to ensure that the details have not changed before you finally agree to them. Changes are inevitable when anyone is trying to arrange meetings where more than one or two people are involved.

♦ **To order goods and services**

In order to prepare for ordering goods and services you will need to gather together all or most of the following information:

- the name of the company where the goods or services are to be ordered from
- the telephone number of the company where the goods or services are to be ordered from
- the details of the order.

Most of this information is likely to be available from the catalogue or advertising literature that the company distributes.

♦ **To pass on information to others**

To prepare to pass on information it is very likely that all that is required is to:

- identify the name and telephone number of the person concerned
- obtain details of the information to be imparted.

Although in most cases the information that you have to impart is general, there will be other times where the information could be sensitive and should only be given to the person directly and not left as a message.

To gather information from others

To prepare for gathering information from others you are likely to need all or most of the following details:

- the information you are to gather
- the question you will need to ask
- a possible starting point where the information might be found.

Gathering information can be relatively easy or may prove to be long-winded and difficult, depending on whether it is readily available or you have to chase around in order to find it. If you are gathering information for another person you should encourage them to be specific as to what is required.

The sensitivity of the information

General information can be released without affecting or causing embarrassment to anyone. But information that could cause offence or embarrassment to a person or organisation should be considered sensitive.

Calls where sensitive information is involved are usually only addressed to named people. All calls should go directly to the person concerned and the information only passed to the said person. The same will be true if you are requesting sensitive information; the person who has the information should confirm your status to accept such information before they give it to you.

When is the best time to make the call

The old saying, *'there is no time like the present'*, might be true in some cases, but it is not always good advice for making calls. Your timing will probably depend on your reason for making the call. Calls to colleagues where you want to give or gather information are probably best made during the normal working day, where possible avoiding lunch and tea breaks. Calls to place orders or make arrangements again are best made during the normal working day. But calls where you are trying to sell your organisation's goods and service to homeowners are best made when they are likely to be available and that is usually in the early evening.

Many organisations now operate in the global market and may well deal with suppliers and customers overseas. In this case although you may have been asked to contact a supplier or customer as soon as possible, remember that it is inappropriate to telephone them in the middle of their night. Where this does happen you may need to inform the person making the request that it will probably be more appropriate to send a fax or email, due to the time difference between the two places.

How urgent is the call?

If you work in a front office or reception area it is very likely that you will be asked to make calls on behalf of quite a few people. These people may be your line managers or people in a supervisory role and they will all see their own personal requests as urgent and expect you to put them on top of your priority list. To get the full credit that you deserve for your work, you will need to be an expert juggler in order to satisfy every one of their demands.

Some organisations and government offices set standards that allow people to classify the priority they require for their requests. These standards give the different criteria that need to be met for each grade of priority. The normally accepted grades are: immediate, priority and routine.

Immediate requests are dealt with as soon as possible. Priority requests are normally dealt with within four hours. Routine requests are normally dealt with by the end of day if they are asked for in the morning, or by the close of the following day if they are requested later on. Routine requests may be upgraded to priority if they are not dealt with in the allotted timescales, but under normal conditions they will only be dealt with when there are no higher priority requests outstanding.

If your organisation does not adopt agreed standards and you are constantly facing the dilemma of balancing requests from different people, you may need to ask your line manager or supervisor to give you guidance as to what is priority.

Case study – Eileen's experience

Working in the reception area of Rayner Engineering I am the first face any visitors to the company see when they arrive at the office. I welcome them, get them to sign in, and arrange for them to be picked up by the people they have come to visit. I also deal with all the incoming telephone calls where the callers do not know the extension they require. Callers can dial the extension numbers direct, so it is only the callers that ring the main works number that I have to deal with.

Because staffing the reception is not a full time job in itself, I am also given the task of arranging meetings and booking hotel accommodation for the staff if they are required to work away at any time. I also have the responsibility of taking bookings for the two conference rooms in the building.

Some of the managers hold meetings with their staff all over the country and I am asked to arrange the meetings, which can be on consecutive days for the full five days in the week. Each meeting will be in a different location and they will require accommodation for the meeting and hotel accommodation for the evening before the meeting. Sometimes I begin to fall over myself because I find I cannot get a conference room at one location on a particular date but I can get hotel accommodation; I am continually juggling with dates and rooms.

If I don't keep notes of what I am trying to achieve and what I have booked and haven't booked the whole process would be in total confusion.

Check it out

♦ Do you have a switchboard?
♦ Are you given any other work to do, besides operating the switchboard? If so, what other responsibilities do you have? Make a list of them for your portfolio.
♦ Do you make telephone calls on behalf of anyone else? If yes, do you make notes in preparation for making the calls?

Keep some examples of the notes you make as evidence for your portfolio.

Making telephone calls

This section does not tell you how to make a telephone call, as you have been doing that for years. Instead we will be looking at how you handle the call from the point where the person answers your call.

Calls to a named person or title

If the call is to a known person you should start by asking to speak to the person concerned by name or title. If you are asked to give the purpose of the call, you should give it without disclosing the details; for example, 'I have a message from Mr Simons regarding the meeting tomorrow'.

When you are connected to the person concerned, you confirm their identity and then you state your name, your role in the organisation and the reason for your call. This should be done clearly and concisely. You can then confirm that it is convenient to continue with the call. If not, you arrange an appropriate time to call back. If you do this then it is important that you do call back at the agreed time. Failure to call back as agreed can annoy a busy person who has made arrangements to be available to receive the call. There may be occasions where you have agreed a suitable time to call back, but due to unforeseen circumstances the person is not available or it is still inconvenient to accept your call. This is likely to be due to work pressure.

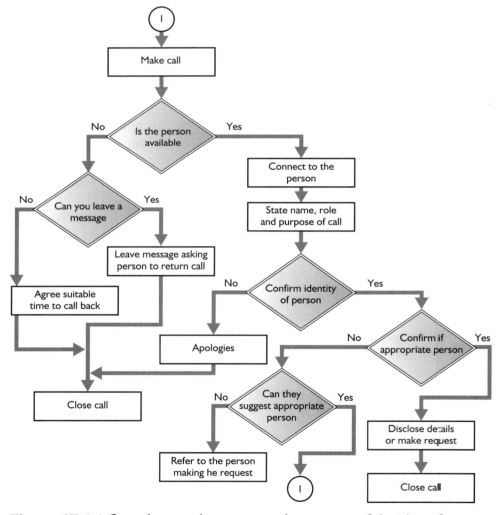

Figure 17.1 A flow chart to demonstrate the process of deciding if you should disclose sensitive information

When disclosing information or making requests you should express yourself clearly, concisely, and avoid the use of jargon. Similarly, when receiving information you should use your active listening skills, test your understanding of what is being said, and record the information accurately. You should always ensure that you end on a positive note.

Where sensitive information is concerned it is important that you have confirmed the person's identity and established they are the appropriate person to talk to before you disclose the information.

Calls to an organisation or company

Calls of this type are far more straightforward, as they are usually of a general nature where you are making calls to make bookings or appointments, or place orders for goods and services. The call is made to an organisation or company and not to particular person. Whoever answers the call will take your details and make your booking or appointment or take your order.

You will need to confirm that the telephone number you have called is able to deal with your request; then it should be straightforward for you to give the details of the request to the other person. When the other person has dealt with your request you should say thank you for the service and close the call.

Types of sensitive information
What is sensitive information

The dictionary definition of the word **sensitive** in this context is *subject to restriction of discussion to prevent embarrassment or to ensure security*. Therefore sensitive information is anything that a person or organisation would prefer not to be generally disclosed.

There are degrees of sensitivity: at the one extreme there is information that could cause mild embarrassment or irritation if released, but at the other extreme there is information that could have serious consequences for the individual or organisation if it became general knowledge.

There are two basic types of information that can be considered sensitive; that concerning individuals and that concerning the organisation. It is possible that there will be times when you will be asked to deal with one or both and it will be your responsibility to ensure that they are handled properly, kept securely and not inadvertently disclosed to anyone else.

Sensitive information concerning individuals

Any information that contains details that can be cross-referenced to a particular person or group of people can be considered personally sensitive, for example information containing staff details or staff medical records.

Any accidental release of information relating to staff or their personal details could be embarrassing to both the organisation and the people involved. Staff details that could be classed as sensitive information might include:

- personal details
- salary details
- promotion prospects
- redundancies
- staff changes
- staff appraisal details.

All of this is information that the organisation and the people involved would prefer to remain confidential. The release of some of these details could cause friction between individuals, particularly where money matters are concerned, or between groups of people where staff changes or redundancies are concerned.

People are also very secretive about their medical details and are reluctant for other people to know their personal history and details, such as medical history, sick leave record or sexual preference.

You will need to treat any information that is classed as personally sensitive with the greatest of care and ensure you don't disclose it to anyone other than the person nominated. You should also be aware of the **Data Protection Act** and its implications for anyone releasing such sensitive information, even as harmless gossip. (See Unit 11 for more details concerning the Data Protection Act.)

Sensitive information concerning the organisation

The release of commercially sensitive information could have very serious consequences for the organisation and its personnel. This could include:

- expansion plans
- sales figures
- price structures
- promotional plans
- advertising plans
- production methods.

The list is endless as anything that could be used by a competitor or rival should be considered commercially sensitive.

For example, you can imagine the effect on your organisation of a rival company using sensitive information that you have inadvertently disclosed in order to under-cut your special prices that were to be released as part of a new sales promotion campaign. By promoting their goods and services first at a low price they have defeated the whole of your organisation's campaign.

Handling sensitive information

In an attempt to prevent sensitive information falling into the wrong hands, some organisations and government agents use a method of classifying the information in terms of how damaging its disclosure could be to the individual or organisation. Procedures are then put in place to ensure the information is handled appropriately, so preventing its disclosure by accident. Most organisations adopt the following categories for protecting sensitive information:

- unclassified
- restricted
- confidential
- secret
- top secret.

Unclassified information is usually readily available from various sources and can be accessed by anyone who is interested. Its disclosure is very unlikely to cause any embarrassment to anyone.

Restricted information is for use only within the organisation that generated it, and could be of interest to a competitor or rival company. Its disclosure could cause some embarrassment and possibly minor damage to the organisation.

Confidential information has the potential to cause damage to the organisation if released and therefore its disclosure should be limited to those people in the organisation who need to know about it. Secret information should be limited to senior management only and could have serious implications for the organisation if released.

Do's and don'ts

It is extremely unlikely that you would be asked to deal with anything above the restricted classification, therefore these suggestions reflect the requirements of the restricted category.

Do's

- Always confirm the person's identity and establish that they are the appropriate person to talk to before disclosing the information.
- Always ensure that sensitive information is securely locked away before leaving your work area.
- When passing on the sensitive information always record the fact that you have completed the task. It is useful to record the time, date and the name of the person who you informed. This can help avoid problems with people who claim they have not received the information.
- If you are unable to pass on sensitive information you should always inform the person who made the request that you have encountered problems. They may be able to offer an alternative solution.

Don'ts

- Don't leave sensitive material lying around on your desk or work area. This is particularly important when you are working in a reception area where visitors may see it.
- If the person you are requested to give sensitive information to is not available, don't leave the information with a third party for them to convey to the person.
- Don't leave sensitive information in a voice bank or on an answering machine. These could be accessed by other people.
- Don't entrust other people to relay sensitive information on your behalf if you were given the task.

Check it out

◆ Do you handle sensitive information? If so, what types of sensitive information do you handle?

◆ What precautions do you take to protect the sensitive information?

Your organisation's standards with regards to service and quality of calls

People today expect a high quality of service. In order to satisfy this expectation organisations will document procedures with regards to the service and quality standards they expect you to achieve. Customers will not put up with mediocre service without complaining and with more and more organisations in competition, the only distinction between many of them is the quality of service they offer to their customers.

Earlier in this chapter we looked at how you were the interface between people visiting your department or organisation, both in person and via the telephone and how your attitude to the callers not only reflected on you personally but also on the people you front and work for. Being pleasant, courteous and helpful gives the visitors a positive image of the organisation. But if you take the visitors for granted, regard them as a nuisance or an inconvenience, and make no attempt to meet their needs they leave with a negative impression of the organisation.

Outstanding customer service does not happen by accident; it requires careful planning, commitment and dedication. Everyone in the organisation will need to be focused and prepared to make the extra effort to maintain and improve the standards laid down by the organisation. Customer requirements are always changing and everyone will need to strive for continuous improvement if the customer is to remain totally satisfied.

If you do not meet the customer's expectations, they may withdraw their business from your organisation and go elsewhere. If you meet their expectations, they are likely to continue with your organisation and you will get their repeat business. However, if the caller's expectations are *exceeded* because of the quality of your customer service, then your organisation will almost certainly get the repeat business and may draw in new business as well as the word spreads of your exceptional service.

Remember
Bad news spreads faster than good news.

If a customer receives poor service from your organisation they are likely to tell more people about it than if they had received exceptional service. People tend to reserve good news for their more immediate friends and colleagues.

Your organisation should have service standards that you are expected to uphold.

Think about it

Put yourself in the customer's shoes and ask yourself the following questions:

1 If I were the customer, how would I want to be treated?
2 What kind of service would I expect?
3 What would make me feel that I had received exceptional customer service?

Check it out

Find out if your organisation has a defined set of service standards that you are expected to work to. If it does, find out what they are called and make a note of them. If they are detailed, write down where they can be found.

17.3 Report faults in telephone equipment

It is assumed that two of your prime functions are manning a front office reception area and operating a telephone switchboard for your particular department or organisation. Here you will be ideally situated to take on the responsibility for co-ordinating all telephone faults for your department or organisation. If given this responsibility, you will be the focal point for all telephone fault reports where you will record the fault details, report the faults to the appropriate service provider and monitor progress until the faults are cleared.

WHAT YOU NEED TO KNOW OR LEARN

◆ how to recognise a fault in telephone equipment
◆ your organisation's procedures for reporting telephone equipment faults
◆ your organisation's service agreement with your telephone service provider
◆ how to assess the priority to be given to a fault in the telephone equipment
◆ possible contingency plans to maintain communications until the fault is cleared.

How to recognise a fault in telephone equipment

A telephone is an essential part of both our business and private lives. We rely heavily on it for distributing information, and for gathering in information from others. Businesses rely on the telephone for providing the means by which vital information and data are transported between locations. This can be in the form of data links connecting computer systems together, fax machines and voice communications.

What constitutes a fault?

We usually say we have a fault when something stops working or it reacts in a way we did not expect. When using a telephone you expect to be able to complete a certain sequence of events – pick up the handset, listen for a dial tone, dial a number, the number to ring etc. If at any point in this process you are unable to go to the next stage, you have a fault. The same will be true when you are using the telephone system for sending or receiving data or faxes. If the system will not let you use it properly, you have a fault.

Common types of fault reports

The fault reports you receive are likely to vary for each of the type of services you operate. The most common faults reported for normal telephone service are:

♦ unable to dial/no dial tone/unable to make calls
♦ cannot receive calls/telephone not ringing
♦ calls faint/calls very faint/unable to hear
♦ calls noisy/lots of interference.

The most common fault reports for fax lines are:

♦ unable to dial/no dial tone/unable to send faxes
♦ cannot receive faxes/fax machine not ringing
♦ faxes are very faint
♦ dark lines along faxes.

The most common fault reports for data links are:

♦ cannot send data
♦ cannot receive data
♦ high error rates
♦ data totally corrupt.

In the lists above you can see that some fault reports have been listed together, because of the various interpretations different people put on the same basic problem. For example, if you are unable to make a call because when you pick up the handset it appears to be dead, some people will report the fault as unable to dial, others as no dial tone, and a third as unable to make calls. All three are right but they have all put their own interpretation on what is wrong.

Depending on the type of environment where you work, you may even get fault reports that you are able to deal with yourself. For example, if you work in an environment where you use plug in head sets to handle calls, it is very likely that the organisation will carry a number of spare sets. Therefore if one of these headsets develops a fault it can easily be changed for a good one from stock, and the faulty one reported as a non-urgent routine fault. If your organisation adopts such a practice, all faulty headsets should be labelled as such, and segregated from the good spare stock until they have been repaired and tested.

Co-ordinating fault reports

The majority of fault reports you will receive will be single reports and there will no connection between them, in other words they are isolated fault reports. Occasionally you will receive a number of reports, usually in quick succession, which may be indicative of a major fault developing. This may not be very obvious initially but as the number of fault reports increases you may be able to see a pattern developing. This may be all the extensions in one particular part of a building, extension numbers in a particular range, or a number of reports saying calls to outside lines are noisy or faint.

Your organisation's procedures for reporting telephone equipment faults

Many organisations will have set up formal arrangements whereby all fault reports are made to a central point. Others may have informal arrangements where it is assumed that as receptionist or telephone operator you will be the most knowledgeable member of the staff to take charge and deal with all telephone fault reports.

Check it out

Find out if your organisation has a formal or informal telephone fault reporting procedure. If there is a formal procedure, where can it be found?

♦ What does it say?
♦ Does your organisation operate an informal arrangement? If yes what would you do to formalise it?

Fault reporting points

An effective reporting point should be accessible and staffed throughout normal office hours, to allow a rapid response if necessary. The person who staffs the reporting point and co-ordinates the reports should know and understand the following:

♦ the method of recording the fault reports
♦ the procedures to follow when fault reports are received
♦ the fault reporting details for each particular service provider
♦ the service level agreements with the service providers
♦ the criteria for assessing whether a fault is priority or routine
♦ possible contingency plans for occasions when major faults occur.

Methods of recording fault reports

Whatever recording method you adopt, it should enable a fault report to be tracked from the original report until it is finally cleared and the service restored. It should also enable you to identify repeat fault reports where the same piece of equipment or line is concerned, as this may indicate the existence of deeper problems. As an example, take a particular extension that is regularly being reported as noisy, but every time a telephone engineer attends to the fault they always report the line as clear as the telephone instrument has been replaced. This obviously clears the immediate problem, but the odds of every telephone connected to this extension going faulty after such a short time is extremely high. This could indicate that there is a more serious problem that is not being diagnosed which is causing all the telephone instruments to go faulty on a regular basis.

The method of recording fault reports is up to the individual organisation, whether this is a log book or a computer-based system, but it should contain most or all of the following information:

◆ organisation's fault reference number
◆ time and date reported
◆ details of fault as reported
◆ time and date passed to service provider
◆ fault reference number from service provider
◆ classification of fault (priority or routine)
◆ time and date fault cleared
◆ what action was taken to clear the fault.

Ref No	Received		Details of Fault Report	Reported		Class	Provider Ref No	Cleared		Clear Details
	Date	Time		Date	Time			Date	Time	
001/01	1/3/02	13:30	X3456 no dial tone	1/3/02	14:40	R	CR103	1/4/02	11:20	Telephone changed
002/01	1/4/02	12:20	Black lines along faxes 347823	1/4/02	15:00	R	CR206	1/6/02	16:15	Fax machine cleaned
003/01	1/8/02	8.30	Unable to make calls X6745	1/8/02	9:05	P	CR476	1/8/02	18:15	Cable fault repaired
004/01	1/8/02	8:35	Unable to make calls X6012	1/8/02	9:05	P	CR476	1/8/02	18:15	Cable fault repaired
005/01	1/8/02	8:50	Unable to make calls X6758	1/8/02	9:05	P	CR476	1/8/02	18:15	Cable fault repaired
006/01	1/8/02	9:00	Unable to make calls X5623	1/8/02	9:05	P	CR476	1/8/02	18:15	Cable fault repaired
007/01	1/8/02	9:30	Unable to make calls X5002					1/8/02	18:15	Cable fault repaired
008/01	1/8/02	9:35	Unable to make calls X5432/5027					1/8/02	18:15	Cable fault repaired
009/01	1/8/02	10:45	Unable to make calls X6902					1/8/02	18:15	Cable fault repaired

An example of a fault logbook

From the example of a typical fault logbook you will see that the first two fault reports were isolated reports with very little to connect them, therefore they were treated correctly as routine faults. However on 8 January the fault co-ordinator received four fault reports in quick succession, all reporting the same basic problem. He or she obviously became suspicious that a major problem was developing; as a result the fault reports were quickly passed to the service provider with a priority classification. This intuition paid off as the problem was a cable fault that had a wider impact than was originally suspected, with more fault reports being received later.

By recording all fault reports in a logbook the type of problem highlighted above can easily be seen. If each fault were passed on to the provider without being recorded the problem above would not have been recognised so soon.

Check it out

♦ Does your organisation keep a telephone fault report logbook?
♦ What information does your organisation record?

Make a note of this for your portfolio.

Your organisation's service agreement with your telephone service provider

Since the liberalisation of the UK telecommunications sector your organisation's choice of who provides its telecommunications services has increased considerably. Until the 1980s there was in effect only one provider, British Telecom (BT), to provide a full package of available services. Since then more and more companies have entered the market; some of these companies are small and operate in their own locality and others are major organisations operating internationally.

Telephone service providers

These days your organisation may well use several organisations to provide and maintain your telecoms service; your network access may be provided and maintained by one and the internal network and structure by another. It is even feasible that your telecoms system may have dual network access; each provided and maintained by a different organisation. This will give your organisation some resilience should either network access route fail. This is extremely important in an industry that relies so heavily on its telecoms network and system.

Although above we have assumed that the provider of the system is also responsible for its maintenance, this is not always the case. Some small companies may be able to provide the service, but do not have the resources to maintain the service within agreed service limits.

In order to run a successful telephone fault report facility you will need to know who is responsible for what, and who to contact in the event of having to report a fault. You will also need to know what level of service your organisation is entitled to when a fault is reported.

Service level agreements

Service level agreements are the contracts between your organisation and your suppliers or customers. They set out the terms and conditions both parties are expected to adhere to in the supply or receipt of goods or services.

Service level agreements that have been drawn up for the maintenance of telecoms networks and systems usually cover such items as:

♦ the length of the agreement
♦ the charges for the service
♦ fault reporting procedures
♦ service response times
♦ your organisation's responsibilities
♦ ending the agreement
♦ limitation of liability of the maintainer.

The drawing up and signing of the agreement is normally carried out at a senior level within your organisation, but it will be up to you to work within the agreement. Certain details within the service level agreement (such as the length of the agreement, the charges for the service, ending the agreement and the limitation of liability of the maintainer) are outside the scope of this qualification. It is very unlikely that they will have any impact on your responsibilities. Although you will have no say in the terms and conditions of such items as fault reporting procedures, the service response times, and the organisation's responsibilities, you may well be responsible for their implementation.

When an organisation signs a contract with a company for the maintenance of its telecoms systems and networks, the company will supply it with procedures detailing how to report faults. These procedures will contain the telephone numbers your organisation can use for reporting faults. Most companies will provide 24-hour cover but will expect your organisation to restrict reports outside normal office hours to urgent or serious faults only. Companies usually give one telephone number for reporting faults in normal office hours and a second emergency number should it be necessary to report a fault outside these hours.

The company will also supply you with a list of response times it will achieve in reacting to your fault reports. These response times will vary, depending on whether the reported fault is service affecting or non-service affecting. Service-affecting faults are those faults that cause disruption to the normal working of the telecommunications networks and systems, and require fast response times to minimise their effect. However, the response time for a non-service affecting fault can be longer as no one is directly affected by the fault. The company may also give guidelines on the type of faults that it will accept as priority faults and if you exceed these guidelines the company may impose additional charges for every fault that was inappropriately reported.

The company will also list your organisation's responsibilities in relation to the network and systems. These could include avoiding any misuse of the equipment, adhering to any health and hygiene requirements, using the correct grade of consumables and maintaining an agreed stock of these consumables.

Check it out

Who maintains your organisation's telephone systems and equipment? Copy out the table below and fill in the gaps.

How many companies provide the maintenance cover? . . . .

. . . .

Name of company: . . . .

Contact numbers: . . . .
  Within office hours: . . . .
  Outside office hours: . . . .

What is the company responsible for? . . . .

. . . .

Give details: . . . .

. . . .

What are the agreed response times? . . . .

Does your organisation have any responsibilities in the terms of the contract? . . . .

List them here. . . . .

. . . .

Did your organisation's telephone maintainer give guidelines on the type of faults that it would accept as priority faults? If so what are they? . . . .

. . . .

How to assess the priority to be given to a fault in the telephone equipment

Earlier in this chapter we discussed some of the most common type of faults you could encounter. We will now take some of these faults and try to determine what priority should be attached to each fault.

In general the priority you give to a fault will depend on the effect the problem is having on the service offered by the office or organisation. To start we will consider two distinct classes of faults: non-service affecting faults and service affecting faults.

Non-service affecting faults

Non-service affecting faults have no impact on the service you offer to your customers or callers. They are usually cosmetic in that they do not affect the operation of the particular piece of equipment or system. They could include broken cases or covers, frayed or twisted cords or unlit lights that show the status of the equipment. In themselves they do not affect the working or output of the system or network. They could also include faulty items of equipment that have been exchanged by the person reporting the fault. Such equipment exchanges allow the service to be restored quickly and leaves the faulty item to be repaired at leisure. Faults in this category are usually reported as low priority routine faults.

The priority given to a fault will depend on whether it is affecting the service

Service affecting faults

Service affecting faults are those types of faults that have an impact on the service you can offer to your customers and callers. Their effect can range from the complete shutdown of the operation to relatively minor problems where an extension telephone is not working. Such faults can be either reported as priority or routine depending on the severity and nature of the problem.

What one organisation considers a routine fault another organisation may consider to be a priority. For example, imagine that two organisations both lose the use of a single workstation. The first organisation may have a total of 200 workstations, therefore the loss of one will only have a minor impact on the service that organisation can offer. However, the second organisation only has a total of ten workstations, therefore the impact of losing 10 per cent of its call handling capacity could be devastating, particularly in a busy period. The first organisation is likely to report their loss as a routine fault, but the second may well be seeking urgent priority help to restore service.

There may also be situations where the initial impact on the service your organisation can offer is only slight but from past experience you know that faults of this nature can develop and have a major impact on the service. In such situations you may be justified in discussing the situation with your maintainer and reporting the fault for priority attention.

Faults requiring routine attention

Routine faults can be handled by the normal fault process where the response times are acceptable to your organisation; these account for between 90 to 95 per cent of all reported faults. The effect such faults will have on the service you are able to offer is usually minimal or at most minor. The type of faults that can be handled in this way could include:

♦ the vast majority of non-service affecting faults
♦ faults that affect one or two extensions
♦ faults where the impact is minimal or minor
♦ faults that only slightly restrict the level of service you can offer and the level is considered acceptable.

The majority of common faults reported for normal telephone services are routine faults, unless there are more similar reports; in which case if the number indicates a more serious problem then priority action is necessary. A number of reports of people being unable to make calls or unable to receive calls could indicate problems with the telephone switch or a possible distribution cable fault developing. Faint or noisy calls are also indicative of a possible cable fault developing.

Fax line faults are similar to telephone faults in the majority of cases and should be treated as routine faults. Faint faxes and dark lines along faxes are both indicative of the fax machine requiring a clean or service.

Problems with data links are more complex as the loss of a low capacity link may have little or no effect in the overall network, or it could have major implications if that particular link carries vital information between buildings or locations. A drop in the speed that data are transferred between locations may be acceptable for one organisation or be intolerable to another. Some organisations may prefer to operate a link at a slower speed rather than lose that link if it were reported and taken out of service for repair. So you can see that how and when you report a fault on a data link may well depend on how problematic the fault is and whether the organisation is willing to accept inferior service until a time that suits them.

Faults requiring priority attention

Priority faults are those types of faults that create an unacceptable degree of difficulty in maintaining the service your organisation offers to its customers and callers. They require urgent action in order to restore normal service. On average they only account for a small proportion of the total faults you are likely to report.

Case study – Maryam's experiences

On Monday as I walked into work from the bus stop on Bramhall Lane I saw some council workmen cordoning off the wide grass verge at the junction with the industrial estate. I had seen plans showing how they were going to widen and improve the entrance to the estate. They were driving metal spikes into the footpath and erecting red and white ribbons to keep people away from the area they were working in.

At about 11.00a.m. I started to get one or two reports that some of the lines into the building were noisy and there appeared to be someone else speaking on the lines. I checked all our outgoing lines and two of them were noisy, so I reported them to the BT fault desk as routine faults, where they gave me a reference number.

In the early afternoon I received several other reports that some people were experiencing problems of noise and interference. I explained that we had problems with two of the lines but they had been reported and were being dealt with. I had several other reports of problems after this so I decided to check all the lines again. This time I found eight of the fifteen were noisy, so I decided to call BT again and raise the faults to priority. I rang their fault report line and quoted the reference number I had been given before; the girl said that BT had already raised the faults to priority status because they had other reports from customers on the industrial estate experiencing similar problems.

When I left work that night BT engineers were working in the area where I had seen the council workers hammering metal spikes. They had excavated a big hole and were examining cables that went though the pipes.

Next morning when I arrived at work the BT engineer was already here testing all our lines. When I asked what had happened, he said the council workmen had driven a spike straight through the main cable serving the industrial estate. He said they had worked all night restoring the cable, but everything appeared to be OK now.

1 Was Maryam right in reporting the original fault as routine?
2 Was it necessary for Maryam to attempt to raise the fault status to priority. If so why?
3 Could Maryam have done anything differently?
4 Would you have expected or have asked for a reference number when you report a fault?
5 What are the advantages of this?

Possible contingency plans to maintain communications until the fault is cleared

Contingency plans are put in action to restore or to maintain service in the event of a fault causing disruption to the normal service offered by your organisation. The plans can be very simple or very complex. Some organisations will have drawn up plans in advance so that should the problem arise the plan can be implemented without delay; while others will rely on the ingenuity of their employees to react to the situation and make the most of the resources remaining. In reality, most organisations have plans in place to cover the minor problems but feel that it is unrealistic to have plans to resolve major problems.

Contingency plans should be practical, successful in restoring the service and cost effective. Plans that cost the organisation more money to implement than is likely to be saved by their implementation are not viable propositions.

Possible contingency plans

The best contingency plans are usually the simplest as they can be implemented at a moment's notice without fuss and everyone knows and understands their involvement. All contingency plans, even the simple ones, need to be tailored to the requirements of the individual organisation. We will start by looking at some of the common contingency plans which organisations use to maintain their telecommunications service. These include:

♦ exchanging faulty equipment for a working spare
♦ taking faulty equipment out of service
♦ switching to night service
♦ diverting calls.

♦ Exchanging faulty equipment for a working spare

This is probably the most effective and most commonly used contingency plan. It is where an organisation keeps a serviceable stock of items available, so that if an item is found to be faulty it can be exchanged for one of the serviceable spares.

Many organisations operate this type of contingency plan for the exchange of faulty headsets. Agents who find their headset is faulty can exchange it for one that works. This may sound very simple but it requires everyone using the system to follow laid down procedures if the system is to be effective. People exchanging faulty items need to be careful that they do not mix up the faulty item with the good ones; otherwise the next person may well exchange their faulty item for that left by the previous person. To avoid this happening all faulty items need to be clearly marked as faulty and segregated from the working spares. It is also essential that the system is regularly monitored by the person responsible for maintaining the stock of serviceable spares. Faulty items need to be repaired where possible or new items purchased in order to replenish the stock and maintain it at an acceptable level.

You may find that there are other items of equipment where your organisation holds a stock of serviceable spares that can be used to replace faulty items. If so, it is likely that the procedures it adopts to control the stock is basically the same as that outlined above.

◆ Take faulty equipment out of service

Removing equipment from service is effective as it avoids anyone experiencing the problems associated with the faulty equipment, but it does restrict the service you are able to offer until the fault is cleared. Taking one incoming line out of service, out of a total of twenty, may have very little impact on the service offered to your callers unless it occurred during a particularly busy period. However, as a contingency plan, it will need to be tightly monitored to avoid further lines being taken out of service that may have serious consequences for the service you offer. It will also be necessary to ensure that lines that have been taken out of service are restored as soon as practically possible.

◆ Switch to night service

Many receptionists use the night service facilities available on most switchboards to switch all incoming calls to nominated extensions when they finish for the night or need to take a break. Most telephone systems are capable of being programmed to divert incoming calls to any internal extensions instead of them being answered at the switchboard. To be effective it is assumed that these extensions will be staffed and the calls will be answered.

These facilities can also an effective way of restoring service should a fault develop with the switchboard; by switching to the night service, incoming calls can be answered and service to the callers restored.

◆ Diverting calls

This type of contingency plan is appropriate where you have to divert calls to another telephone or location in order to overcome problems with their original destination. It can be very effective in resolving a vast array of problems. It can range from a telephone extension that is found to be faulty and so all calls are diverted to another close by; or a major problem that involves transferring all calls from one call centre to another when the original centre has all its access lines cut.

Check it out

◆ Does your organisation have contingency plans for when faults occur? Explain how and when they are implemented.

Keys to good practice

✓ When making or receiving telephone calls, always treat the caller as you would like to be treated.

✓ If you have any doubts about the sensitivity of information, always err on the side of caution but consult your manager.

✓ When placing a caller on hold, check at regular intervals that they wish to remain on hold.

✓ Always make a note of the caller's name whenever it is given as it will save you embarrassment if you have to ask for it to be repeated later

✓ Where necessary ask the caller to spell their name and address.

✓ When reporting telephone faults always ask for a reference number as proof of the report.

✓ Be aware of contingency plans before they need to be implemented.

Check your knowledge

1 Name three things you need to gather from the caller before you can process their call.
2 What are the two types of sensitive information?
3 Give three examples of sensitive information and say what type of information it is.
4 List five types of information you will require in order to make a telephone call.
5 What constitutes a fault in telephone equipment?
6 List six items that are usually contained in a service level agreement.

Test your Knowledge – Answers

Unit 1 (page 54)

1 Any four of the following:

- know your area of responsibility
- ensure all reference material is to hand and that it is current and up to date
- ensure you have the necessary computer access
- ensure you have the sufficient consumables items available to last the shift. e.g. Pens, pencils, paper
- ensure your headset is working and adjusted properly.

2 Example: **E**cho, **X**-ray, **A**ble, **M**ike, **P**apa, **L**ima, **E**cho

3 Finishing on a positive note encourages the caller to call again. This is best achieved by thanking them for their custom and confirming that they are satisfied with the outcome of the call.

4 RNID stands for Royal National Institute for the Deaf.

5 Calling the person by their name personalises the call and you are then able to address the caller directly.

6 You would use an open question when you are trying to encourage a caller to talk and give you as much information as possible, or when you need to expand the discussion.

7 Closed questions can be used to obtain a decision or to confirm details, but they can also be used to make a choice or to select an option.

8 Different types of questions can be used to help you ask additional questions that delve deeper into the area you are interested in. This is best achieved by asking a closed question and then asking the person to explain the reason behind his or her choice.

9 A probing question is most appropriate when you require more information than the caller has originally given you, or to lead the caller to consider other possible options outside of those originally considered.

10 The first three of the following, but the forth is also important:

- keep the caller informed at all stages of the call, including when they are placed on hold
- check that the other person is available to take the call, if so, pass on as much information as possible to avoid the caller having to repeat the details
- give the caller the name and telephone number of the person to whom they will be transferred
- thank the caller for holding and tell them you are about to transfer them.

11 Businesses can legitimately monitor a call without permission if they are:

- checking whether or not communications are relevant to the business
- monitoring calls to confidential, counseling help lines run free of charge

12 Callers have a right to expect you to limit your collection of information to that which is relevant for a particular use. This use should be specified at the time, and the information given must only be used for this purpose.

Information you collect in this way should be held in confidence and used only for the business of the caller and should not be disclosed to anyone other than the officers, directors or employees of your organisation with a specific need to know.

Any infringement of this might result in you being liable under the Data Protection Act.

13 Any eight of the following:

- try not to panic or close the call immediately
- try not to lose your temper
- don't be tempted to react in a similar way
- try not to take the remarks personally
- don't become upset
- be patient
- listen to what the caller is saying; giving verbal nods to reaffirm you are listening.
- try to calm the situation by addressing the caller by name
- if the caller does not calm down, clearly advise them that unless they are prepared to continue the discussion in a civil manner, you will have no option but to terminate the call
- if the caller calms down and you are able to continue but he or she is not satisfied with your answers to their questions, offer to pass the call to a colleague or supervisor, or offer to call them back when you have investigated further
- if, despite a warning the aggression and abuse continues, then you may have no alternative but to terminate the call.

Unit 25 (page 110)

1 Defined service levels enable an organisation to achieve consistency, as they govern the level of service that an organisation offers its customers.

Such consistency can only be achieved if quality standards are also set as they control the way that people are expected to work so that the defined service levels can be met.

2 The key purpose of quality management is to enhance an organisation's capacity to improve its performance and develop excellence for its customers.

3 Understanding what your organization expects of you means that you are able to perform consistently and identify any opportunities for improvement.

4 In today's climate, you should be taking an active approach by assuming responsibility for your own performance and looking for ways in which you can improve that performance. To do this, you will need to monitor your own performance.

5 A self-development plan is a document that details your intention to undertake any developmental activities that you may need to address any deficiencies that there may be in your performance. It could include further training that may be required or just the opportunity to gain greater experience.

6 Six pieces of Heath and Safety Regulation and their effect on you:

- The Workplace (Health, Safety & Welfare) Regulations 1992 – they govern the working environment that you are expected to operate within.
- The Management of Health & Safety at Work Regulations 1999 – these ensure that your organisation manages health and safety within the workplace and maximises the well being of all its employees.

♦ The Provision and Use of Work Equipment Regulations 1998 – they ensure that your organisation makes sure that any equipment it expects you to use as part of your job role is suitable, safe and properly maintained.

♦ The Health & Safety (Display Screen Equipment) Regulations 1992 – these help to make display screen work safer and more comfortable.

♦ The Safety Representatives & Safety Committees Regulations 1977 – these allow recognised trade unions to appoint employee safety representatives who have certain rights.

♦ The Health & Safety (Consultation with Employees) Regulations 1996 – these ensure that your employer as a duty to consult employees in good time on a range of matters affecting their health and safety at work.

7 A hazard is anything that can cause harm, such as chemicals, electricity or working from ladders.

8 A risk is the chance, high or low, that somebody will be harmed by a hazard.

9 Setting up your workstation to suit your own personal needs will ensure that you are comfortable while you work. This will minimise any risks to your well being from repetitive strain injury (RSI) or eye strain.

10 A Repetitive Strain Injury (RSI) is a soft tissue injury in which muscles, nerves or tendons become irritated or inflamed. They occur when repeated physical movements cause damage to tendons, nerves, muscles and other soft body tissues. It can be a serious and painful condition that can occur in young, physically fit individuals and it can leave people permanently disabled or unable to perform certain tasks. It is far easier to prevent the condition than it is to cure it once it is contracted.

11 You may have listed any six of the followings things:

♦ Adjust the height of your chair until your forearms are parallel to the keyboard when typing and your wrists are in a neutral position.

♦ Ensure that your eyes are at the same height as the top of your screen.

♦ Make sure that your thighs are parallel to the floor and that your feet rest firmly on the ground or a footrest.

♦ Locate the keyboard and mouse close to you so that you do not stretch to reach them.

♦ Leave a space in front of your keyboard so that you have somewhere to rest your hands when you are not using the keyboard.

♦ Position your screen and keyboard in the best position for your task.

♦ Ensure that the seat of your chair is short enough from front to back to enable you to make contact with the backrest and adjust the backrest so that it provides adequate support for your back.

♦ Remove any clutter from under your desk so that you have sufficient leg room.

♦ If you copy type, use a document holder.

♦ Try to take regular breaks away from your computer.

12 You may have listed any three of the following things:

♦ Changes in mood or behaviour which can lead to deteriorating relationships with colleagues

♦ Irritability

♦ Indecisiveness

♦ Absenteeism

♦ Reduced performance

13 The Working Time Regulations 1998 were brought in to protect workers from being forced to work excessive

hours. They also make the provision of paid annual leave mandatory and include rights to rest breaks and uninterrupted period of rest.

14

- ♦ Assess the situation – do not put yourself in danger.
- ♦ Make the area safe.
- ♦ Assess all the casualties and attend first to any unconscious casualties.
- ♦ Send for help without delay.

15 The **R**eporting of **I**njuries, **D**iseases and **D**angerous **O**ccurrences **R**egulations 1995 – these regulations require the reporting of work-related accidents, diseases and dangerous occurrences. The information gathered as a result of this piece of legislation enables the enforcing authorities to identify where and how risks arise and allows them to investigate serious accidents.

16 You should check your answer with your manager.

17 You may have listed any four of the following:

- ♦ Providing your colleagues with accurate information on time.
- ♦ Sharing new information with your colleagues.
- ♦ Considering how your actions may affect other people.
- ♦ Being open and honest.
- ♦ Being a reliable member of the team.
- ♦ Doing a good job.
- ♦ Doing your fair share of the work.
- ♦ Lending a helping hand.
- ♦ Respecting other people for the knowledge and experience they may have.
- ♦ Listening to what others have to say.

Unit 26 (page 129)

1 To evaluate how well the organisation is operating you compare, rank, and grade information by the use of specific qualitative or quantitative factors. These factors include mental and physical skills, degrees of responsibility, and working conditions.

2 Analysis would be based on looking at both the 'qualitative' and 'quantitative' factors affecting your organisation. Some of quantitative factors are:

- ♦ Number of agents logged on and available to take calls.
- ♦ The amounts of time agents log out for whilst on shift.
- ♦ Total number of calls taken during the period specified. (Normally measured in the total number of calls taken per hour or day, either collectively or by individual agents).
- ♦ Total number of missed or lost calls.
- ♦ Average waiting times for calls to be connected to an agent.
- ♦ Average call time.
- ♦ How many calls are referred for further action or escalated to a higher level.
- ♦ Types of calls received. (Usually listed by product or service required).
- ♦ Number of inbound calls taken by individual agents.
- ♦ Number of outbound calls made by individual agents.
- ♦ Amount of time agents take completing administration between calls. (Wrap time).

3 Analysis is done by measuring performance against the targets set by your organisation, or measuring your performance against your job description.

4 You can identify areas where potential improvements can be made by looking at existing problems within your organisation, or if you don't have any problems that you can use as a starting point then look at existing systems and procedures and see if any of these can be improved upon.

5 You would consider the questions; 'What if' and 'So What' to each of the potential improvements you have identified.

6 Check your answer with your manager.

7 If you do not have a formal system it would be logical to list the potential improvements in an order of priority as to which you think is the best and then the second best and so on. For each potential improvement you would want to include the following information:

♦ What the potential improvement is.
♦ The background as to why you think the existing system needs improving.
♦ Why you think this is an improvement over the existing systems.
♦ The benefits, advantages and disadvantages of the potential improvement.
♦ Impact on the organisation.
♦ The achievability of the potential improvement.

8 Your team leader would be the best starting point but check your answer with your manager.

9 By considering the 'impact on' questions you can prioritise which are the best potential improvements to recommend. These could include:

♦ Impact on the customer.
♦ Impact on the quality of call handling.
♦ Impact on the quantity of calls handled.
♦ Impact on operational efficiency.
♦ Impact on individuals within the call centre.

10 When considering the feasibility of your ideas you would want to consider the following factors:

♦ Time scale to implementation? – Is it going to be out of date before we can get it in place?

♦ Will our existing technology cope with it? – Will current call centre applications allow this to be implemented using our existing systems?
♦ Will it be accessible to all or limited? – Who are the improvements targeted at and will it lead to discrimination or affect staff morale?
♦ Is there going to be a balance between the benefits to customers, call centre agents and call centre operations?
♦ Will it have an impact on our competitors and how do we think they will respond?

11 Some of the formats for presenting information that could be used are:

♦ Hand written notes.
♦ Word-processed notes.
♦ Tape recordings to illustrate voice procedures.
♦ Video recordings.
♦ Role-plays using agents.
♦ Acetates for use with an overhead projector.
♦ Lists or points for discussion on white boards, chalk boards or flip charts.
♦ PowerPoint presentations or other IT applications using slide shows.
♦ Existing lists, tables and statistics extracted and printed from the call management systems

12 You would state the advantages/ benefits and disadvantages to the organisation. The benefits could include:

♦ Benefits to the customer.
♦ Benefits to the quality of call handling.
♦ Benefits to the quantity of calls handled.
♦ Benefits to operational efficiency.
♦ Benefits to individuals within the call centre.

- Financial benefits.
- Safety benefits.

13 Check your answer with your manager.

Unit 2 (page 160)

1 Empathy is the ability to identify yourself mentally with a person so that you can understand them better.

2 The five factor that prevent us from listening are:

- Environmental distractions
- The third ear syndrome
- Jumping ahead
- Emotional filters
- Day dreaming

3 Five different types are questions include:

- Closed questions
- Open questions
- Probing questions
- Direct questions
- Hypothetical questions

4 Summarising is used to ensure that you have fully understood what you have been told. To summarise a conversation, you first need to listen carefully to what the person is telling you and then re-state back to them a condensed version of what they have said.

5 Alpha; Bravo; Charlie; Delta; Echo; Foxtrot; Golf; Hotel; India; Juliet; Kilo; Lima; Mike; November; Oscar; Papa; Quebec; Romeo; Sierra; Tango; Uniform; Victor; Whiskey; X-Ray; Yankee; Zulu.

6 The Data Protection Act 1998 came into force on the 1st of March 2000.

7 Data must be:

- fairly and lawfully processed
- processed for limited purposes
- adequate, relevant and not excessive

- accurate
- not kept for longer than necessary
- processed in accordance with individual's rights
- kept secure
- not transferred to non-EEA countries unless the data is adequately protected

8 Individuals have the right to:

- gain access to their data
- seek compensation
- prevent their data from being processed in certain circumstances
- opt out of having their data used for direct marketing
- opt out of fully automated decision making about them

9 You will need to check your answer with your manager.

10 You will need to check your answer with your manager.

11 You are more likely to get the customer to buy-in to any solution that you may propose if you:

- explain each of the alternatives clearly to the customer
- describe the advantages and disadvantages of each option
- answer any questions that your customer may have about each option
- allow the customer time to consider the proposal

12 You will need to check your answer with your manager.

13 You will need to check your answer with your manager.

Unit 6 (page 181)

1 It is usual to take down the caller's name and possibly their telephone number and/or address. You will also need to find out the reason why the caller has contacted your organisation. The key information that you require will vary depending upon your job role – for example, if you are responsible for taking hotel bookings then you may well also need to obtain the caller's credit card details. You should therefore check your answer with your manager.

2 You will probably need to bear in mind the following:

  ♦ when the caller expects the arrangements to have been made by
  ♦ what could happen if the arrangements are not made immediately
  ♦ the urgency of the task
  ♦ the effect of these arrangements on any others that may need to be made

As it is likely that the way you determine and set priorities will vary from job to job, you will also need to check your answer to this question with your manager.

3 Again, we can give no definitive answer to this question as it will depend on the nature of your job role and how your organisation operates. You will therefore need to check your answer with your manager.

4 Check your answer with your manager.

5 Check your answer with your manager.

6 You should never make promises to the caller that you can not keep as you could be starting a process that could have a significant impact on you; the caller; and your organisation. What may have been a difficult situation to start with could become a complete disaster if you make a promise that you can not keep.

7 The extent of your customer's legal rights will depend upon the nature of your organisation's business. You will

therefore need to check your answer with your manager.

8 Check your answer with your manager.

9 If you exceed the caller's expectations by providing them with excellent customer service, the customer is likely to want to do business with your organisation again. Your organisation is therefore more likely to get repeat business. It is also possible that your organisation will draw in new business, as it is quite likely that a satisfied customer will tell their friends and family about their experiences. It is therefore possible that making sure that the customer goes away satisfied could lead to an increase in the number of people who think positively about your organisation which, in turn, could increase your company's turnover.

10 You should always monitor actions that you have initiated because you can never be sure that the actions will be completed otherwise.

11 Thinking ahead can help to ensure that any potential problems are spotted and dealt with before they become an issue.

12 Check your answer with your manager.

Unit 7 (page 222)

1 In February 2002 there were 91 million credit and debit cards in the UK.

2 Visa

3 MasterCard

4 Switch

5 Switch

6 To process a credit card transaction you will need the following:

  ♦ name and address
  ♦ type of card

- the number of the card
- the name and title displayed on the card
- a contact telephone number
- the order
- the address the goods are to be sent to

7 To process a bank transaction you will need the following:

- bank sort code
- account details
- customer's name and address
- answer to the security question you asked
- details of the transaction

8 The main causes of credit card failure are:

- being unable to confirm the caller's identity
- the card has expired or is pre-dated
- the card has been reported lost or stolen
- the transaction value exceeds your organisation's floor limit
- the caller requests the payment be split between two or more cards
- you are offered a type of card your organisation is not licensed to accept
- the card has been stopped by the credit card company or bank

9 A floor limits is a transaction limit under which transactions can be processed without authorisation from the card issuing company. This limit is agreed on between the organisation and the relevant bank.

All transactions whose total value is below the floor limit can be agreed by the organisation without prior authority from the card issuing company. But transactions whose total value is about the floor limit will need to be authorised by the card issuing company before they can be accept by the organisation.

10 When dealing with a customer who offers a stopped card, you should:

- be polite
- explain that you are unable to accept the card for payment as the card as been refused
- refer the caller to the company or bank that issued the card
- never get involved in discussing the reason why the card was refused
- try and leave the caller on a positive note

Unit 9 (page 275)

1 Check your answer with your manager.

2 The six steps of the sales process are:

1. Analyse the customer's needs.
2. Offer solutions.
3. Sell benefits.
4. Handle questions.
5. Handle objections.
6. Close the sale.

3 The Telephone Preference Service is a service which exists to help those customers who do not want to receive cold calls from organizations. It was set up in 1995 and is managed by the Direct Marketing Association.

4 It is unlawful to make unsolicited direct marketing calls to individuals who have indicated that they do not want to receive such calls. All call centres must keep an in-house 'Do Not Call' list that contains the numbers of any customers that have indicated that they do not wish to be contacted again.

5 The DMA Code of Practice is a document issued by the UK Direct Marketing Association that sets standards of ethical conduct and best practice that its members must adhere to as a condition of membership.

6 How predictive dialling works:

- When a number of agents are logged into the same campaign, information is held on a network server with links to all agents. The network server has a link to a predictive dialling engine, which may be a physical device (hard dialler) connected directly into the Public Switched Telephone Network (PSTN) or it may be a piece of software (soft dialler).
- As agents become available, the server and the dialler decide which order to dial the campaign numbers in and then initiate the calls.
- If there is no answer after a defined number of seconds, the dialler hangs up. For those calls that connect, the dialler strives to filter out such things as answering machines and puts the remaining calls through to agents.
- At the same time as the connected call is being put through to the agent's headset, details of the called party are brought up on the agent's screen.
- The dialler monitors the results of all the calls, such as the percentage of no answers, busy signals, etc., and it also measures agent performance in terms of average talk time. It then uses this information to calculate how many lines it should be dialling out on. At times of high no answer levels the dialler initiates several calls for each agent who is either waiting or about to finish a call.

Predictive dialling has the following benefits

- Many more calls can be made in a much shorter period of time than an agent dialling manually can make.
- Numbers are not missed – if the dialler encounters a busy signal or no answer, it will dial the number again later.

- The system can also keep track of an entire campaign's progress in real time, which would be virtually impossible to do manually.
- Diallers can be fed 'Do Not Call' lists.

7 The three most important questions that you should ask yourself before starting a telemarketing/telesales campaign are:

- What do I hope to accomplish?
- Who am I going to call?
- What am I going to say?

8 You should set very specific sales call objectives because:

- You will achieve definition of purpose.
- The objectives will direct and guide the call.
- The customer will know why you have called.
- You will not waste any time as your efforts will be focussed.
- You will be able to measure results on every call.

9 Objections tend to arise from:

- the customer having insufficient information
- the customer's particular circumstances
- procrastination on the part of the customer
- the price or running costs of the product or service.

10 A good introduction should:

- identify you
- put your listener into a positive frame of mind
- allow you to effectively move on to the next part of the call

11 You should ask the customer for permission to continue with the call because they will not pay attention to you if they are busy. Your call is likely to be an intrusion into the customer's busy day, so if you are considerate and find out if it is convenient for you to continue with the call, the customer is more likely to listen to what you have to say.

12 Good listeners:

- Give their full attention to the person who is speaking.
- Make sure that their mind stays focussed
- Let the speaker finish before they begin to talk
- Listen for main ideas as they are the most important points that the speaker wants to get across
- Ask questions if they are not sure that they understand what the speaker has said.

13 The four steps for overcoming objections are:

- Empathise with the customer.
- Clarify your understanding of the customer's concerns.
- Present the customer with a solution.
- Gain the customer's agreement.

14 The five stages of buying are:

- Problem recognition.
- Information search.
- Alternative evaluation.
- Purchase decision.
- Post-purchase evaluation.

15 The two central objectives of selling are:

- Stay in control of the conversation.
- Try to put yourself in a position where you are able to close the sale.

Unit 11 (page 305)

1 Most common answers are:

- A monitor or Visual Display Unit
- A system unit
- A keyboard
- A mouse
- A printer

Other acceptable answers are:

- a floppy disk drive
- a zip drive
- a CD-ROM drive
- a DVD drive
- a CD writer
- a DVD writer
- a modem or
- a scanner

2 You may have listed any two of the following items:

- All the computers in a network can communicate with each other.
- Data and information can be shared by many users.
- Several users can also share a printer.

3 Three forms of data storage are:

- Random Access Memory (RAM)
- The computer's hard drive.
- An external storage medium such as a floppy disk, CD-ROM, DVD or zip disk.

4 A Digital Versatile Disc or DVD stores the most amount of information.

5 Logging on is the process of identifying yourself to the computer by giving your user name and password.

6 There are six obligations.

7 Tailoring your workstation to your own personal needs will ensure that you are comfortable while you work which will minimise any risks to your well being from repetitive strain injury (RSI) or eye strain.

8 You need to save your work so that data is not lost when you switch off your computer. Saving your work regularly whilst you are working will also minimise the amount of data that could be lost due to a system failure.

9 To avoid the possibility of not being able to access your data if anything happens to the original version of the information.

10 The Data Protection Act 1998 exists to protect the rights of individuals and to ensure their privacy. It was brought in as a response to people's concerns about who has access to information held about them and whether the information kept is accurate and up to date.

11 Data needs to be kept secure so that only people who are authorised to see or use the data have access to it.

12 You can minimise the potential for damage by:

- ◆ keeping your workstation clean
- ◆ always shutting your computer down correctly
- ◆ avoiding the possibility of introducing a computer virus

13 You should check your answer with your manager.

14 If not, you should check with your manager.

Unit 17 (page 341)

1 You need to know:

- ◆ the callers name
- ◆ where the caller is from and who they represents
- ◆ the purpose of the call

2 There are two types of sensitive information, which are:

- ◆ information concerning individuals
- ◆ information concerning the organisation

3 Any three of the following:

Commercially sensitive information could include:

- ◆ expansion plans
- ◆ sales figures
- ◆ price structures
- ◆ promotional plans
- ◆ advertising plans
- ◆ production methods

Personally sensitive information could include:

- ◆ information containing staff details or
- ◆ staff medical records.

4 Any five of the following:

- ◆ why do you want to make the call
- ◆ who do you want to call
- ◆ what do you want to say
- ◆ what information do you require to make the call
- ◆ is the information sensitive
- ◆ when is the best time to make the call
- ◆ how urgent is the call

5 The five categories of sensitive information are:

- ◆ unclassified
- ◆ restricted
- ◆ confidential
- ◆ secret
- ◆ top secret

6 We usually say we have a fault when something stops working or it reacts in a way we did not expect. When using a telephone you expect to be able to complete a certain sequence of events – pick up the handset, listen for dial tone, dial a number, the number to ring etc. If at any point in this process you are unable to go to the next stage, you have a fault. The same will be true when you are using the telephone system for sending or receiving data or faxes. If the system will not let you use it as it should, you have a fault.

7 Any six of the following:

- ◆ the length of the agreement
- ◆ the charges for the service
- ◆ fault reporting procedures
- ◆ service response times
- ◆ your organisation's responsibilities
- ◆ ending the agreement
- ◆ limitation of liability of the maintainer

Glossary of call handling terms

Abandoned calls	These are calls that have arrived at the **Automatic Call Distributor** but where the caller has hung up before an agent has been free to answer. These are sometimes also called **lost calls**.
Adherence factor	A measure of how closely agents adhere to their schedules for breaks and lunches.
Agent ID	The code allocated to individual agents which enables them to log into the **Automatic Call Distributor**. The system uses this identification code to track the performance of agents.
Agent group	Agents may be placed in groups, based on the type of calls they will be dealing with, which enables the **Automatic Call Distributor** to route calls to an appropriate group depending on the nature of the incoming call.
All trunks busy (ATB)	This is when all the telephone lines are in use at the same time – other callers will get the engaged tone when this happens.
Annual monthly trends	The percentage increase or decrease in calls over a twelve month period.
Answer detect	The ability of the telephone system to detect and identify network tones when automatically making outbound calls. The system is able to identify and filter out calls that do not connect (ringing tone or engaged tone) or calls that result in a connection to a fax or answering machine. Only live calls are routed through to an agent.
Auto attendant	This is where an **inbound call** is answered by a recording that asks the customer to either press buttons on the keypad or say which extension they want. The system then automatically routes their call.
Automatic Call Distributor (ACD)	A telephone system capable of handling large volumes of calls, which automatically routes the next call to the agent who has been waiting for the longest period. This type of telephone system is flexible and can be programmed in a variety of ways, such as routing certain types of calls to specific agents (or groups of agents) or giving certain types of caller priority. The ACD is also capable of producing an array of management reports.
Automatic Dialler	Sometimes also called an **Outbound Dialler**. An automated dialling system – several different types are available with different levels of sophistication. See **screen dialling**, **power dialling** and **predictive dialling**.
Automatic Number Identification (ANI)	A system feature that allows the caller's telephone number to be forwarded at the same time as their call so that the caller can be automatically identified. This is sometimes also called **Calling Line Identity (CLI)**.
Available	The agent's status when they are logged on to the **Automatic Call Distributor** and they are ready and waiting for an **inbound call**. May also be called **idle** or **ready**.

Average Handling Time (AHT)	This is the average of the time spent on a call (**talk time**) plus any work that follows on from a call (**wrap up**).
Average speed of answer (ASA)	The average length of time that calls spend in the queue.
Average Talk Time (ATT)	The average length of time that an agent spends speaking with a caller. It is measured from answering a call to hanging up.
Back busy	Deliberately busying out lines during peak times so that some callers get an engaged tone rather than ending up holding for an unacceptable length of time.
Blending	Where a **call centre** uses the same agents for both inbound and outbound calling, utilising troughs in call volume to make **outbound calls**.
Blockage	When all the **exchange lines** are engaged (in use) and therefore blocked to all other callers trying to get through. Usually measured as a percentage of the total time.
Call centre	A place where calls are handled by individuals who are specially trained to resolve those calls as part of a one-stop shop.
Call data	Information about calls that can be found in management reports.
Call screening	Where the caller is initially interrogated by either an **auto attendant** or an **interactive voice response** to determine the best call handling options to use before transfer.
Call seconds	The amount of time that **exchange lines** are occupied. Measured in seconds and calculated in sums of 100 (36 centum (hundred) call seconds equates to one hour or one **Erlang**).
Caller tolerance	The length of time that callers are prepared to wait in a **queue** for an available agent – usually described as high or low.
Calling Line Identity (CLI)	A feature which enables the caller's own telephone number to be forwarded at the same time as their call, to facilitate identification.
Centum call seconds (CCS)	36 centum call seconds equate to one hour or one **Erlang**. They are used to measure the amount of time that exchange lines are occupied.
Contact management	Software programmes that record the outcome of each call (inbound or outbound).
Cost per call	This can be calculated by dividing the full cost of the entire call centre operation by the number of calls handled. If this is then compared with the revenue per call, the profit (or loss) factor of the call centre can be calculated.
Cost per call minute	This can be calculated by dividing the full cost of the entire call centre operation by the average length of a call (in minutes) multiplied by the number of calls handled. The figure obtained can be used as an effective benchmark in comparisons with other **call centres**.
Cost per call second	The same calculation as in cost per call minute but calculated in seconds rather than minutes.

Customer Relationship Management (CRM)	The use of a variety of methods and contact strategies to enable the building of lasting and profitable relationships in order to retain the best customers and generate profitable revenue.
Daily index factor	A weighting given to each day of the week that allows accurate monthly forecasts to be allocated to each day.
Delay announcements	The recorded messages played to callers while they are in a **queue**.
Delay of Delay	The average delay experienced by callers who have been placed in a queue.
Dialled Number Identification Service (DNIS)	A facility that allows more than one telephone number to terminate in a single **queue**. This facility allows the system to identify the call volumes made to each number by recognising the different numbers dialled.
Double jacking	Where two people can both participate in the same call as they are both connected to the same telephone terminal or **turret** at the same time. Used extensively in training to 'shadow' a new agent.
Erlang	A formula created by A. K. Erlang, a Danish engineer. It is a measure of telephone traffic. One Erlang equates to one hour of telephone traffic.
Erlang B	Another formula created by A. K. Erlang that calculates the number of exchange lines needed to accommodate a specified call volume. It assumes that no callers will retry if they get an engaged tone.
Erlang C	A further formula created by A. K. Erlang that can be used to forecast call volumes, taking random call arrival into account. It assumes that calls will **queue** when there are no agents available to answer calls. This formula is used extensively in **call centres** for call forecasting, staff scheduling and to measure service level achievement.
Exchange lines	Another name for telephone lines or **trunks**.
Extended Erlang B	The same formula as Erlang B except that the assumption is now that callers will retry if they get an engaged tone.
Full time equivalents (FTE)	The number of agents required, expressed in terms of the total person hours required, divided by the number of hours a full time agent would normally work. This figure is used to facilitate salary budgets and hiring approvals.
Gate	A group of agents that handle one or more specific types of call.
Half hour segment index factor	A weighting allocated to each half hour of the day so that daily call forecasts can be accurately predicted.
Headset	A telephone set with a mouth and ear pieces that enables hands-free operation.
Hunt group	A means of distributing calls. There are two systems:
	1 where calls are distributed in the same order each time – the first extension will always receive the next call unless it is busy, in which case the system will 'hunt' for the second extension, etc.

	2 a 'round robin' – where the second call will automatically hunt to the second extension and the third call will hunt to the third extension, etc. This methods leads to a more even distribution of calls.
Idle	A description given to agents who are logged on available and waiting for a call to come in. Sometimes also called **available** or **ready**.
Inbound calls	All calls received by a **call centre**.
Intelligent routing	Where callers are routed based on a number of parameters such as: ♦ information about the caller ♦ **queue** status ♦ agent status ♦ the current situation. Sometimes also called **skills-based routing**.
Interactive voice response (IVR)	Where an **inbound call** is answered by a recording that asks the customer to press buttons on the keypad in response to a menu of options. The system can then search for specific information, based on the numbers selected, which is then converted into the spoken word. For example, an account balance.
Interactive web response (IWR)	Where a customer transacting business over the Internet is able to transfer to an agent in the call centre and continue their enquiry over the telephone.
Interflow	When calls flow out of the **Automatic Call Distributor** to another source. May be used when all agents are busy and calls have stacked up past pre-set parameters or for night service arrangements. Once they have been interflowed, calls cannot be brought back into the **Automatic Call Distributor**.
Intraflow	When calls are flowed from one **agent group** to another so that they can be handled more quickly.
Line utilisation	A report produced by the **Automatic Call Distributor** that shows the **occupancy** of each **exchange line** during the requested period of the report.
Lost calls	These are calls that have arrived at the **Automatic Call Distributor** but where the caller has hung up before an agent has been free to answer. These are sometimes also called **abandoned calls**.
Management information services (MIS)	Reports produced by the **Automatic Call Distributor** that show data on agents and **agent groups**; **inbound** and **outbound calls**; and **exchange lines**.
Mean monthly trend	The percentage increase or decrease in call volume over a one month period.
Music and messaging on hold	Playing messages and music to calls in the queuing system to tempt callers to hold for longer. May also be used when callers are placed on hold during the handling of their calls.

Night service	Used when the **call centre** is closed. It could consist of a message given to callers; a diversion to another **call centre**; or a diversion to a voice mail box.
Occupancy	The percentage of time that individual agents (or the average of all agents) are actively occupied during **talk time** and **wrap up** time. It does not include **ready** time.
Outbound calls	All calls that are made by a **call centre**.
Outbound Dialler	Sometimes also called an **automatic dialler**. An automated dialling system – several different types are available with different levels of sophistication. See **screen dialling**; **power dialling** and **predictive dialling**.
Outsourcing	Where an external company is contracted to provide **call centre** services.
Overflow	Where calls are flowed from one **agent group** to another so that they are handled more quickly.
Pattern	Sometimes also called a **queue** or a **split**. A holding pen for calls.
Pooling principle	The principle that dictates that the larger a **call centre** is, the more efficient that each agent becomes in terms of **occupancy**.
Power dialling	Where the telephone system dials as many calls as it has lines available. It then uses **answer detect** to enable it to put through any live calls to agents. If no agent is available when a call is answered, it will simply drop the call which causes a 'nuisance call' – this type of system is therefore not very popular.
Predictive dialling	Similar to **power dialling** but more sophisticated. The system uses a pacing algorithm that regulates the number of **outbound calls** made based on the probability of an agent being available. This system minimises the number of 'nuisance calls'.
Preview dialling	Uses screens of data downloaded from a central database. The agent then initiates the call usually by using a pre-programmed button on the keyboard or screen.
Queue	A 'holding pen' for calls that are waiting for an agent to become free.
Queue time	The number of seconds that a call waits in a **queue** before handling.
Ready	A description given to agents who are logged onto the **Automatic Call Distributor** and are available and waiting for a call to come in. Sometimes also called **idle** or **available**.
Recorded announcement (RAN)	An intercept message that is controlled by the **Automatic Call Distributor** using parameters such as the **ring time** or the time of day (for night messaging).
Ring time	The time taken from dialling to a call to be answered by either a live agent or a **delay announcement**.
Seasonality variation	The variation in call volume due specifically to seasons during the year.

Screen dialling	Where the agent selects a number on the screen using a mouse to point and click and the system then dials the number for them.
Screen popping	The system tries to identify each call and checks the customer database for a match. If a match exists, the data for that record is displayed on the agent's screen just before the call arrives at the agent's **headset**.
Service agency	A bureau that offers a **call centre** service either as an **intraflow** facility or by handling the complete operation.
Service level	The percentage of calls that a **call centre** expects to handle in a specific number of seconds.
Shrinkage	The percentage of time when scheduled agents are unavailable to take calls because of breaks, lunches or training.
Short calls	Usually calls with less than five or ten seconds talk time. The defining time period is set by the **call centre**.
Skills-based routing	Where calls are identified and then routed through to the most appropriate agent. For example, calls from a foreign country would be routed through to an agent who speaks the appropriate language. Sometimes also called **intelligent routing**.
Speed of answer	The time from a call arriving at the **Automatic Call Distributor** to when it is answered by an agent.
Split	A group of agents handling one or more specific types of call.
Talk time	The time in seconds that an agent is talking. It is measured from the agent answering the call to when the caller hangs up.
Top and tail recordings	Where greetings and goodbyes are pre-recorded so that they sound fresh and enthusiastic all day.
Trunk	Each telephone or **exchange line** is called a **trunk**.
Trunk hold time	The length of time that a call is active, from the caller completing dialling to the caller hanging up.
Turret	The telephone console used by agents.
Unavailable	An agent's status when they are logged into the **Automatic Call Distributor** but are not available to take calls. For example, during breaks or training.
Workload	The call volume measured in hours. One hour of workload equates to one **Erlang**.
Wrap up	The time spent, after the caller has hung up, completing work associated with a call.